REA

FIR ON

New H Primary

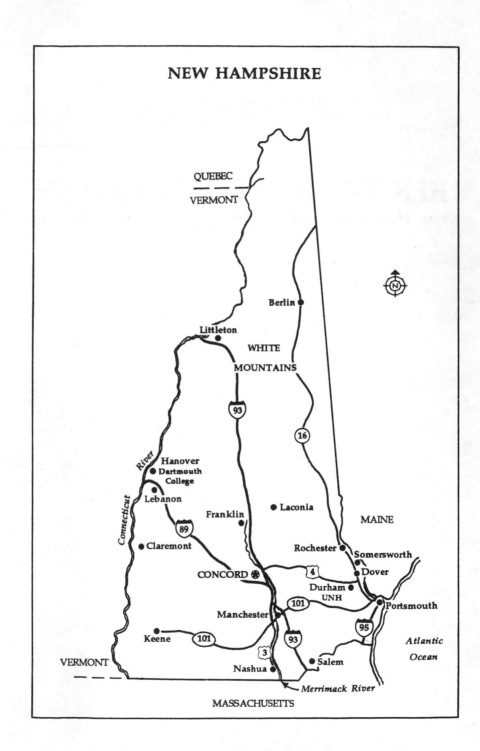

NEW HAMPSHIRE

QUEBEC
VERMONT

Berlin

Littleton

WHITE
MOUNTAINS

93

16

Connecticut River

Hanover
Dartmouth
College

Lebanon

Franklin

Laconia

MAINE

89

Claremont

Rochester

Somersworth

4

Dover

CONCORD

Durham
UNH

Portsmouth

101

Manchester

95

Keene

101

3

93

Nashua

Salem

Atlantic
Ocean

VERMONT

Merrimack River

MASSACHUSETTS

FIRST IN THE NATION
New Hampshire and the Premier Presidential Primary

Charles Brereton

Foreword by Mark Shields

Peter E. Randall
PUBLISHER

PORTSMOUTH

1987

To my mother and stepfather

© 1987 Charles Brereton
Printed in the United States of America
ISBN 0-914339-20-6

Peter E. Randall Publisher
Box 4726, Portsmouth NH   03801

The author gratefully acknowledges permission for the use of material from the following:

Theodore H. White, excerpted from The Making of the President 1964. *© 1965 by Theodore H. White. Reprinted with permission from Atheneum Publishers.*

Gary Warren Hart, excerpted from Right from the Start: A Chronicle of the McGovern Campaign. *© 1973 by Gary Warren Hart. Reprinted with permission of Times Books, a division of Random House Inc.*

Library of Congress Cataloging-in-Publication Data

Brereton, Charles
     First in the nation : New Hampshire and the premier presidential
primary / Charles Brereton : foreword by Mark Shields.
          p.   cm.
     Bibliography: p.
     Includes index.
     ISBN 0-914339-20-6
     1. Primaries--New Hampshire.   2. Presidents--United States-
-Election.   3. United States--Politics and government--1945-
I. Title
JK2075.N42B72 1987
324.5'4--dc19   87-28478
                                                                CIP

If you want to see the beginning of it, you have to go where the snow is deep and the people are few and only a fool or a politician would expect to see the beginning of anything important. The custom, then, is to fly from Washington to Boston and, in Boston, to rent a car and seek out the road that follows the Merrimack River due north into the snowy hills and unreality.

That way lie the beauty and the gentle madness of New Hampshire in the winter of its presidential primary.

Charles McDowell Jr.
from *Campaign Fever*

Also by Charles Brereton

First Step to the White House (1979)
New Hampshire Notables (1986)

Contents

Foreword

NOT EVERYBODY LOVES New Hampshire and its influential first-in-the-nation presidential primary. According to New England's most popular columnist, *The Boston Globe's* Mike Barnicle, New Hampshire residents are so backward and sluggish that it takes them two hours to watch "Sixty Minutes." The egocentric self-importance of the New Hampshire voter is regularly lampooned in the latest edition of the story about the taciturn farmer who is asked by the out-of-state reporter his opinion of Candidate Rockefeller/McCarthy/Muskie/Ford, etc. In his best Pepperidge Farm delivery, the farmer answers: "Don't know; I only met him twice."

This persistent criticism of New Hampshire contains more than a trace of envy, which is not entirely irrational. After all, in determining among all the willing national candidates who will eventually become president of the United States, no other state can approach New Hampshire in clout. In our presidential politics where change is the only permanent reality, New Hampshire endures as the reliable constant. Every four years, New Hampshire's primary makes the state the center of the political universe. And every four years, the New Hampshire primary responds to all that attention by making a president. Every one of the winners of the last nine presidential elections began that political year by winning the New Hampshire primary.

There is a historical imperative to this record: To understand American presidential politics, you must begin with an appreciation, and preferably an understanding, of New Hampshire and its role. With the special affection of an adopted son, Charles Brereton understands New Hampshire, its people and, yes, its peculiarities. With a knowledge of primary politics second to none, Brereton writes movingly about New Hampshire, even shattering a few stereotypes along the way.

Consider, for starters, the relative importance of California and New Hampshire in presidential campaigns. In the nominating contest where the field is narrowed from more than a dozen hopefuls down to the two nominees, one of whom will be the next president, New Hampshire matters a lot and California hardly at all.

True, if California were an independent nation it would have the sixth largest gross national product in the world; California does have a population larger than either East Germany or Canada. But in presidential pre-convention politics, California can usually be safely ignored. Consider these facts: In 1976 when outsider Jimmy Carter won New Hampshire and the White House, the California primary was won by a margin of 1.2 million votes by the state's governor, Jerry Brown. That same day Ronald Reagan, who lost the nomination to Gerald Ford, won the California primary. In 1980, President Jimmy Carter turned back Edward Kennedy's challenge in New Hampshire and at the New York convention, but Kennedy carried the California primary just as Gary Hart did on his way to a second-place finish at the 1984 convention. Of course, by November, California with one-sixth of the electoral votes needed to win the White House becomes a Critical Battleground. But by then the nation's choice is limited to just two.

The case against New Hampshire's wielding such disproportionate influence is based on more than envy. It is a small state geographically remote without either a large city or substantial minority population. Not even the state's most chauvinistic fans (in whose ranks reside Charles Brereton) would argue that New Hampshire is representative of the nation. It has consistently been more white, a lot more Republican and, in recent years, a lot more prosperous than the country, often boasting the nation's lowest unemployment rate. In terms of population growth, New Hampshire is a Snow Belt state with a Sun Belt-style expansion.

The extraordinary influence of New Hampshire on nomination politics is a joint product of the calendar and an essentially unreported press conspiracy. First, the calendar. Because of the 22nd amendment to the Constitution which limits a president to two terms, every politician in shoe-leather knew that the 1988 race would be wide-open, the first since 1960 without an incumbent in either party. That's why in September of 1985 at the Michigan Republican convention, the fledgling Bush, Dole and Kemp campaigns were all in attendance. Since then, we have had straw polls and national surveys to take the temperature of the electorate. And finally after all the speculation and the machinations, real voters go into a polling place and make a decision. No more theorizing and temporizing, New Hampshire voters speak and, at long last, the political reporters have results to report. All the fabricated, synthetic, straw polls are consigned to the rubbish; an authentic election has been held. New Hampshire is the real Big Apple; if a candidate can't make it there, then he almost certainly won't be around to make it anywhere.

The press conspiracy which reinforces New Hampshire's primary is not sinister, but it is real. New Hampshire, most political reporters would admit, is fun. Only a hour and a half from Boston, two thirds of New Hamphire's population live in the southern half of the state. Beyond convenience, there are pleasant familiarity and some predictability. The Sheraton Wayfarer in Bedford is the press and political command post and a candidate's schedule seldom travels more than a couple of hours from Bedford. It is a great place to catch up on old friends from earlier campaigns, to have a cup of anything, and swap a lie or two. Among the figures from earlier campaigns are New Hampshire former chief executives. No state's ex-governors are wooed so fervently by presidential candidates. It was a major coup for challenger Ronald Reagan in 1976 to capture the support of former governor Hugh Gregg. But even with it, Reagan lost to Jerry Ford. Four years later, Hugh Gregg endorsed George Bush who, after an upset victory in the Iowa caucus, lost to Reagan in New Hampshire. The New Hampshire primary for out-of-office public figures is the political equivalent of baseball's designated hitter rule; it allows former stars to compete after their active playing days are over.

But the most persuasive argument for keeping New Hampshire first is a serious one. In New Hampshire, presidential candidates must campaign "retail," in a brand of person-to-person politics that requires candidates to answer real questions, some silly, from voters. There is something admirably democratic about a presidential candidate standing at a factory gate, pleading his case to blue-collar Americans who pack a lunch and punch a clock. In that democratic exchange, the candidates and maybe the country are the beneficiaries.

Because of its size, New Hampshire provides the underdog with his chance. Here, an underfinanced and undercovered long-shot, through stamina, determination and time, can "retail" the electorate. The underdog cannot simply be overwhelmed by the favorites' big media buys and swollen campaign treasuries. The same could be argued for any small state and there is probably a good argument for rotating that first-in-the-nation primary among the smallest states. But New Hampshire has it now and shows no sign of sharing it with anybody else. So New Hampshire in presidential politics is where for all the real contest begins and for many it ends.

None of us will probably ever know New Hampshire's political history as well as Charles Brereton. But by reading what he has so well written, we will begin to grasp some of the flavor and a lot of the national significance of the New Hampshire primary.

Mark Shields

Introduction

A BUMPER STICKER SEEN INFREQUENTLY in the Granite State proclaims "New Hampshire is the Center of the Universe." Many people snicker at the boast—but not the individuals who want to be president of the United States. Every four years at the outset of the presidential race, the national spotlight concentrates on this heavily forested, granite-strewn wedge of northern New England.

New Hampshire's first-in-the-nation primary is the initial direct expression by voters of their choice to occupy the Oval Office for the next four years. Although populated by just over a million residents–41st in the nation in size–New Hampshire is the key that unlocks the door to the presidential nomination and eventually to the White House.

Between 1916 and 1948 New Hampshire's voters could only choose delegates to the national conventions. But since the inception of a presidential preference poll in 1952, every winner of the presidency–Dwight Eisenhower, John Kennedy, Lyndon Johnson, Richard Nixon, Jimmy Carter and Ronald Reagan–began his march on Washington with a victory in the New Hampshire primary. In addition, the primary delivered a clear and concise message of "no confidence" for two incumbent presidents—Harry Truman in 1952 and Lyndon Johnson in 1968. Both men, beleaguered by a war in Southeast Asia and low public opinion ratings, announced they would retire just a few weeks after New Hampshire's decision.

The primary also turned long-shot Senators Estes Kefauver, Eugene McCarthy, George McGovern and Gary Hart into serious contenders after initial victories (Kefauver in 1952 and Hart in 1984) or stronger-than-expected showings (McCarthy in 1968 and McGovern in 1972). An outright or moral victory in New Hampshire has often helped to unleash an outpouring of media attention, contributions, endorsements and volunteer help in other states, fueling the vital momentum to sustain and expand a presidential nomination bid.

New Hampshire's prominence every four years has little to do with the size of the electorate. (Out of the millions of votes cast in the primaries each quadrennium, New Hampshire's contribution has averaged only 172,444 since 1952.) Rather, the significance of the New Hampshire determination can be traced to two factors. First, it is first. Second, it is probably the world's most extensively covered election relative to the number of votes cast.

If Utah, Idaho or South Dakota had been the starting gate for the presidency, the media might not have taken the same interest. The first primary is significant not simply because of its position on the calendar, but also due to the state's proximity to major media centers such as Boston, New York City and Washington, D.C. Television and radio networks, magazines, wire services and newspapers that cover American presidential campaigns have beaten a well-worn path to a place just a few hours away.

New Hampshire is an editor's dream: The snow-covered landscape reminiscent of the nation's roots; an antiquated though endearing citizen democracy called Town Meeting; the ethnic groups that add vitality to the mill towns along the state's rocky rivers; the rapidly growing economy of the southern tier, built upon high-tech industries. And reporters induce ubiquitous, tight-lipped Yankees to reluctantly roll off a "country quote" into the often-frosty air.

Critics of the pre-eminent primary contend the state is unrepresentative, that it is too conservative, small, rural and white to merit all the attention it reaps. The primary has drawn some caustic comments: "That deep, frozen, inconclusive, misleading carnival of political egotism"; "New England's oldest winter carnival"; "the tattle of jesters which we have come to believe is the pronouncement of kings"; "the state's private practical joke on the rest of the country"; and a "quadrennial coldwater fiesta to hook the tourist dollar."

The 1949 revision in the primary law placed the candidates on the ballot and catapulted New Hampshire into the world's spotlight. This change dovetailed with an improving air transportation system that enabled ambitious politicians to stalk votes. Equally important was the introduction of television into millions of homes, providing the medium by which candidates could bypass party machines. This new relationship contributed to the demise of political bosses and paved the way for non-political figures such as General Dwight Eisenhower to become president.

New Hampshire's small population checks the media's power, allowing the candidates to frame and deliver their messages directly to the voters—without the massive media filter that dominates the process in the most populous states. Not until 1978 did candidates for statewide office first use TV spots in their campaigns. Campaigning the old-fashioned way—via service clubs, schools, community forums and factory gates—may appear to be too frivolous for those who seek the leadership of the Free World, but such techniques present opportunities for the voters to directly size up the aspirants. The primary also provides a level playing field for all the hopefuls. The outcome of the vote is not necessarily favorable to the candidate with the largest campaign war chest.

Critics allege that New Hampshire is unrepresentative of the nation and should not be permitted to have the first direct judgment of its presidents. The state has few minority voters, but the accusation of non-representativeness can be turned on its head: What state in the nation *is* representative?

We might conclude that, due to its vast size, California is the most representative state. However, could we reach the conclusion that, if California and not New Hampshire were at the front of the presidential primaries, the nomination process would prove more idyllic?

The New Hampshire primary represents, along with the Iowa caucus, the best opportunity for candidates to venture outside the major media centers and the Washington Beltway. Candidates campaign in direct contact with the citizenry, not only in TV studios, airport tarmac press conferences and rallies, and fundraising parties patronized by America's wealthy elite who bankroll presidential campaigning. The voters gain an opportunity to learn about the candidates, and the candidates to learn about those they hope to govern.

The record of New Hampshire is one of success, and perhaps too much of it. Its unique ability to attract the candidates and the media has given rise to so many usurpers that the primary process has been "New Hampshirized": other states have shifted away from caucuses and conventions to primaries, especially primaries held in early March.

The presence of too many primaries forces the political parties to address the problems of the length, cost and debilitating effects of the nomination system. Some would argue that a primary in every state on a single day is the democratic and progressive ideal. Yet such an election would not enhance the democratic process. The expenditures to mount a national campaign would be enormous—and viable candidacies would be a select few.

New Hampshire has managed to develop precedents and a common law concerning the primary. The state is small enough in population and geographic area that the populace has a chance to meet and hear all the candidates several times. This opportunity for comparison shopping, as it were, does not exist in the mega-states of the nation. It surely would not exist if a national or series of regional primaries were in place.

Undoubtedly the media play a significant role in the New Hampshire vote, yet their presence is limited in contrast to what transpires in larger states. The media's role is subordinate—the candidates' fates are still determined in large measure by their direct exposure to the voters, and not what the media filter conveys.

Without question there is significant economic value to holding the first primary. Yet the initial primary in New Hampshire in 1916 was not structured to attract candidates; their names were not even on the ballot during the first 32 years of the primary. It was not an election enacted to draw television coverage, for television had not been invented. The success of the New Hampshire primary has been so profound it has made presidential primaries too common and hence campaigns have become too long, arduous and expensive.

Rather than create a national primary, the political parties should structure their rules to restore an equilibrium between primaries and caucuses. This change would strengthen the role of the parties and reduce the power of the media. It would behoove the Congress of the United States to enact legislation mandating free television time for presidential and congressional candidates to alleviate the most burdensome financial commitment candidates confront.

If a national primary were to replace New Hampshire's part in the nomination process, the long shots, the poorly financed, those lacking the anointment of powerful media, political, or business and labor organizations could be blocked from making a breakthrough into the national political consciousness. A national primary could set the nomination process back a hundred years. Are 19th-century political bosses who controlled and manipulated the nomination system to be replaced by a handful of 20th-century media moguls who can determine the outcome of a national primary?

Democracy means more than permitting every eligible citizen the right to vote. It should include some manner for those seeking the presidency to directly present themselves to some segment of the electorate. The New Hampshire primary provides such a forum.

1952
Vote Heard 'Round the World

IN THE EARLY MORNING HOURS of a September day in 1938, a hurricane originating in the West Indies was advancing off Cape Hatteras at 45 miles per hour. By mid-afternoon it became evident that the storm was going to slam full-force into New England. What followed was the most destructive storm ever to hit the area, leaving in its wake the greatest property damage that had occurred in a single storm anywhere in the world.

Along the coast, forty-foot storm waves swept everything away; winds up to and above a hundred miles an hour carried the destruction far inland. Torrential rains swelled rivers and streams, already rising from four straight days of downpour.

The sun rose the following morning to a cloudless sky. The devastation took with it more than 600 lives and decimated the property of an estimated 100,000 families. Economic loss totaled more than a quarter of a billion dollars.

The hurricane blew down billions of board feet of timber, while the leaf pulp turned houses green. Six hundred thousand acres of forest were a tangled mass of wreckage, providing a potential for disaster possibly worse than the storm itself. In some places the blown-down trees were piled to a height of thirty feet and more. Every rainless day that passed increased the flammability of broken branches, leaves, pine needles and trunks.

To arouse the public and the government to these dangers, the lumber industry embarked on a plan of action to salvage the fallen timber. A White Mountain lumberjack-turned-

1

executive in his late thirties named Sherman Adams soon came to the forefront of the drive.

Adams was small and lean, hardly fitting the image of a North Country lumberjack. What he lacked in physical attributes he more than compensated for in energy, tenacity, ambition and intelligence. By the time of the 1940 election, at the urging of some friends and fellow lumber company executives, Adams was elected to the state legislature. On re-election in 1942, he was unanimously selected speaker of the House. His rapid climb up the political ladder continued in 1944, when he was elected to the United States Congress from the state's Second (western) District.

Both Adams and his wife Rachel disliked Washington, and he was frustrated with the slow pace of Congress. He returned to New Hampshire after just one term and sought the Republican nomination for governor, but lost in the primary by a scant 185 votes to the incumbent.

After a two-year hiatus from politics, Adams won the 1948 gubernatorial nomination without significant opposition, but the general election proved to be another matter.

The outgoing Republican administration was embroiled in a scandal. One week prior to the vote a grand jury handed down indictments against the state comptroller and a contractor, charging them with 123 counts of attempting to defraud the state of New Hampshire and obtaining money under false pretenses.

Although a substantial embarrassment to the outgoing Republican administration, the scandal had no connection with candidate Adams. He beat his opponent, a Dartmouth College history professor, by 11,000 votes, a narrow margin in a state that the Republicans had dominated since the days of Abraham Lincoln. In spite of a disregard for public relations (the hallmark of his career) Adams was re-elected in 1950 by more than twice the margin of his first victory.

One piece of legislation signed by the former lumberjack would have ramifications for his own career and the role his state would play for years to come in presidential politics: the 1949 law to change the way the Granite State conducted its first-in-the-nation presidential primary.

Until 1878 New Hampshire conducted its state elections annually on Town Meeting day, the second Tuesday in March. After the biennial election was implemented the date was shifted to November. Until that change was made, the yearly March returns from the state were closely monitored by the nation's press, since they were the first partisan vote and were regarded as an important index of popular feeling. Reporters from a number of metropolitan papers wrote numerous accounts of the spirited campaigns. During the Civil War, when President Lincoln needed public approval of his conduct of the war, the endorsements from the North Country were watched with great interest in Washington.

The development of the New Hampshire presidential primary traces its roots to the reform efforts that swept the state at the beginning of the 20th century. At the time the political system was dominated by the Republican Party, which in turn was controlled by the Boston and Maine Railroad. Their dominance centered on the nominating convention, which featured a device guaranteeing that the wish of the convention was also the wish of the B & M: the proxy.

At the infamous 1906 Republican state convention, the noted author Winston Churchill sought the gubernatorial nomination. His progressive supporters ran into the B & M machine and the proxies they had obtained from delegates by gifts, outright purchase, barter or exchange. (One historian wrote that proxies "were treated like mutual tickets at a Cuban horserace.") The resulting outrage soon led to the banning of the proxy and the passes the railroad distributed to its political supplicants.

The final blow to the power of the B & M was the institution of the open primary, first enacted for the 1910 state election. Robert P. Bass, elected governor that year, had led the fight in 1909 for the new system of popular vote by the people to nominate candidates.

The Bass administration, although noted for its progressive reforms, failed in 1911 to expand the primary law to include election of delegates to the national conventions by a vote of the people. Notorious conventions were still dominated by the B & M and its corporate allies.

By 1913 the Bull Moose split among the Republicans the previous November placed the Democrats in control of state government. The new primary law was enacted with virtually no opposition. It was originally scheduled for the third Tuesday in May of 1916, a date late enough to allow the political situation to develop. But in the legislature's 1915 session, someone with an eye for the dollar calculated that if the date were moved up to coincide with Town Meeting day it would be necessary to hold

one less election in a presidential year. Yankee frugality caused
the Granite State to alight on the second Tuesday in March for
its primary.

In 1916 the primary followed Indiana's by a week and
was the same day as Minnesota's. After that it was always first,
but between 1916 and 1948 the election was hardly noteworthy.
The nature of running for the presidency had not developed into
today's four-year, carefully choreographed, multimillion-dollar
mass-media production. Even if that had been the case, New
Hampshire's original primary law was in a sense only "half a
primary." The electorate could not directly choose whom they
wanted in the Oval Office. Their choice was restricted to delegate
hopefuls—essentially prominent state politicians who ran either
pledged to a candidate or uncommitted. The early primary was
nothing more than a popularity contest for politicians competing
for a seat on the floor of the national conventions. The voter
would have to wait until 1952 for a full choice.

In the wake of cries of protest by the press and politicians
that the 1948 delegate fight between Dewey and Stassen partisans had proved inconclusive, the 1949 legislature passed a law
instituting the "beauty contest" provision. A candidate or
would-be candidate could add his name to the ballot if a proper
number of voter signatures were secured, and it would remain
there unless a disclaimer was filed with the secretary of state by
the candidate.

The 1949 revision included one other change. Delegate
candidates would be allowed to compete in the category
"favorable" without the consent of the candidate, adding more
flexibility and enabling the voter to discern a potential delegate's
inclinations beyond the unpledged slate.

The seemingly insignificant change of tacking on a beauty
contest would bring another hurricane to New Hampshire in
1952—this time a political storm, once again finding the ambitious and well-positioned Sherman Adams standing in its path.

Until he was thrust upon the world scene by World War
II, the career of Dwight D. Eisenhower largely followed a path
from one drowsy Army post to another. But overnight he was no
longer a professional soldier in a time of peace, but the recipient
of an authority and prominence which have been delegated to few
others in history.

The prospect of the presidency was first seriously mentioned to him by a West Coast journalist named Virgil Pinkley in

1943. The Eisenhower response was direct: "Virgil, you've been standing out in the sun too long." In 1944 the gossip back home had President Franklin Roosevelt selecting Eisenhower as his running mate in the event the Republicans nominated General Douglas MacArthur. While attending the 1945 Potsdam conference, President Harry Truman reportedly told him, "General, there is nothing that you may want that I won't try to help you get. That definitely and specifically includes the presidency in 1948."

Truman, as it turned out, had another plan that year. However, when the 1948 primary season commenced, a Draft Eisenhower boomlet started in New Hampshire. A slate of delegates pledged on his behalf was to be filed, and the then-publisher of the *Manchester Union Leader*, Leonard Finder, loudly beat the drums trying to stir up support. He got an unequivocal no, and the general-turned-Columbia-University-president played no role in the 1948 election, not even bothering to vote.

In February of 1951, at President Truman's request, Eisenhower left Columbia and returned to active duty as the head of NATO forces in Europe. At his Paris post, the stream of president-makers that had started at Columbia continued unabated. Massachusetts Senator Henry Cabot Lodge, who had first discussed the idea of Eisenhower running for president in 1950, broached the subject again in July. Even the freshman senator from California, Richard Nixon, stopped by for a half hour chat while in Europe. Two New Hampshire politicians also made the pilgrimage: Senator Styles Bridges and Congressman Norris Cotton, who had succeeded Sherman Adams.

Another visitor to Paris that summer of 1951 was Robert Burroughs of Manchester, a former Republican National Committeeman. An insurance company executive and designer of pension plans for a number of large East Coast corporations, Burroughs had cut his teeth on New Hampshire politics while chauffeuring his father in a Cadillac convertible during a successful congressional campaign in 1917. Although he had worked on pension reform legislation with Republican Senator Robert Taft of Ohio—a likely candidate in 1952—Burroughs shared the feeling of many Republicans that Taft could not win. After the 1948 Dewey debacle, the Republicans had been locked out of the White House for two decades; they desperately wanted a winner—and General Eisenhower, not Taft, looked like the man.

Burroughs wrote to Eisenhower requesting an interview when he made a vacation trip to Scotland. Eisenhower informed him that he would be wasting his time, but agreed to a meeting on August 1st. One of the general's top aides, Major General Wilton B. Persons—an acquaintance of Burroughs—informed him that he was not the first to approach the general about running for the presidency. "They've come from both parties and none of them have managed to persuade him...their arguments just haven't been good enough. Some of them have tried to push him too hard," Persons related to the New Hampshire visitor. In his very Southern manner, he added, "The general don't take shovin'."

At their meeting on August 1st, Burroughs discovered Eisenhower was quite agitated about a scandal involving cheating among West Point cadets. It struck close to home, for Eisenhower was a former West Pointer. Greatly disturbed that any cadet would violate the honor system, Eisenhower discussed the scandal throughout the hour allotted to Burroughs who found no opportunity to talk about the presidential campaign.

However, in their extended meeting Burroughs cleverly played incidents of corruption in the Truman administration off the West Point scandal. In the most publicized incidents, government officials were given gifts of mink coats and freezers by corporations in hopes of favorable treatment on government contracts. Burroughs asked Eisenhower if, since Truman was the commander in chief, was not the present dishonesty of those cadets related to the climate of corruption emanating from the capital? If Eisenhower were president, Burroughs asked, wouldn't he then be in a position of leadership to clean up the mess in Washington—to create a climate in which future scandals might be avoided?

The arguments impressed Eisenhower, who later told Burroughs: "Those were the first reasons which were presented to me by anyone who came to see me with the same purpose you had, the first ones that appealed to me at all."

However, the general then launched into a series of reasons why he did not want to run. For years he lacked a normal home life. During the war there were periods when he did not see his wife or son for months. The family did not appreciate the public limelight, and it certainly would not be reduced if he became president. He told Burroughs, "When I get back to the apartment I will ask my wife whether she would like to go down to the dining room for dinner or have it sent up to the apartment. Probably she will say, 'I just can't face another reporter with a notebook or any more photographers with those flashbulbs, so let's have dinner sent up here and have a quiet evening by ourselves.'"

At the end of the interview Burroughs reminded Eisenhower that, because of his war record and his national popularity, he might be the only person in a position to become president who could alleviate the corruption in Washington. The general agreed to seriously consider adding his name to those in the New Hampshire primary.   However, there was no doubt about the general's reluctance to actively seek the nomination— in the embryonic stages of the campaign, the office would truly have to seek the man.

On October 16, 1951, at a press conference attended by more than 200 reporters and photographers, Senator Robert Taft announced his candidacy for the Republican nomination for president; it would be his third attempt. Now in his early sixties, and with bitter defeats for the party nomination by Wendell Willkie in 1940 and New York Governor Thomas Dewey in 1948 behind him, this would be his final attempt to follow in the footsteps of his father, who had been elected the 26th President in 1908.

In the fall of 1951 Senator Henry Cabot Lodge began to pull together the initial elements of the national Eisenhower organization. The plan called for Eisenhower's announcement from Paris by January that he would be amenable to a genuine draft, and he would return to campaign for the nomination by the end of March or beginning of April. An office was opened in Washington with the main responsibility of maintaining contact with the "Eisenhower for President" clubs then mushrooming all over the country.

After months of indecision, Governor Sherman Adams announced on September 30th that he was supporting General Eisenhower. He was "almost sure" that the general would allow his name to go on the New Hampshire ballot.

(When asked why he threw his support to Eisenhower, Adams said, "I became rather intrigued with the idea of a person who actually wasn't a politician, whose party wasn't even a matter of record and who had no intention or desire to become president, but who had more qualifications perhaps than any other American for that particular job.")

In the hope of deciphering the general's still unknown party affiliation, Adams had the New Hampshire attorney general write to the county clerk in Abilene, Kansas, to try to discover his political identity from the voter list in Eisenhower's home town. That settled nothing, for the clerk parsimoniously wrote back on the bottom of the original inquiry that the general "has never voted in this county as far as I know..." and that, "I don't think he has any politics."

At a November meeting arranged by Governor Dewey, Lodge was selected campaign manager. He accepted with reluctance, for he faced re-election to the Senate in 1952. (Gearing up to oppose the incumbent was youthful three-term Massachusetts Congressman John F. Kennedy, who had already stumped in 311 towns and cities in the Bay State, confidently laying the groundwork for one of the major upsets in a turbulent political year.)

With the New Hampshire filing period for candidates approaching, Lodge and Adams had to secure some assurance that Eisenhower would allow his name to be put on the ballot so that they would not be left out on a limb, to the peril of their political careers. On the day after Christmas, William A. Robinson, an executive with and later publisher of the *New York Herald Tribune*, returned from Paris, where he had spent Christmas day with the Eisenhowers. His message from the general: he would not repudiate having his name entered in the New Hampshire Republican primary; Army regulations kept him from political activity of any kind; he would return in June; and upon his return he would not lift a finger for the nomination.

Lodge was already in a panic over the general's absence from the political front. An examination of the correspondence in the Eisenhower Library in Abilene, Kansas, shows just how uncertain Lodge had become about attempts to win the Republican nomination from a military position in Paris. On December 3rd, in a letter written from his home in Beverly, Massachusetts, Lodge invited the general to attend a Republican Party conclave to be held in San Francisco on January 17th, 18th and 19th. In extending the invitation he wrote that it would "be the greatest single opportunity to meet party leaders. There will be nothing equal to it until the convention in Chicago in July." Lodge was quite blunt about the prospects of the draft: "People want to know what you think from your own lips and no amount of speaking by Senator Duff or myself or by anyone else can possibly take the place of you. The talk about a draft is no good any more."

On Sunday morning, January 6th, at a press conference in Washington timed for maximum impact on the following day's newspapers, Lodge released a letter he had written to Governor Adams asking him to place the general's name on the New Hampshire ballot. Lodge said Eisenhower had "personally assured me" that he was a Republican and he had also "assured many people he would accept the nomination."

Lodge was certain his statement would not be repudiated, and he referred reporters to call Eisenhower's Paris headquarters for confirmation—a bold gamble designed to force the matter.

The general wanted to be spared the problems and burdens of the approaching campaign. He wanted to concentrate his energy on settling the rivalries and nationalistic differences among the 12 NATO sovereignties he was trying to lead. He also wanted to keep a line drawn between being a draftable public figure and an actual candidate. He had named retired General Lucius Clay as his sole liaison between himself and the politicians trying to draft him. The Lodge press conference had done considerable damage to the distinction Eisenhower was trying to maintain, and Clay told Herbert S. Parmet, author of *Eisenhower and the American Crusades*, (Macmillan, 1972), that the general was so furious he came close to issuing a statement of withdrawal from the New Hampshire primary.

That winter no one knew the potential Eisenhower had as a national leader. It was certain, though, that New Hampshire would be a good place to launch the draft movement. But, according to one journalistic account, Eisenhower harbored the hope that he would be in a position to accept the nomination of one party only because the other party proffered it also (a modern-day George Washington). That hope would never be fulfilled. The looming presence of Robert Taft in 1952 would guarantee that the famous general would need to scramble for the nomination just like any other candidate.

Nineteen fifty-two was to be a rarity in primary politics, for a contest on both sides within New Hampshire was developing. The coonskin-capped senator from Tennessee, Estes Kefauver, fresh from his well-publicized chairmanship of the Senate Special Committee to Investigate Interstate Crime, had decided to start his challenge to President Truman in the Granite State. But he was given no chance of success; he was considered an inconsequential side show—not much different from the Democratic Party in New Hampshire as a whole at that time.

Robert Taft's decision on entering the 1952 first-in-the-nation primary was a matter of consternation as he carefully weighed the arguments for and against his entry. Although it was a move he regretted after his defeat, his entry placed a stamp of legitimacy on the primary itself. It also served as the first battleground of a fight for the Republican nomination which had no equal in length or intensity since the "Rough Rider," Teddy Roosevelt, failed to deny William Howard Taft the nomination he had handed over a quadrennium before.

In his two previous attempts at the presidency, Senator Taft had studiously avoided every primary he could. The cold, forced harshness of his speaking voice and his stiff attitude failed to generate warmth. All his public life he had struggled with his introverted nature, and as a speaker he always failed to use the staples of American political oratory to win converts to his cause. He expected that his long years of legislative leadership would win over the common man; but, more often than not, the voters were interested in not what a candidate said or did, but how he said it or what he promised to do.

One biographer noted that Taft's critics "enjoyed describing him as a chemistry professor, a small-town bank president, possibly a Sunday school superintendent or vestryman. He seemed unapproachable—a cartoonist's dream, a party leader's despair." Finally, there was the baggage of Taft's principles which were sincere but more suited for the twenties, not for the tumultuous and drastically changing forties and fifties—times when he sought to lead an emerging and then dominant world power.

The primaries—exhaustive, wide open, expensive and unwieldy—were not made for the ultimate insider, the man who had spent so many hours marshalling his arguments and conservative cohorts on the Senate floor in opposition to the New and Fair Deals. The disparity between an open primary and the caucus/convention system was as wide as the difference between a board of directors meeting and a labor union rally at the front gate of the same factory. Taft, the scion of an American political dynasty that rivaled the Rockefellers and Kennedys in the 20th century, knew where his destiny lay.

However, there was one characteristic he adequately possessed, a prerequisite for the primary trail—combativeness. It was an ingredient that helped him to minimize in his mind the advantages the Eisenhower forces enjoyed in New Hampshire: the support of Governor Adams and much of the top echelon of the party; an eastern seaboard state with an international border, a proximity not conducive to Taft's isolationist sentiments; and a state just a brief plane ride away from the major media centers of the East Coast with publications and publishers hostile to the Taft candidacy.

Through the early part of January, Taft held fast and resisted the pressure to place his name on the ballot, preferring to wait for a Midwestern contest. But his East Coast campaign manager consulted with the senator's supporters and encouraged Taft to put his name on the preference poll. The *Manchester Union Leader*, by then in the grip of publisher William Loeb, had begun to trumpet Taft's candidacy, and the anti-Adams forces, eager to hand the acerbic governor a setback on March 11th, lobbied for Taft, too.[1]

Finally, on the day before the close of filing, Taft acceded to entering the beauty contest. The decision was hailed by his campaign manager as "absolute fearlessness...Bob Taft has never run from a fight, and, even though he has the great disadvantage of running in a state that has been carefully selected as the first and most secure arena for General Eisenhower, he shows no hesitancy."

---

[1] The Eisenhower-Taft primary contest was to a certain extent a continuation of the bitter Charles Tobey-Wesley Powell Senate GOP nomination fray in 1950. Tobey, seeking a third term, barely defeated Wesley Powell, a former aide to Senator Styles Bridges. Powell, an ardent conservative and anti-Communist as well as one of the most controversial figures to grace the northern New England landscape, is given credit by some for encouraging Taft to enter the primary. He met with Taft in Washington in early January, but he insisted in an interview for this book that his purpose was not to egg Taft on, but actually to warn him not to expect any help from his colleague in the Senate, Styles Bridges. Taft had hopes that Bridges would assist him, if not with an outright endorsement, at least with some subterranean assistance. Many of Bridges' supporters backed Taft, but the senior senator maintained his declared neutrality throughout. One of his former aides recalled his saying at the time: "Why should I get involved—either one has to come and do business with me."

Taft's decision was based on the premise, "I thought we had everything to gain and nothing to lose." An upset victory in the beauty contest could have been a devastating blow to the fledgling Eisenhower draft, possibly destroying it altogether. A narrow loss for the general in such hostile territory could be construed as a "moral" victory, since he was not given much of a chance at the outset.

Throughout the month of February a campaign by surrogates was waged from one end of the state to the other. A group of prominent congressmen, senators and governors from around the nation scurried about in support of the absentee general. The Taft forces were dependent on more home-grown talent, attempting to hold public attention with rallies and debates engaging the Eisenhower partisans. But the final week Taft took a bold gamble by embarking on a three-day, 28-city tour over 500 miles of the snow-covered state.

While Estes Kefauver wandered about virtually unnoticed, Taft's tour created a minor sensation and provided a break in the long winter monotony. With a fresh six-inch snowfall covering the ground, Taft kicked off the tour with a press conference in Manchester. Accompanied by two busloads of reporters, the caravan moved its way up the Merrimack River Valley, stopping at the capital city of Concord and a series of dilapidated mill towns. By mid-afternoon the procession swung northeast to the Lakes Region. Taft did his best to avoid or tolerate the tomfoolery that afflicts a presidential hopeful at virtually every stop. At one point that first day he refused to don an Indian headdress for the photographers.

The farther north he moved, the more strident became his attacks on the Truman administration and its flaws—the corruption, alleged subversion, shortages, the Korean war, labor strife and rising prices and taxes—Taft made it clear he intended to "shun a me-too campaign which won't even convert a handful of New Dealers. We cannot slip into office behind a curtain of generalities. We can only win by a presentation of definite issues which will arouse the enthusiasm of our fellow Republican workers."

Taft was not mincing his words or trimming his sails. Time and again he promised to wage a fighting campaign, and in the city of Claremont he pledged to "liquidate" the secretary of state, Dean Acheson.

At the concluding rally of the second day in Manchester, the *Union Leader* reported that 1500 people listened as:

> Taft then lashed out with both fists at Ike, for the first time when he inquired if General Eisenhower would be willing to "make an all-out attack upon the administration, of which he has been a part, for the disastrous results (of its foreign policy), the loss of China and the 100,000 American casualties in Korea?" Turning to corruption in government, Taft asked if General "Ike", in view of his close association with the present and previous Democratic administrations, and the constant advancement "he has received from them," would feel inclined to "present that issue in the perspective and with the force it deserves."

The Taft tour was not entirely comprised of hard-hitting orations against his major opponent (who remained in Paris, aloof from the tussle) or attacks on the Truman administration. The trip put his personality on display, and he was much the loser for it.

The 1952 primary found the owner and editor of the *Peterborough Tanscript*, Paul Cummings Jr., in the Taft camp—in spite of the fact much of his family favored Eisenhower, including his cousin, the largest customer in his printing plant. Peterborough had been a hotbed of Eisenhower activity, and once Cummings heard about Taft's plans to stump the state, he thought he had found the one thing the Eisenhower adherents could not do—"Let's produce the body and bring the candidate to town. We'll really show this Ike crowd."

So late in the second grueling day of Taft's tour during the final weekend before the vote, the Ohio senator and his entourage pulled up in front of Peterborough's town hall. A crowd of almost 300 people greeted him. Cummings hoped his candidate would take the time to make contact. It was not to be, as he wrote in an editorial in the next edition of the *Transcript*:

> Taft's stiffness, and lack of ability to unbend was never more evident than here. Though advised of the strong pro-Eisenhower conditions existing in Peterborough, he still came up with a standardized five-minute talk, a quick rush for his car and on to Milford. If he'd taken the eight to ten minutes he spent in town to speak briefly, shake

some hands, let the voters get a feel of him, and sign autographs for the eager youngsters (and oldsters) whom he brushed by with a send-them-to-my-office remark, he might have won some friends and influenced some people....

Cummings conceded, "It just deflated the Taft drive here." Taft lost the town 489-273.

Another reporter observed an incident confirming that Taft's warmth was a intense as the heat of a mid-February snowstorm. Taking a break from campaigning, the senator stopped by a coffee shop. The waitresses gathered around him to shake his hand and exchange pleasantries, a campaign ritual. Oblivious to them, he curtly ordered, "Coffee, please, and make it hot." All the waitresses, the reporter claimed, later voted for the general with the warm smile and famous war record. Taft was to learn, as so many others would in subsequent New Hampshire primaries, that it was not enough to make an appearance and expound on one's views—you had to make "contact" also.

However, the Ohio senator was present, at least—not in lofty isolation across the Atlantic. He was talking issues not relying on his supporters to recycle comments from years past, as the Ike partisans had to do. He was discussing the state of the economy, a significant concern in a state witnessing the closing of its textile mills, which were moving South. And he was asking where the general stood on controversial issues, such as the Taft-Hartley Labor Relations Act and the nation's China policy. James Reston, writing in *The New York Times,* noted:

> In short, while Messrs. Lodge, Adams and Stassen can ask questions of Mr. Taft, the Ohio senator is here to answer them. But when Mr. Taft asks them questions about what Ike thinks about this and that, they are forced on too many occasions to reply that they "think" the general believes thus and so, and they "understand" he told a visitor or wrote a letter in which he stated his views.

Taft's tour had wiped the grin off the faces of the Eisenhower backers, and all the momentum was moving in "Mr. Republican's" direction. The experts predicted a tight race. Lodge felt the Draft Ike crusade had gone into its worst tailspin. Their earlier incautious remarks that the state was "in the bag" allowed Taft to claim a moral victory of sorts if he collected even one delegate, and an actual victory if he carried away a few more, even less than a majority. The great "expectations game" that would cause such consternation in many a New Hampshire primary henceforth was underway. To try to turn the tables psychologically on Taft, Lodge proclaimed in a visit to the state that an Ike defeat would not be a disaster, and Adams commented that, in light of Taft's personal campaigning, it would be a "political miracle" if Eisenhower managed to win.

The atmosphere that election year was saturated with foreign affairs: the war in Korea, the growing tensions with the Soviet Union, and the role that America would play in the world just past the mid-point of the 20th century. Taft was vulnerable in this area, chiefly because of his isolationist sentiments and sometimes-contradictory views on meeting the Communist challenge. He also possessed a litany of Senate votes that had opposed moves preparing the country for World War II. This record, little known then to the average New Hampshire Republican, would be targeted by the Eisenhower forces to halt Taft's momentum.

The former three-term governor of Minnesota, Harold Stassen, was on the preference poll ballot, in the second of his numerous attempts for the Republican presidential nomination. Due to his internationalist leanings, he was expected to draw votes from Eisenhower, just as the delegates running favorable to General Douglas MacArthur were likely to drain votes from the Taft slate. (MacArthur's name had been filed for the preference poll, but he withdrew it and urged his supporters to back Taft.) Stassen, on leave from his University of Pennsylvania presidency, was stumping the state; he soon began playing the role of inquisitor of Taft's foreign policy record, which included his 1949 votes against the North Atlantic Treaty Organization and the rebuilding of postwar Europe.

Adams took to the state's 12 radio stations and some of its newspapers to respond to Taft's criticism of the general's role at the Potsdam conference. Adams stated, "It was at Potsdam when General Eisenhower first criticized the foreign policy of the United States by emphatically stating that it was not necessary for the United States to make any concessions whatever to the Soviet Union to get them to go into war with Japan." Labeling Taft an isolationist, the governor added "The senator has made it clear that he has no real basic understanding of our obligations and responsibilities in the world today."

The nomination procedure is virtually uncontrolled by any federal regulation, and thus the chase for delegates is entirely within the province of every state, subject to legislative, party, and executive control and influence. Nineteen fifty-two would result in a series of bitter and prolonged delegate credential fights, mostly among Southern Republicans. In New Hampshire, the Taft camp raised allegations that Governor Adams was thwarting state law to benefit his candidate. The New Hampshire attorney general, an Adams appointee, had ruled that, while all the delegate candidates would be rotated alphabetically, the four names on the preference poll would not be, since the beauty contest was only advisory in nature. Thus, Taft's name would be listed last on every ballot, after Eisenhower, Stassen, and even an obscure St. Louis lawyer, William E. Schneider.

The Taft forces cried foul, and some independent observers contended that the ruling violated the spirit, if not the letter, of state law. Before Taft could effectively protest the decision, many of the 350,000 ballots had been shipped to the voting places around the state. Taft decided not to take legal action, since it would put the state to the added expense and trouble of printing new ballots if the courts ruled the initial batch illegal.

A flood of out-of-state pamphlets attacking Eisenhower poured into the state, adding more controversy to the already heated fight. One anti-Semitic tract, entitled "Special Eisenhower Edition," linked Eisenhower to "the revolutionary under-cover machine known to the FBI and the politically wise as the Anti-Defamation League of B'nai B'rith." The pamphlet also cited the general's friendship with former *Union Leader* publisher Leonard Finder, one of his original backers in the state, and raised the loaded question: "Is Eisenhower Jewish?" When the Taft group failed to disown some of the scurrilous material floating around the state, they were accused of condoning such tactics, even if they were not responsible for its production or distribution.[2]

[2] Since the primary was, up to that time, the most expensive election ever conducted in the state, charges of buying the primary eventually surfaced. After the vote the *Manchester Union Leader* alleged without substantiation that big Wall Street international banking houses and other out-of-state sources spent a quarter of a million dollars boosting Eisenhower for the primary. The most reliable sources estimate that Eisenhower spent $65,000, Taft $50,000.

The first returns came from two tiny villages that conducted their voting just past the stroke of midnight on March 11th. They proved inconclusive. The village of Waterville Valley held a midnight supper and cast all seven ballots for Eisenhower. The town of Millsfield was the next to report—Taft 4, Stassen 1, Eisenhower 0.

(In making arrangements to cover the midnight Waterville Valley vote, a wire service reporter called the telephone company and asked to have the line into the remote village tested and cleaned up. This simple request became garbled, and word spread that President Truman planned to come to the century-old Waterville Inn for an election-eve speech. In the ensuing excitement, every tree branch scraping the line for 10 miles through the White Mountain National Forest was cut away by telephone company personnel brought in from as far away as Keene. The president never showed, but the village enjoyed the best telephone service in its history. However, the residents were not enamored with their sudden notoriety and refused to hold another midnight election for years.)

As many New Hampshirites awoke on the morning of March 11th, they were greeted with rain, snow and sleet. One hundred thousand Republicans were expected to make the trek to the polls, starting the first turn of the wheel in presidential selection. Taft's spirits were high, set on the capture of four of the 14 delegates to lay the claim of a moral victory. His state campaign manager was even bolder—he was certain Taft would capture six delegates and win the preference poll outright by 5,000 votes.

The Eisenhower Special had been slowed, but the New Hampshire Republicans would soon place it back on track, full steam ahead.

The smaller, more rural and usually conservative areas are generally the first to tabulate their votes in the primary, and, as expected, Taft shot into an early lead as the returns started to filter in. Unexpectedly, however, he captured the vote in Manchester, considered an Eisenhower stronghold. Due to his own aggressive organization and the editorial support of the *Manchester Union Leader*, Taft captured 12 of the city's 14 wards.

The tenuous 500-vote lead Taft had compiled was wiped out as the first ward of the capital city of Concord reported in. From that point on the Eisenhower momentum proved unstoppable; by 2:00 a.m. the *Union Leader* called Ike the winner, and an hour later Taft's campaign manager threw in the towel. Taft had failed to capture even one of the 14 delegates, and was trounced in the beauty contest—46,661-35,838—losing all of the ten counties in the state and all but one of the 12 cities. Most surprising of all, Eisenhower carried 138 out of the 223 towns, which were supposedly Taft Country. True to style, Taft said of the results: "I am somewhat disappointed."[3]

As politicians and the media spent the next day assessing the returns, Eisenhower, returning from a trip to Germany, was met at Orly airfield in Paris by a small band of reporters. Regarding the primary results, the general commented, "I was naturally touched. More than that, I was deeply moved." Wrestling with his emotions, he looked across the airfield into the setting sun and said, "Any ordinary American would be if other Americans felt that way about him."

The New York Times, avidly pro-Eisenhower, was moved enough by the returns to print a full page of editorial comment from 43 newspapers around the country. The *Louisville Courier-Journal* noted, "One of the proudest of Taft's boasts ('I can win. I've never lost.') already is wasted away on the snowy air of New Hampshire."

But the Granite State victory alone would not secure the general's commitment to return to the United States. That would take a primary one week later—the so-called "Minnesota Miracle." Harold Stassen, that state's former governor, was the only major candidate listed on the ballot. He won the primary with 120,000 votes and most of the delegates. However, an unauthorized write-in for Eisenhower received 108,000 votes, almost overwhelming Stassen. These two primaries moved the general to send a letter to Truman asking permission to resign his NATO post. His request was granted on April 12th, effective June 1st.

After the premier primary, Governor Adams busily traveled the nation, addressing rallies on Eisenhower's behalf in Vermont, New Jersey, Massachusetts, New Mexico, Nevada,

---

[3] Harold Stassen drew 6,574 votes, MacArthur's unauthorized write-in 3,227. A total of 136,179 New Hampshirites turned out, almost double the number of the 1948 primary. Of the 96,507 Republicans voting, Eisenhower won a majority, 50.2%, to Taft's 38.6%. (See appendix for all primary results.)

Oregon and Montana. The standard Adams address included attacks on Taft's conservative credentials, especially his support of a public housing program to subsidize the construction of 810,000 housing units at the cost of several billion dollars; his support for subsidizing high school districts to the tune of $300 million a year—a measure "not calculated to preserve the rights of states in their own public education institutions," Adams charged; and backing of a bill for federal subsidies to state health programs that "offers a good introduction to socialized medicine." Adams argued that the Ohio senator "had contributed his share of sponsoring schemes which are pure economic experimentation and which water down states' rights."

In calling for the nomination of a man "who can win," Adams commented on a political pundit's observation that, in 1952, the Republicans had to decide whether it was more important to obtain "a workable peace in the world and security of the nation against Communist aggression, or, on the other hand, whether the great question is saving America from a system of soft socialism." Adams believed, "In naming a candidate we yield neither objective this year."

Adams closed his speeches with a flourish:

> Eisenhower did not campaign in New Hampshire. He will not campaign in Nevada. He is over there standing between you and the weapons of the Soviets. He is watching the Soviet submarines which threaten our coast with guided missiles and the Soviet planes waiting to cross Canada to drop atom bombs on our homes. He is watching the pulsating wickedness of a Communist system that keeps ten million slaves in captivity, that tears children from their deported mothers' arms, and whose clenched fist right now is poised to batter down the American home and Church of God.
>
> There is a vacant chair in many of your homes tonight, belonging to a boy away at camp or over in Germany, or maybe sleeping under one of the white crosses on Korea's Heartbreak Ridge. There will be more if we continue to *lose* the peace. That vacant chair by your fireside is the same vacant chair that is in this campaign. Both *your* sons and General Eisenhower cannot be here to speak for themselves because they are over there defending little children here, our town and city halls, our little

white meeting house, and all the things that are to us most precious.

Two days prior to the official opening of the Chicago convention in a sweltering July, Adams was selected by Lodge, Dewey, former General Lucius D. Clay and Herbert Brownell to be the floor manager of the Eisenhower forces. Although he had attended only one previous convention (in 1944), Adams proved a master at the back-breaking work needed to monitor closely the 17 assistant floor leaders and every significant floor vote. Eisenhower, in his suite at the Blackstone Hotel, was impressed with the no-nonsense job Adams performed, his coolness under fire and his incredible endurance.

After the general's nomination at the end of the first ballot, Adams participated in a meeting of 25 top party and Eisenhower leaders to select a running mate. At the meeting, they ratified a choice already made by Dewey and Lodge and concurred with by the general—the vice-presidential candidate would be the 39-year-old freshman senator from California, Richard M. Nixon.

The selection of Nixon was a classic case of ticket balancing. Young and from the West, Nixon balanced the older, Eastern nominee. His fervent efforts at ferreting out alleged Communists in government and his hard-hitting partisan campaigns endeared him to a constituency that badly needed to be incorporated under the Eisenhower banner—the Taft forces.

Adams, who was "on the verge of collapse," vacationed in Wyoming's Grand Tetons prior to returning to New Hampshire. On a mid-July morning, he received a call from Denver. It was Eisenhower asking him to serve as his right-hand man for the general election. Adams returned to the Granite State, secured a leave of absence as governor until the election, and assumed his post in Denver late in July. Adams had come far from obscurity in just over six months. He would go much farther in the next six years.

The presidential nomination process has undergone significant change since the days of the congressional party caucuses, which anointed the nominees in the first few decades of the 1800s. The party conventions, firmly established by the middle of the 19th century, were an improvement of sorts, but they too became a brokerage house between the state conventions (frequently boss-controlled) and the general election.

The tide of progressivism brought more reform to the nation than any other era, and the presidential primary was one of its most enduring accomplishments. The primaries were colorful and heated on occasion (witness the Taft—Roosevelt clash in 1912), invaluable for launching the presidential hopes of some (Franklin D. Roosevelt's delegate victory over Al Smith in the 1932 New Hampshire primary) or for destroying the nomination dream of others (Wendell Willkie's trouncing in Wisconsin in 1944 or Harold Stassen's setback by Tom Dewey in Oregon in 1948). Yet these were largely unconnected dramas, for the primaries would not develop a sustained significance and energy until after the middle of the 20th century.

The 1952 presidential election set a precedent of sorts, for a new era of politics was dawning—an era increasingly dominated by electronic media, more citizen participation, and a process made more mobile and flexible by an improved transportation system. The progressives' democratization of the nominating procedure underwent a revival of interest in 1952. Even though two decades would pass before a direct link between winning primaries and winning delegates would be completely forged, a pioneer needed to blaze the trail. For the Democrats that man would be the first-term senator from Tennessee, Carey Estes Kefauver.

Estes Kefauver, born in 1903 in the rolling eastern hills of Tennessee at the foot of the Great Smoky Mountains, was the son of the local hardware store owner. Educated in the local schools, Kefauver received a degree from the University of Tennessee in Knoxville in 1924 and a law degree from the Yale University Law School in 1927. That year he was admitted to the Tennessee bar. After joining a law firm in the city of Chattanooga, the young lawyer wrote a series of articles for the *Chattanooga News* on reforming the system of county government and changing the state's outdated constitution, which drew considerable attention in the community. Kefauver later acknowledged those articles helped launch him on the road to public service.

In 1938 Kefauver started a pattern that would dominate virtually all his election campaigns—he took on an entrenched politician, in this case a state senator, who was backed by the local machine. He barely lost—by 307 votes out of 15,000 cast. His growing reputation caught the eye of the state's governor, who appointed him commissioner of Finance and Taxation.

After four months, he resigned to run for the seat left vacant by the death of the congressman from the Third District. Backing Roosevelt's New Deal and the Tennessee Valley Authority, he won the seat, defeating a Republican isolationist.

During his nine years in Congress, Kefauver distinguished himself in two areas: modernizing of the congressional machinery and as the chairman of the subcommittee to investigate the economic concentration of big business. (Lobbyists who failed to relish Kefauver's searching reports of monopolistic practices paid him a compliment with the phrase: "In Kefauver we antitrust.")

In November of 1947 he announced his intention to run for the Senate, launching a campaign that stands as a classic example of one man's crusade to challenge an entrenched boss. Poorly financed, volunteer-supported, he managed to generate backing from unions, women's and Negro groups, and business and professional associations. All through the winter and spring Kefauver traveled the roads of the Volunteer State with his wife Nancy and a few aides. Twenty to thirty stops a day were scheduled, but—thanks to Kefauver's determination to stop wherever he could gather up a few voters to hear his pitch—the count usually doubled. His wife and aides noted thousands of names of the people he met, sending follow-up letters asking for their support on primary day. Yet all this work in such a large state failed to provide the momentum in a bitter three-way race that included an incumbent Democratic senator and a judge backed by Edward H. Crump, the boss who controlled the city of Memphis and the surrounding county.

Late in the campaign, while trying to tag Kefauver as a Communist, Boss Crump compared Kefauver to a "pet coon." Kefauver was able to turn the charge into a public relations coup of considerable proportions. He took to traveling with a caged raccoon and said, "I may be a pet coon, but I'll never be Mr. Crump's pet coon." The coon was later replaced with a coonskin cap, in which the candidate with the "Sunday smile that he can turn loose seven days a week" was photographed everywhere. The gimmick was as unsophisticated as it was popular and proved to be one of the most successful in American political history. Kefauver later wrote, "My own audiences grew with the fame of the coonskin cap. The coonskin cap merely dramatized a grim, determined campaign on the part of thousands of people to free themselves, once and for all, from one-man rule."

In the largest primary turnout in the history of the state up to that time, Kefauver won with more than 40% of the vote and went on to an easy victory in November.

A novel circumstance enabled the first-term senator from a border state to become a national figure and presidential contender in just three years. Due to his chairmanship of the Senate Special Committee to Investigate Interstate Crime and its nationally televised hearings in 1950 and 1951, Kefauver became overnight a national hero and secured the base to strike for the presidency in 1952.

Two years prior to the 1952 election President Harry S Truman had written himself a memo indicating that he would not seek another term in the White House. Truman had revealed his plans to some of his staff in November of 1951, but, as the first primary approached, his plans were still a secret to the public. Truman was thus free to keep his opposition off-guard and explore his options, the most important of which was to find a suitable heir. (Supreme Court Chief Justice Fred Vinson and Illinois Governor Adlai Stevenson were at the top of his list, but both refused to run.)

At a press conference the last day of January, the president was clearly annoyed that his name had been entered in the New Hampshire primary without his consent. Asked about his plans, Truman bluntly stated that he thought the primaries were just so much "eyewash" and that he could have the nomination merely for the asking. Such a gratuitous remark drew criticism from all over the state, which was just beginning to bask in the limelight cast its way.

Truman also announced he would withdraw from the New Hampshire primary. His statement drew mixed reviews in the nation's newspapers, but created immediate and harsh reaction throughout New Hampshire. Governor Adams was quoted the following day in the *Concord Daily Monitor*:

> When the president of the United States sneers at our system of free elections, he belittles one of the fundamental principles of free government. He brings discredit, not only upon his office, but upon his capacity to fill it.
>
> His remark is one more proof that the Democratic Party, once styling itself the people's party, has by the admission of its chief, become the party of rule by

regulation, by executive order, by direction, and no longer thinks itself responsible to the people of this country.

The Keene Sentinel reacted as vehemently:

The primaries are indeed eyewash. They are meant to clear the eyes of the delegates of the trash thrown in them by professional convention-rousers. They rest the blood-shot eyes of delegates who have been subjected to the pressures of machine politicians and allow them to see more clearly....It's time the voters, not the smoke-filled rooms of convention halls, decided who was to get the nomination.

The pro-Eisenhower, strongly Republican *Concord Daily Monitor* ran an editorial entitled "The Boss is Insolent," which read in part:

What the president was saying is that he is the boss of a national political machine, held together with the patron-age and favors bought with taxpayers' money, and that this machine will do whatever he bids, regardless of what is best for the people, or of what the people themselves may think best.

What the president was saying is that the sovereign state of New Hampshire can go to Hell.

Five days later Truman would perform a full back flip and plunge right into the "eyewash" after all. He wrote the New Hampshire secretary of state, Enoch D. Fuller, "I had thought it would be better for my name not to appear on any ballot at this time as a candidate for president until I am ready to make an announcement...the chairman of the Democratic National Committee and many good Democrats in New Hampshire are of the opinion that my name should be left on the ballot. At their suggestion, therefore, I shall not ask you to take my name off the list."

Thus, the New Hampshire showdown between the Tennessee insurgent and President Truman was a maze of plot-ting and planning that ended with a bold gamble by one and a reluctant entry by the other. As it turned out, Truman could have saved himself some embarrassment by agreeing to a "hands off" policy that was proposed at the last minute. One evening Kefauver found himself on the same plane with the pro-Truman

Democratic National chairman, Frank McKinney. Kefauver offered to withdraw from the beauty contest if Truman would do the same; thus the matter would be left to the voters. But the Truman partisans, eager to thrash the upstart senator in his first outing, turned down the offer.

Any final chance of an accommodation between the two men ended with a series of remarks Kefauver made in his first primary campaign appearance before the Nashua Chamber of Commerce. Without mentioning Truman by name, the Tennessean noted that the primary was not "eyewash at all, but rather take it as a democratic method for you to express your choice of nominee to the highest office in your power to give." In an implied attack on Truman's early association with the Kansas City Pendergast machine, he told the group, "The ordinary course of a man up the political ladder in the United States is by successive steps from the locality and then may or may not proceed to the state and national level of office and politics. In the locality, however, the moral tone of his later service as governor, senator, ambassador, or president has usually been set." In commenting on foreign affairs, the digs at Truman continued: "Just as we do not gauge our domestic politics on the whims of racketeers, so we should not gauge our foreign policy on the whims of Stalin."

Kefauver would generate thousands of friends and millions of votes along the primary path that year, but with these remarks created one powerful opponent, a man who would destroy his presidential hopes at the national convention.

During the final month before the vote, Kefauver made two trips to New Hampshire, becoming the first candidate to adopt the person-to-person technique that has since become ritual. In many of the towns and even some of the cities, he was the first in-the-flesh Democratic aspirant for a major office residents had seen in some time. He was not soon forgotten due to the prominence of the post he was seeking.

An oak of a man at 6'3", he would stick out his huge hand and say, "Hello, I'm Estes Kefauver and I'm running for president. I'd appreciate your vote." He did not follow the usual political dictum of tracking down a few "key" people—to Kefauver everyone was key. He had a great instinct for working the ground level of politics, he ambled along countless main streets greeting shoppers and clerks, worked the assembly lines in factories, attended teas in private homes and receptions in hotel meeting rooms.[4]

Eugene Daniell, a Republican state senator who had unsuccessfully challenged Adams for governor in 1950, stepped across party lines to support Kefauver in 1952. He helped recruit part of the delegate slate and traveled with the candidate. Daniell remembers: "Kefauver was without question the finest person-to-person campaigner ever to hit this state. He would go into a town cold turkey and come out of it a short time later with a dozen strong supporters. It was a wonder to behold."

The senator was extremely popular with women who saw in him a courtly and gallant Southerner who had "chased all them criminals" and who was the only person in his party courageous enough to take on an unpopular president. Tom McIntyre, an attorney in Laconia and a former mayor of the city (he would be elected to the United States Senate in 1962, the first Democrat in 30 years from the state), recalled the day he first met Kefauver and how his wife Myrtle signed on board. They were with some fellow Democrats at the ice car races on Lake Winnipesaukee on a February day as the senator and Mrs. Kefauver came off the ice:

> We were standing there in a small circle and he wanted to make a contact before he turned around and headed back to Concord. Estes said, "Well, Tom, are you gonna help me?" And I said, "Senator, I'm the county chairman and I must remain neutral." And he next looked over at Hugh Bownes and asked him the same thing, but I spoke up for Hughie, "He can't help you because he's

[4] The person-to-person stumping was not without its peril or amusing incidents. One day Kefauver was visiting Lebanon and as he stuck his hand through the hole of a movie theater box office to shake the hand of the ticket seller, he got stuck. The small crowd laughed as he tried to free himself. A few minutes later an unsmiling Kefauver managed to escape. Upon arrival in a new town, he would automatically jump out of the car and start pressing the flesh. One day he approached some people saying: "I'm Estes Kefauver, I'm running for president—how'm I doing here?" One fellow answered him dryly: "You're doing fine here, but you'd better get back to New Hampshire where the primary is—this is Vermont!" In his zeal he had inadvertently wandered across the Connecticut River into the Green Mountain State.

the city chairman." This kind of hurt look came over this big Tennessean's face, and suddenly from the outer perimeter of our little group this voice said, "I'll help you, Senator." He looked over and saw Mrs. McIntyre, and he just gently moved everyone aside and stuck out his hand and said, "Madame chairman." That was it. They were off and running.

The New Hampshire Democratic Party was labeled in some quarters a "machine," but in reality it was a house of cards. Strong on paper as well as in rhetoric, it turned out to be ill-equipped to handle Kefauver's underground campaign. The Democrats had not won a statewide office in two decades, and, in spite of the fact that Franklin Roosevelt carried New Hampshire in 1936, 1940 and 1944, little was done to build a vigorous party organization off the strength of his coattails.

The major problem facing the minority party was the existence for generations of a bitter feud between the more rural Yankee Protestant leaders, some of whom traced their political lineage back to Andrew Jackson, and the insurgent Catholics, largely French and Irish, who had worked the shoe and textile mills in Manchester, Nashua and the other industrial cities in the state.

With much pain and turmoil, the ethnic groups slowly wrested control away from the Yankees, only to be followed by in-fighting between the French and Irish. The two groups fought their most intense brawls while endeavoring to control the Hillsborough County government, one of the few governmental entities then subject to Democratic takeover. On occasion the Democrats would come close to a statewide victory, uniting around a Yankee Protestant from another county, but their problems were exacerbated by Republican Senator Styles Bridges, who often had his hand in recruiting straw candidates to disrupt Democratic primaries and guarantee the nomination of the weakest possible candidate.

Only in the final 10 days did the Truman backers finally swing into action, opening a headquarters in Manchester, installing a phone bank and importing political figures to speak on the president's behalf. Sixty-five thousand leaflets were distributed throughout the state, focusing on the state's 45,000 labor union members. The newspapers and radio stations ran Truman ads, and on election eve Congressman John McCormick of Massachusetts delivered a radio broadcast on behalf of the "Man from Missouri."

But they ran into problems. While the CIO labor unions backed Truman, the AFL groups sat on their hands, succumbing to pressure from Washington. Bickering broke out in Manchester between the party regulars and the labor people, and, to ensure the complacency of their efforts, they were boldly predicting a massive victory for the president, by as much as a 70-30% spread in the beauty contest.

The White House was aware of the problems the "machine" was having in delivering for the president thanks to Dennis O'Brien, an employee of the Maine Development Commission, who made a number of trips into the state and sent his reactions to the White House. On February 25th O'Brien wrote that "Kefauver is going to get more votes than you think. He has had a good press, and is a beneficiary of peculiar local conditions that may not exist elsewhere."

He remarked that:

> Little Democratic activity is visible, and the "pro-Truman" forces seem indifferent, and strangely silent. They appear to be making the fatal error of the Dewey camp in 1948: apathy and over-confidence. Since election falls on so-called "Town Meeting day," the small towns will turn out heavily. K. is strong in them, through his campaign tactics. These tactics consist, in miniature, of doing precisely what Mr. Truman himself did four years ago, on a more "personal basis" here. Go straight to the people. As follows: Mr. K. arrives in town, walks up and down main street, stops John Native, sticks out his hand, announces "I'm Ephas Kappas," and goes into his pitch with a reporter handy. The natives, confused and flattered, are "buying."

By the latter part of February it had begun to dawn on the state Democratic leaders that Kefauver was making some progress and thus it was time for some work. National Committeeman Emmett Kelley promised on February 22nd, "State Democratic leaders, practically all of whom are on the Truman bandwagon, will leave no stone unturned to guarantee a victory for President Truman." (Kelley would be one party pol who would never warm to the senator from Tennessee. He once denigrated Kefauver's ability to generate press coverage by remarking, "Kefauver would stick his nose into a horsefeed bag to get his photo in the paper.")

Lacking a candidate, they turned to surrogates. One was John L. Sullivan, the Democratic nominee for governor in 1934 and a Washington attorney who was once Navy secretary. In early March he addressed a meeting of 500 people at the University of New Hampshire in Durham. Sullivan would use the tactic that was tried for another Democratic president 16 years later—the "Communists are watching New Hampshire" pitch— that had little impact in both cases. He said, "In my opinion if the Democrats of New Hampshire fail to give a vote of confidence to our president the effects in Europe will be very bad indeed and the news, when it reaches the Kremlin, will be the best news it has received in a long while."

Besides the late start, the lackadaisical organizing, and the lack of assistance from the White House, the Truman candidacy was plagued by overconfidence, and at the same time always on the defensive. O'Brien, in a second letter, wrote:

> If we were dealing in "ifs," President Truman could come up to New Hampshire and make *one* strong speech, and thereby devastate this television-spawned "competition." But he doesn't design to do so, and the New Hampshire lieutenants in charge, so far, can't provide even pale carbon copies of *his* inimitable, picturesque style. As a result, your cause suffers....New Hampshire Democrats are failing to "sell" their administration aggressively. Instead of this endless defensive, and all that arrant [sic], moss-backed nonsense, why not sock it right to those frugal, thrifty New Hampshire natives. Right in the spot where they know it best, and understand it most. Their pocket-books! Let them [leaders (?)] banish their unjustified temerity. They've got a story to tell—a GOOD story—and all they've got to do is tell it.

Every political analyst was predicting an easy Truman win. An Associated Press account on March 7th showed Truman receiving 65-75% of the vote. Without identifying his source, James Reston in *The New York Times* reported "best opinion was that the president would win."   William V. Shannon in the *New York Post* followed along: "Kefauver has only a slim chance of getting even one of the eight" convention votes.

The fact that so many professional assessments would prove wrong indicated the pundits did exactly what they promised they would not do after their humiliating experience in the '48 Dewey-Truman race: They continued to talk to politicians and other reporters who spent their time talking to each other and reinforcing their miscalculations.

One columnist who openly bid for the warm dish of crow was Stewart Alsop. He quoted Emmett Kelley's "Truman landslide" and he gave Kefauver an "outside chance of capturing just one delegate." He reasoned that Kefauver had transgressed "one of the great, built-in rules of American politics....that you simply do not challenge an incumbent president in your own party."

Alsop's defense in part was that he was misled even by Kefauver, deeply despondent over the poor turnouts he was receiving. In the city of Keene (population 15,600) only 30 people bothered to come out. In the mill and labor city of Claremont (12,800) 60 people turned out in a large hall, whereupon they were all invited down to the front for an informal chat. And an evening address in Nashua drew far fewer people than a Taft speech had that morning.

In his not-for-attribution interview Alsop later said Kefauver was "quite honestly convinced that he had no real chance....Everybody was wrong as usual."

Kefauver had managed—unbeknownst to himself, the press or the politicians—to stumble onto the stage in a manner that quietly turned on the party rank-and-file. It would only become obvious after the ballots were tabulated.

It was a clear and convincing victory: Kefauver received 19,800 votes to Truman's 15,927. He carried eight of the 10 counties and all the delegates. The constituency that made the difference nationally for Truman in 1948—labor—failed him this time. In the state's 12 cities Kefauver won 11,856 to 10,345.

Kefauver said of the surprise win: "The results indicate that a good energetic campaign and supporting group can beat a strong machine....There is a need for new vigor and ideas in the Democratic Party." Other interpretations of the results varied. Some attributed it to a clear refutation of the president and a desire to clean house; others saw it as a victory of personal style for the Tennessee senator. Whatever the reasons, the results sent shock waves through the Democratic Party and the nation.

In the end his New Hampshire upset may have done Kefauver more harm than good. Myrtle McIntyre would reflect later: "He actually was quite upset the night that he was winning the primary against Truman. He didn't want to win—he wanted to make a darn good showing. But he won and when he did that got all the pols nationwide mad at him."

Tom McIntyre was with Kefauver in the Eagle Hotel in Concord as the returns came in. He recalls, "The telephone rang and Estes found out—we were just sitting there talking—the game was all over—and Berlin had gone for Kefauver. Immediately I said, 'and that means you beat Truman.' And that was a very fatal mistake of his for we were there in that convention and every top dog senator in Washington didn't care very much for Kefauver for running over the old man. That hurt him plenty."

While Kefauver basked in the glory of his upset victory and started to campaign nationally for delegates, on March 29th Truman announced, "I shall not be a candidate for re-election. I have served my country long and, I think, efficiently and honestly. I shall not accept a renomination. I do not feel that it is my duty to spend another four years in the White House."

Without significant opposition, Kefauver was able to waltz through most of the other primaries. He garnered 3,166,000 of the 4,909,000 votes cast in the Democratic primaries; going into the Chicago convention he had the most delegate strength. He also led in the rank-and-file polls as their selection for the nomination.

On the initial convention ballot Kefauver led with 340 votes to Illinois Governor Adlai Stevenson's 273; however, he was far short of the 616 needed to nominate. Kefauver picked up strength on the second ballot, but not as much as Stevenson did. Kefauver added 22 1/2 to reach his high point of 362 1/2, while Stevenson moved up 51 1/2 to 324 1/2. By the third ballot, aided by the withdrawal of New York Governor Averill Harriman at Truman's behest, Stevenson received the nomination with 617 1/2, just a whisker over a majority.

As a still-bitter Kefauver would point out a half year later in an article in *Collier's*:

> What happened? I had aroused the implacable enmity of certain politicians, including some defeated hacks and various political yeomen who were taking orders implicitly

from the outgoing Truman administration. There were a number of reasons for their enmity, none of them very inspiring. Some resented my call for new, young, vigorous leadership in places where the party had fallen into stodgy and selfish hands. Others were angry because I had announced for the nomination before Mr. Truman made his intentions known. Still others were irked because I did not withdraw from the New Hampshire primary after Mr. Truman decided to let his name be entered. My victory in New Hampshire, of course, didn't help....Being thus committed to "stop Kefauver," these "machine stalwarts," who were all-powerful behind the convention scenes, disregarded what the people and largest bloc of the delegates said they wanted. They chose a man who was virtually a political unknown on the national scene, a man who publicly insisted he did not want the job, and who had refused to enter a single primary. His selection was said to be a "draft," but some observers have remarked that it was a mighty peculiar draft, with such stalwarts as Truman, Jake Avery, Sam Rayburn, Scott Lucas *et al* blowing on the fire, and minor wood carriers tossing in their bits of kindling.

In spite of complaints and criticisms of the convention management for the manner in which Kefauver and his supporters had been treated, the result was more than just a stop-Kefauver drive. Anti-Kefauver sentiment, strongest in the South and the urban delegations in the North, made up a substantial part of the opposition; Stevenson was in all likelihood the only figure around which the party could unite in 1952. A walkout by the South was a strong possibility if either Kefauver or Harriman were selected; the northern liberals surely would have bolted if Georgia Senator Richard Russell had been given the nod.

The nomination proved of little value anyway, for no Democrat could have beaten Eisenhower that year. The Republican victory margin was massive—6.6 million votes and the Republicans carried the Electoral College 442-89. For the first time in two decades the nation prepared to inaugurate a Republican president.

On election night Robert Burroughs was invited to join a select group of people to watch the televised election returns with General Eisenhower in New York's Hotel Commodore. During the campaign Eisenhower had asked Burroughs to act as a liaison with Indian groups in the West to gain their support. The general wanted to know the results of his Indian mission, and, according to Burroughs: "I started to tell him but he interrupted me, 'I'm punch-drunk right now, but I want you to come up to the house on Morningside Drive tomorrow. I'd like to hear all about this, and I have a couple of other questions I want to ask you too.'"

Burroughs had been entrusted to use his own judgment in making any promises to the Indians and, asked the next morning what he'd done, he replied: "I made only one promise, and you said you'd live up to any promise I made that I felt was in their interest. I promised them that if you were elected president, Dillon Myer (then the head of the Bureau of Indian Affairs) would go out." The Indian leaders Burroughs had consulted with felt that Myer was in an ivory tower. He rarely consulted with them, although he always promised to do so, and was insensitive to their problems.

Eisenhower's reaction was: "I'll tell you something terrible. He's one of the closest friends of my brother Milton. But I'm going to keep your promise. He'll go out." By March Myer had resigned his post.

Eisenhower also wanted to know everything Burroughs knew about Sherman Adams. Burroughs had known the former lumberjack for more than three decades (they attended Dartmouth College together), and he told the general quite a bit about Adams and recommended him highly.

A few weeks later, as Adams was winding up his campaign work in New York City, Eisenhower called the governor into his office and told him: "Well, I've been thinking about you. I could visualize you as a member of the Cabinet, but I need somebody to be my assistant in running my office. I'd like you to continue at my right hand, just as you've been in the campaign. You would be associated with me more closely than anybody else in the government."

Adams returned to New Hampshire to spend Thanksgiving with his family, to attend to his remaining gubernatorial chores, and consider the offer. He consulted with Herbert Hill, the Dartmouth College history professor who had opposed Adams for governor in 1948. Hill remembers that visit to Adams' office:

There was a whole bunch of people waiting to see him, many of whom I knew. One of them said, "I guess you have to be a Democrat to see the governor." Adams wanted to ask me, since I was an old friend, my opinion of whether or not he should go serve in the White House. I said, "You have no choice, Sherm. It's your duty. You've got to do it. You may regret it, it may turn out badly, but you've got to do it."

Adams never recollected formally accepting the offer. He simply remarked to the president-elect: "I'd better go down to the White House and see about planning a staff office there." He began the task of transition and recruitment of the White House staff, and he worked with a special committee on the reorganization of the executive branch headed by Nelson Rockefeller.

The day following the inauguration Adams was sworn in as the assistant to the president. What had begun with such uncertainty a year before in the snows of New Hampshire had finally been transformed into the concrete and powerful reality of the presidency of the United States.

1956
Repeat Performance

FOR YEARS, ARGUMENTS ABOUNDED as to what sobriquet to bestow upon Sherman Adams: the Rock, the Second President, the Great Stone Face, the Boss, Eisenhower's "No" Man or just plain Sherm the Firm. Yet there was no debate over the power he wielded in the Eisenhower White House. Installed just a dozen or so paces from the president's office in the West Wing, the former governor was a direct descendant of the general's World War II chief-of-staff system. Author Louis Koenig wrote that Adams:

> exercised more power than any other presidential assistant in modern times. He made decisions and performed acts which presidents, since the establishment of the Republic, have been given to doing themselves. Indeed, it is demonstrable that his power and impact upon the national destiny have exceeded that of not a few presidents of the United States.

Eisenhower abhorred much of the detailed work demanded of the president. He had virtually no interest whatsoever in engaging in the rough-and-tumble of partisan and power politics; and he despised patronage. He avoided at all cost having to read the voluminous reports pouring forth from the Washington labyrinth. He only desired the time and freedom to chart the general course of his administration—all the while leaving his schedule free enough to engage in golf, bridge and social evenings with his non-political associates.

With a broad range of power never specifically delineated by the president but understood by the two, and subsequently by the White House staff, the Cabinet, Congress and the news media, Adams was literally the "Right-Hand Man." He guaranteed that the difficult task of winnowing down the government reports to one-page synopses for the president was accomplished and that the various departments working on programs met when necessary. Adams also made certain that as much of the decision-making as feasible was done in the agencies and Cabinet departments or, if not there, then by him before it would pass on for the president's judgment. He kept operations moving briskly and, during the president's frequent absences from Washington, he would become the acting president.

Oblivious to fatigue, hardened by his lumberman years, and finished to a fine edge with more than a decade in the heat of political warfare, Adams was one of the few people in the administration with substantial political experience, the power to make decisions and the courage to carry them out, no matter who got stepped on.

Since Eisenhower was "the imperturbable gentleman of good will who saw no evil and spoke no evil," Adams was the "no" man. When someone needed a rap on the knuckles or a dressing down or a dismissal, Adams was always there. If the circumstances called for a shot at the political opposition, Adams would step briefly into the public spotlight and lob a volley—a task he shared with Vice President Nixon. If an Eisenhower decision drew criticism, Adams could expect much of the harping to be directed his way.

His patronage power was massive. In the first two and a half years of the administration, Adams's office processed 60,000 appointments; the final choices in most of the top selections were narrowed down by him. The disgruntled office seeker knew whom to blame for the judgment, and Adams had one more group to add to a growing collection of enemies. As keeper of the gate, Adams had the final say on who was allowed to see the president, and either he or one of his aides would monitor most of the president's meetings.

The blunt, brusque manner of the former lumberjack endeared him to few, particularly among the backslapping, gregarious and genial sorts on the Hill who were always ready to sit down for a drink and a story or two. The scoop-conscious media, depending on tidbits of this and that for color in their copy, received nothing but a stone wall of silence from the taciturn and aloof Yankee. He was there, after all, to serve one man—Dwight D. Eisenhower—and not Congress or the Washington press corps.

Although his style and power upset many and annoyed others, he enjoyed the full confidence of the president. One poll by a national magazine prior to the 1956 election revealed that, of all the men in the nation, Adams was considered the fourth most powerful, behind Eisenhower, House Speaker Sam Rayburn and Secretary of the Treasury George Humphrey: Vice President Richard Nixon ranked ninth.[1]

With Adams safely ensconced in the White House and with Styles Bridges serving as one of the most powerful figures in the United States Senate as the ranking Republican on the Appropriations Committee, New Hampshire's Republicans boasted two home-grown figures with considerable national clout. In addition they controlled the rest of the congressional delegation, the governorship and the state legislature. If not the most Republican state in the nation, New Hampshire was close to being so, and the *rigor mortis* that would set in after the death of Styles Bridges was still years away. In contrast to the pathetic Democrats, the Republicans operated a well-oiled, well-tuned political machine. While Adams was at the pinnacle of power in Washington, he still had to take a back seat at home, where Bridges reigned supreme. Bridges shared with Adams the same aversion for the public limelight, yet he was the kingpin in a tightly structured, hierarchical organization that awarded dedication, loyalty and hard work with steady advancement up the organization ladder. Bridges masterfully handled the patronage allotted to him to build his machine, and he was always on the lookout for fresh young talent to take under his wing, nourishing and expanding his power base.

Very few controversies ever surfaced while Bridges was around to calm ruffled feathers. One news reporter who covered Republican state conventions in the 1950s related how these

---

[1] A morbid joke that made the rounds at the time of the president's 1955 heart attack exemplified Adams's clout:

    Q. "Wouldn't it be terrible if Ike died and Nixon became president?"

    A. "Yes, but what if Adams died and Ike became president?"

conclaves "were more like carefully staged performances in contrast to the wild west rodeo shows the Democrats would throw every two years." William Treat, the Republican state chairman from 1954 to 1958, stated that conducting a convention in those days "was like running a stockholders' meeting in which you controlled 60 percent of the stock or more. There were very few controversies."

Beyond Adams's and Bridges's virtual domination of New Hampshire's political system, the intervening years between the 1952 and 1956 presidential primaries saw the president make two trips to massage the state, and the vice president one.

In June of 1953 the president received an honorary degree from Dartmouth College. He wasn't going to deliver a major address, but since the Canadian foreign minister and president of the United Nations General Assembly, Lester Pearson, would be there also, Adams suggested Ike talk about the relevance of the northern New England educational institution and its role in American-Canadian relations. Eisenhower instead caused it to be a rare occasion: He addressed the controversial politician, Wisconsin Senator Joseph McCarthy, whose aides had managed to push the State Department to ban all books by Communist authors in American libraries overseas. McCarthy's moon was in full orbit, but it was about to set.

Eisenhower spent the first part of his Dartmouth speech talking about college life, patriotism, golf and "fun—joy—happiness, just fun in life." He also promised to "talk a little about courage," which he showed when he abruptly became serious near the conclusion:

> Don't join the book burners. Don't think you are going to conceal faults by concealing evidence that they ever existed. Don't be afraid to go in your library and read every book, as long as that document does not offend our own ideas of decency. That should be the only censorship.
>
>   How will we defeat Communism unless we know what it is and what it teaches, and why does it have such an appeal for men? Why are so many people swearing allegiance to it?

In September 1954 Nixon delivered the keynote address at the Republican State Convention as part of his 48-day, 31-

state drive to try to maintain the slender GOP majorities in the Congress. (Nixon had been telling some of his intimates that it would be his last campaign swing. He was tired of having to serve as the administration's lightning rod with the resulting attacks and abuse. He had promised his wife, Pat, who very much wanted him to take up one of the lucrative law practices or business opportunities being offered to him, that he would leave politics when his vice presidential term expired.) Nixon's effort failed—the Democrats picked up 20 seats in the House and two in the Senate, to regain control of both—but the losses were not severe for an off-year election for the party in power. In the process, the vice president managed to ingratiate himself deeper into the hearts of the Republican regulars, who were most appreciative of his desire to assist the grassroots campaign endeavors.

Asked by Nixon biographer Earl Mazo why he didn't hang 'em up at that time after all, Nixon said: "Once you get into this great stream of history you can't get out. You can drown. Or you can be pulled ashore by the tide. But it is awfully hard to get out when you are in the middle of the stream, if it is intended that you stay there."

A presidential visit to northern New England in June of 1955 began with a day in Vermont, 36 hours in the Granite State, and two days in Maine. Although the procession required the services of 100 Secret Service agents and two planeloads of reporters and photographers, it was a non-political procession that resulted in little news of any substance. The media were so famished for content to fill their stories that, when the president made a casual remark before 15,000 people on the State House plaza in Concord that Sherm Adams was not a third of the way through his stories about New Hampshire, it was interpreted as a subtle reference that he would seek another term, and the press played it as such.

However, true to form, by the next day in Berlin, Ike alluded to a desire to return to the city as soon as he had found another means of livelihood. That was construed to mean that he might not run again after all.

It was a hero's welcome throughout, with large and friendly crowds demonstrating the affection held for the president in the state that helped to put him onto the road to the White House.

In the early morning hours of September 24, 1955 the prospect of a second Eisenhower term was seriously jeopardized.

While vacationing in Denver, the president suffered a major heart attack. Release of the news the next day caused the stock market to plunge its deepest since the Great Depression. The eyes of the nation focused on Fitzsimons Army Hospital outside Denver to see if Eisenhower would live.

With Secretary of State John Foster Dulles masterminding the strategy, the Cabinet decided to send Adams to Denver. All matters for presidential action would pass through him. With the president's re-election prospects looking all but ended, many of the top Eisenhower administration officials wanted to do as much as they could to keep the controversial and untested vice president out of the action. With the demise of Joe McCarthy and the 1953 death of Senator Robert Taft, Nixon was the new hero of the party's conservative wing. His ascension at that time could jeopardize the "modern Republicanism" course that Eisenhower had been steering. Senator Styles Bridges, displeased with the shunting aside of Nixon and the greater powers placed in Adam's hands, telegrammed Nixon: "You are the constitutional second-in-command, and you ought to assume the leadership. Don't let the White House clique take command."

As the president started down the road to recovery and gradually increased his level of activity, the late fall air was pregnant with speculation on who might succeed as the next Republican presidential nominee. Nixon and Adams were on almost every list, as well as the names of Senate Minority Leader William Knowland of California, Thomas Dewey, Governor Christian Herter of Massachusetts, Harold Stassen, United Nations Ambassador Henry Cabot Lodge and the president's brother Milton, president of Johns Hopkins University.

On Friday evening, January 13th, 111 days after the heart attack, Eisenhower convened a secret meeting in his second-floor study in the White House, with about a dozen of his top Cabinet officials and chief aides. The president asked their opinions regarding another term.

The verdict was virtually unanimous: Health willing, he should run again. His advisors pointed to his unique position of being the one man in the nation who could exert a substantial influence for the cause of world peace. If he were out of office and on the sidelines, they said, he would merely become a hindrance to the new president in the area of international relations. They regarded him as unsurpassed in his ability to unite the na-

tion; he had managed to reverse the Republican pattern of
haranguing and opposition set by the New and Fair Deals. Now
the direction was to move toward moderation and constructive
alternatives.

His advisors also felt that his re-election (as in the case of
his election) was vital to the preservation of the party, and thus
the two-party system. His brother, after summarizing the reasons why he should run again, forcefully presented the reasons
why he should not. He had already devoted almost four decades
of his life to public service, and it might be time for him to try to
finally establish a normal home life, to travel and do what he
could for the nation as a distinguished private citizen. However,
it was questionable at that point whether retirement held any
attraction for the president. The boredom of his convalescence
had left him eager to resume his duties and his usual recreational
habits.

On the same day as the advisory meeting, the filing
period for the New Hampshire primary opened. A decision
would soon have to be made on whether Eisenhower's name
would go on the ballot. New Hampshire's secretary of state
wrote inquiring as to the president's intentions, and received the
response: "I do not feel that I should interpose any objections
to such an entry....I must make it clear to all that lack of objection cannot be construed as any final decision on my part
relative to a candidacy for a second term in the office I now hold.
I hope that all who vote in the Republican primaries in 1956 will
carefully weigh all the possibilities that may be involved."

A month later, the president's doctors pronounced him
healthy enough to seek another term. At a morning press conference on February 29th, the president revealed that he would
ask "for time on television and radio. I am going directly to the
American people and tell them the full facts and my answer with
the limits I have so sketchily observed, but which I will explain in
detail tonight so as to get the story out in one continuous narrative. My answer will be positive; that is affirmative."

With that matter finally resolved, the focus for speculation
turned to the vice president. Washington was rife with rumor that
Nixon would be dumped from the ticket and that the president
had publicly urged him to "chart his own course." Privately,
Eisenhower asked Nixon to consider taking a position in the
Cabinet to gain more administrative experience, something Nixon
refused to do.

Some Republican leaders wanted Nixon out because he was regarded as too controversial and a drag on the ticket. Columnist Walter Lippman summed up the anti-Nixon views with the observation:

> The question is whether he represents the central thing which Eisenhower represents, the thing which has given Eisenhower such a hold on the American people. The central thing is that Eisenhower unites the country and heals its divisions. This is precisely what Nixon does not do. Instead of being a national leader, he is a ruthless partisan who divides and embitters the people.

President Eisenhower would run unopposed in that year's first-in-the-nation primary—he garnered 56,464 votes. But the real story of the 1956 primary, a result that would have long-term ramifications for the Republican Party and the nation as well, would be what happened to Richard Nixon on the second Tuesday in March of 1956.

Estes Kefauver was back. In reality, he had never really left. He and his wife had continued their friendship with Tom and Myrtle McIntyre; in 1954 he stumped in the state for McIntyre—then a candidate for Congress—and the rest of the Democratic ticket. Kefauver had been bestowed with the title "New Hampshire's Third Senator," since he was the man the New Hampshire Democrats turned to if they needed assistance in Washington.

His second primary attempt, although still cornerstoned by the famed one-on-one technique, was a much more polished and professional endeavor. One of his original supporters would later complain: "It was no longer a revolutionary movement." Much more care was taken in selecting a full and balanced delegate slate—ethnically and geographically. The crowds were larger than in 1952 and the tours more professionally advanced. His strength was obvious so early in the campaign that the titular head of the party and the frontrunner for the nomination, Adlai Stevenson, decided to avoid the Granite State entirely. Stevenson abhorred the ordeal of the primary circuit, avoiding it as much as possible. He cautiously selected to focus on the Minnesota primary–a week after New Hampshire's–which was regarded as more favorable terrain to contest the master campaigner of the decade.

However, some opposition to Kefauver almost occurred in the beauty contest. One day, Massachusetts Senator John Kennedy called his administrative assistant, Ted Sorensen, into his office. He informed him: "I'm considering running as a New England favorite son in the New Hampshire presidential primary." He did not consider himself a realistic presidential possibility at the time, but he did want to try and unite the six-state New England region under his leadership, to be turned over to the Stevenson candidacy.

Kennedy, not facing re-election until 1958, was eager to actively campaign, and he believed that New Hampshire was "where the action is." But the Stevenson operatives, fearful that such an attempt would only attract more attention to a state solidly lined up for the Tennessean, asked for and received instead an endorsement from the youthful senator prior to the primary.

A write-in effort for the former Illinois governor did transpire, as well as the filing of a favorable slate of prominent Democratic leaders. The Democrats have never avoided a primary fight if they could, and 1956 proved no exception. The Stevensonians hoped to receive 20-30% of the beauty contest votes and to pull in a few delegate aspirants.

But Kefauver's grip on the Granite State proved absolute, Stevenson's absence strangled any hopes his supporters had of hindering the Kefauver drive. In three campaign swings Kefauver rewired many of his 1952 acquaintances, made many new ones, and cultivated the state to the ripeness he had achieved for years previously.

Theodore White, writing in *Collier's*, captured Kefauver's storming of a locale:

> At 10:30 in the morning, Monday, March 12th, a lone sound truck blaring Sousa marches, hillbilly music and the "Ballad of Davy Crockett" pulled into the little factory town of Dover, New Hampshire, and Estes Kefauver stepped out into the snow and began to work. First call was at the office of *Foster's Daily Democrat*—a minute shaking hands with the telephone girls, a minute in the back room with the boys on the desk, then into the barbershop next door. Here he shook hands, told the barber he was Estes Kefauver, hoped the barber would "he'p him out on Tuesday," borrowed a comb to part his hair, refused some hair oil, laughing, because nothing

would make his hair grow again, pushed on up Main Street....In 25 minutes Kefauver had coursed Central Avenue from *Foster's Daily Democrat* at one end to American House at the other, and he had shaken perhaps a hundred hands before he was off to visit a shoe factory....It had taken less than half an hour of Kefauver's technique to rewire Dover's loyalties and explode the charge.

Bernard Boutin, the state chairman for Kefauver, recalled an incident that exemplified the personal touch Kefauver used to such advantage:

Kefauver didn't have the recall for names that a James Farley had, but he did have a little black book that his assistant, Lucile Myers, kept. I remember one lady in Somersworth whose husband had been very ill. We were going along the street in the car and Tom McIntyre said, "You remember so-and-so," and Lucile immediately took out the little black book and gave him a rundown on her. All this happened within the span of one minute. Estes got out of the car and walked up to the woman and started talking with her and asking how her husband was and so forth. That woman—you would have thought she felt that the senator was the greatest thing since the invention of the electric light bulb. It had a tremendous impact, and he did this all over the state.

Kefauver, to virtually no one's surprise, received 21,701 to Stevenson's 3,806 write-ins. He also swept the delegate slate.

Stevenson's nomination dreams were handed a more severe jolt a week later in Minnesota. There the Tennessean trounced him 245,000-186,000, although he had the backing of the party establishment and organized labor. Within a period of just one week Kefauver had rearranged the landscape, jeopardized Stevenson's frontrunner status, and prepared once again to try to accumulate a string of primary victories as he had a quadrennium before.

Bill Dunfey, involved in his family's hotel business, had managed the Stevenson write-in and McIntyre's congressional campaign in 1954. After the Minnesota debacle, Dunfey was invited to Stevenson's Illinois farm to take part in brainstorming sessions aimed at salvaging the Stevenson candidacy.

In trying to decipher what was wrong, Dunfey felt that Stevenson had little comprehension of how the primary process dramatically altered the manner in which the presidential nominee would be chosen:

> We sat there for a weekend and we went through some descriptions of what the presidential primary thing is: "It's a new game, and especially the television aspect of it. Kefauver's playing things to the hilt, and, unless you're willing to change your approach, he's got California all locked up." Stevenson was appalled at what was being prescribed as to what he would now have to do. He just couldn't believe it. Sure, you've got to have a paid television broadcast and you've got to address the Council on World Affairs, but when they see you on the tube, then they've got to see you in person in the primary process. Once that occurs, the linkage comes. If they don't see you in the flesh and they see Kefauver on the tube and at the plant gate or on the town green, he's got the linkage and therefore the election.

The new-model Stevenson rolled up his sleeves, plunged into the remaining key primaries and was able to slowly turn it around: he won by 13,700 out of a half million votes in Florida and by a wider margin in Oregon. In the Golden State grand finale, a permanent lid was put on Kefauver's presidential dreams—Stevenson won by a 2-1 margin. With the securing of the nomination, the dubious honor of competing once more against the immensely popular Eisenhower.

After his defeat to Stevenson in California, Kefauver decided to call it quits. Tom McIntyre recalls, "He called and said, 'Tom, I've got to pull out of the race. I'm out of money to push on any further.' I remember saying to him, and I don't feel this way now, I said, 'From where I sit, senator, you've got a helluva good job as it is.'" Laughing, he said, "I don't know why I said that."

For Richard M. Nixon it was another time of trouble. Not enough to merit a full chapter in his memoir, *Six Crises*, but nevertheless a situation that saw him threatening to leave politics for the third time in four years. It was also a period that stirred the conservative wing of the Grand Old Party to rally and keep one of their heroes in power.

Eisenhower, ever the non-politician, did not feel it was either his responsibility or duty to dictate to the Republican National Convention who his running mate should be, at least not until his own renomination was a reality. As sincere and innocent as the president's position may have seemed, it left Nixon slowly twisting in the wind. With an absence of a clear statement of confidence from the president, Nixon was more than ever before, an inviting target for columnists and pundits. Was Ike of the mind that Nixon's place on the ticket could jeopardize millions of Independent and Democratic votes, they asked? Or was he concerned that the youthful Nixon, with only a decade in public service and no executive experience, might be ill-suited to assume the presidency if one of the president's illnesses proved fatal? Richard Nixon was at yet another crossroads in his career.

He was so dismayed by the "chart your own course" remark and the offer of a Cabinet post that he resolved to leave politics once his term was up. He informed some of his intimates that he would be calling a press conference to make his decision public. When word of this reached the Republican National chairman, Leonard Hall, and the president's deputy for legislative affairs, Wilton B. Persons, the two men rushed to the Capitol and convinced Nixon to delay his decision for a time. They argued that his withdrawal might hopelessly split the two wings of the party, particularly the donnybrook to fill his shoes.

Suddenly, on March 13th, news came rolling out of New Hampshire that dramatically changed Richard Nixon's future. That evening Nixon and his wife were guests at the home of Alice Roosevelt Longworth. After dinner the hostess asked her guests if they wanted to turn on the radio to hear the New Hampshire returns. In *Six Crises*, Nixon wrote:

> I told her not to bother because, since my name was not on the ballot, I did not believe anything of significance as far as I was concerned would happen. The following morning my phone was ringing off the hook. The New Hampshire primary, the first of the 1956 campaign, had returned a surprising, unsolicited write-in vote of 22,936 for me as the vice presidential candidate. It was a reas-

suring comment coming from the voters at a difficult time, and I reappraised the situation in light of the result.

Not only was Nixon's confidence boosted while his resolve to fight to stay on the ticket was strengthened; the returns sent reporters scurrying to find out how this had happened. The write-in vote was a clear indication of Nixon's grassroots support, which was far greater than many people anticipated. Overnight the tone of reports predicting his future shifted from his potential to drag the ticket to the schism that would form in the GOP between the "modern Eisenhower" and "conservative Taft" wings if he were dumped.

At a press conference the day following the New Hampshire vote, the president, growing weary of the lengths to which his refusal to openly endorse Nixon was being interpreted and realizing his options in picking a new running mate had been drastically foreclosed, told reporters:

> Anyone who attempts to drive a wedge between Dick Nixon and me is—has just about as much chance as if he tried to drive it between my brother and me....I will say it in exactly the terms I mean. I am very happy that Dick Nixon is my friend. I would be happy to be on any political ticket in which I was a candidate with him.

This would be, with only one exception, the strongest endorsement the beleaguered vice president would receive from his boss before the convention.

Ike's statement, along with the surprising write-in vote, moved *Time* to conclude, "as far as politicians were concerned, last week was the week that Dick Nixon, for all practical purposes, was nominated."

How this Granite State explosion transpired and the myth, rumors and speculation that revolved around it is a fascinating puzzle to pursue. Rumors began circulating immediately that Styles Bridges and his machine engaged in a massive last-minute mail and phone blitz to drum up votes. Bernard Boutin said: "As I remember it, the question of the spontaneity of the 1956 Nixon write-in subsequently was pretty much disproved. If memory serves me correctly, the engineer of it was Sinclair Weeks [secretary of commerce in the Eisenhower administration] working with Styles Bridges...something in the area of $60,000 was expended to pull it off."

An examination of pertinent files in both the Styles Bridges Collection at New England College and the Sinclair Weeks Papers at Dartmouth College failed to turn up any documentation that an organized effort took place. Dozens of men active in the Republican Party at the time were interviewed about the write-in, but this turned up no evidence that any mass mailer or extensive phone canvass existed. (The speculation on the mailer turned up figures ranging from 20,000 to 100,000 pieces of mail.)

Senator Bridges himself was interviewed on the program "Face the Nation" on March 18th. When asked if the vote for the vice president was spontaneous and unplanned, he responded: "I would say that it was practically spontaneous. I think I expressed the opinion to one person that it was at least 99 1/2 percent spontaneous." Regarding the impact of the write-in, he stated: "I think there's a psychological change since New Hampshire as far as the vice president's concerned."

Bridges' role, always difficult to pin down because he operated in such a secretive manner, indicated that—outside of making a total of 87 phone calls to his "action people" around the state—he did little else. In a story on Nixon's future in its March 26, 1956, edition, *Newsweek* examined the Bridges role:

> The theory that Senator Styles Bridges of New Hampshire, a close friend of Nixon, had conducted a secret write-in campaign was so plausible that some analysts believed it. They theorized that Bridges had thus killed two birds with one stone: He had given Nixon a hand up and at the same time rebuked Sherman Adams, the president's top assistant, ex-governor of New Hampshire and Bridges' political rival, who had been among those favoring postponement of the vice presidential selection.
>
> Bridges said he wished he could take credit for the Nixon endorsement in his home state but couldn't. Dwinell [governor at the time and another Nixon partisan] agreed that New Hampshire Republicans had done their good deed for Nixon without any prompting.

Bridges and another Nixon advocate, publisher William Loeb, had to be extremely careful about engaging in covert activity. Had they done so and been discovered prior to the vote, and the Nixon showing proved disappointing, they might have finished their friend's political career immediately. That may be an exaggeration, realizing how tenacious Nixon was, but such a situation would have given the press pack baying at Nixon's heels more latitude to increase their attacks on him. It also would have strengthened the hand of White House aides who were maneuvering to allow time for some other candidates such as Massachusetts Governor Christian Herter, to come forward while Eisenhower kept Nixon on the back burner.

The returns did move Loeb to pen in one of his front-page editorials:

> With no organized campaign of any kind whatsoever, this unheard-of write-in for Nixon was evidently the spontaneous expression of indignation over the apparent attempt by presidential hatchet man Sherman Adams, the White House palace guard, and such assorted New Deal characters as General Lucius Clay, Paul Hoffman, Milton Eisenhower and the rest of the Republican New Dealers to ditch Dick Nixon from the ticket.[2]

[2] Loeb's claim of spontaneity was later contradicted by none other than William Loeb. In a May 28, 1974, news story in the *Union Leader*, Loeb stated: "The Bridges organization sparked a write-in vote in the New Hampshire presidential primary in March of 1956 which gave the vice president the up to then largest write-in vote ever achieved by anyone in New Hampshire."

The article also noted that Senator Bridges was concerned enough about the polls showing Nixon to be a drag on the GOP ticket that he became the catalyst behind one poll that rated Nixon as having substantial strength.

Bridges initiated a nationwide survey by ex FBI agents with Howard Hughes aide Robert Mayhew in charge. Bridges called Loeb in the spring of 1956 at his home in Nevada, asking Loeb to contribute $2,500 for the cost of the project—which he did.

Harold Stassen, the leader of the "Dump Nixon" drive, had a survey showing Nixon costing the party 8%, or 2.3 million votes. The Bridges poll covering a sample of 48 states told another story. With only a 40% Republican make-up, Nixon was supported for another term with 54.3%; Massachusetts Governor Christian Herter, the most prominent name mentioned to replace the Californian, received 25%; and 20% expressed no opinion.

The Nixon outpouring was triggered in part quite inno-
cently by one of the few remaining liberal-progressive Republican
nuts and bolts specialists—Raimond Bowles, who admitted he
took "an unholy joy in being a maverick." Bowles had helped
run the Senator Charles Tobey renomination fight against Wesley
Powell in 1950, and in 1952 worked on a paid basis in the
Eisenhower primary drive. After organizing the Manchester vote
in the March primary, Bowles moved on to other primary and
convention states and the national convention. When the 1956
primary approached, he was self-employed in public relations
back in his home state.

Feeling "an uneasiness about Nixon," Bowles launched,
on his own initiative, a one-man crusade to have Christian
Herter's name written in for vice president in the primary. (This
effort was made independent of Harold Stassen's national drive
to gain support for the Massachusetts governor.) Bowles contacted Herter's staff and the governor about his plans. He said
the governor was "pleasantly interested." Bowles spent about
$1,000 to circulate a mailer to some 20,000 Republican house-
holds in the First Congressional District and to run a series of
small newspaper ads. (Bowles was also running as a delegate
favorable to Ike, so his ads plugged both ventures.) It resulted in
a "decent little write-in vote." He admitted it helped set off the
Nixon showing: "That was an explosion."

Bowles contends to this day only 4,000 to 5,000 Nixon
votes can be attributed to Bridges' phone calls: "Too much attention is focused on the mechanics. Bridges and his organization couldn't have turned out that kind of a vote with that kind of
an effort. It just doesn't happen that way here. The rest of the
vote is inexplicable except the people decided to do it."

The day after the vote, Nixon called State Chairman
William Treat to express, through him, his gratitude to his supporters. Treat knew of no calls by Bridges, and attributes much
of the breastbeating that took place after the primary to a normal
campaign occurrence, saying, "Defeat is an orphan, while victory
has a thousand fathers."

In part, Nixon's success shared a characteristic with that
of Henry Cabot Lodge in 1964 and Spiro Agnew in 1972—the
name was simple to spell. In addition, Nixon had paid two visits
to the state since his nomination, and his 1954 trip was the first
to the state by a vice president since the days of Calvin Coolidge.
These visits endeared him to the party regulars, who passed the

word around in an unorganized, spontaneous fashion that one of their leaders needed a helping hand.

The party workers who helped make the difference for Nixon that year (and whenever he ran in the Granite State) fondly remember his first trip to New Hampshire as vice president to address the 1954 state convention. Congressman Norris Cotton, who would win election to the United States Senate that November to fill the unexpired term of the late Senator Tobey, liked to contrast Nixon's visit with the one by Eisenhower the following summer. He felt it explained why Nixon held the allegiance of the party stalwarts: When Nixon had finished his address he made it a point to stay around to shake the hand of every single person as they were leaving the hall—a touch politicians of every variety don't soon forget.

During the 1955 Eisenhower trip Cotton spent almost two days riding in the same car with the president, and yet before an audience "the name Cotton never passed his lips," the senator remembered. Ike did mention Bridges and Adams frequently, but neither of them faced re-election the following year. In the town of Whitefield, north of the White Mountains, Bridges mentioned to Cotton he was getting a bad deal. He offered to mention it to the president. Cotton told him, "To hell with him. I'll get re-elected without him. Don't mention a word to him."

Finally at the Dartmouth Grant (a location as remote as possible for giving a political endorsement), Eisenhower managed to say a few words in behalf of Cotton—to a crowd consisting largely of wilderness guides. Cotton concluded that the president was not anti-Cotton, he was just non-partisan. One could never say the latter about Richard Nixon—nor 22,936 New Hampshire Republicans.

Between 1952 and 1956 the once-insignificant "Switzerland of America" had played an important role in helping to launch Dwight D. Eisenhower on the road to the White House. It also helped to save Richard Nixon's place on the GOP ticket, and thus cleared the way for his shot at the top spot in 1960. As the new decade unfolded, the nation's eyes would once again turn to the Granite State. By then, a decision would have to be made about who would follow in Eisenhower's footsteps. The opportunity would arise for the state's long neglected Democrats to help launch a fellow New Englander toward the presidency and into the pages of history.

1960
Kennedy Versus Nixon— Round One

JOHN FITZGERALD KENNEDY possessed a number of assets that would propel him toward the Democratic presidential nomination in 1960: a wealthy and famous family; an ability to speak effectively in public, with invitations by the hundreds pouring into his office; and his mediagenic countenance (and that of his wife Jacqueline), which graced the cover of many national magazines in a publicity build-up seldom matched in American politics. Unlike many of his peers, he comprehended how the growth of the suburbs and the appearance of television in most of the nation's homes was revising forever presidential campaign techniques. With his family fortune at his disposal, he was able to hire an energetic staff, a pollster and a private plane to lay his campaign base.

In his years in the Senate, Kennedy had compiled moderate-to-liberal voting record strong on bread and butter issues—one that would not totally alienate any region of the country or segment of the Democratic Party. Finally, as a Harvard graduate with a Pulitzer Prize under his belt and status as unofficial historian of the Senate, Kennedy managed to blend elements of intellectualism and ambition into one entity.

Yet there were liabilities also. He was young–42–when the election year began, and he lacked administrative experience. In addition, no senator had been elevated to the presidency since Warren Harding. He was from a state that had only 16 Electoral College votes, and the Democratic Party had not nominated a New Englander in more than a century. His controversial father was certain to be an issue; the allegation that the shrewd and ruthless Joe Kennedy was using his fortune to try to buy his son the White House was sure to surface in the course of the campaign. The elder Kennedy's well-known isolationist views as the ambassador to Great Britain just prior to World War II left a residue of public distrust that passed on to the son. Finally, there was the most significant handicap of all: his Catholicism.

As the 1960 election year commenced, Kennedy realized that if the choice of the Democratic nominee ever went to the convention back rooms in Los Angeles in July, he would become just another Estes Kefauver, probably relegated to the second spot for maturing and seasoning. The Massachusetts senator had to use the primaries to maximize his assets and demonstrate his popular appeal, depriving the party bosses the opportunity to launch their machinations on the second ballot. Kennedy also needed to implement a delegate operation in the non-primary states to ensure enough strength to win on the initial ballot.

The foundation for the nomination and the presidency itself was New England. All 114 convention delegates from the six-state region had to be locked in completely. Once that was accomplished, all the other dominoes would begin to fall into place.

Although worth less than a dozen Democratic convention delegates, the New Hampshire primary was of value. Once again occupying the first spot on the primary calendar, the vote would be closely monitored by politicians and pundits throughout the land to see just how fast Kennedy charged out of the starting gate.

A few tepid soundings were made by a number of Democratic hopefuls as to the possibility of taking Kennedy on in his own backyard, but none came forward. Only a handful of unauthorized delegate hopefuls favorable to Adlai Stevenson and Senators Hubert Humphrey of Minnesota and Stuart Symington of Missouri filed in the Granite State.

The Kennedy camp wanted the beauty contest portion of the ballot as unfettered as possible, and decided to challenge the ballot petitions of Paul Fisher, a ballpoint pen manufacturer from Chicago; Elton Britt, a country music singer and the self-proclaimed "world's smoothest yodeler" from Damascus,

Maryland; and Lar ("America First") Daly, a bar furniture salesman from Chicago and perennially unsuccessful presidential aspirant who campaigned in a dandy Uncle Sam outfit.

Fisher had enough valid signatures to be placed on the ballot, but Britt's and Daly's were successfully challenged. With the aid of Concord and Manchester city officials, the Kennedy campaign discovered that both had listed a number of non-registered or non-existent voters and used the names of deceased voters on the petitions.

The challenge was not exercised until Bernard Boutin, the *de facto* Kennedy chairman, contacted the senator and explained the situation. Kennedy was at first reluctant to appear to strong-arm people off the ballot, but he was won over by Boutin's argument that only those with valid legal petitions should go on—and ensure a genuine test by keeping the publicity seekers away. Neither Daly nor Britt decided to appeal the secretary of state's decision to keep them off the ballot.

Thus, at the outset the 1960 New Hampshire Democratic primary looked like a ho-hum affair. But by the time the votes were tabulated, the primary once again provided interesting copy, color and controversy until the Wisconsin primary pitted Hubert Humphrey against John Kennedy.

John Kennedy and his associates had done their homework. His stroking of the Granite State during the 1950s almost equaled that of the Eisenhower-Nixon team. In the fall of 1953, a year after his victory over Henry Cabot Lodge and seven weeks after his marriage, Kennedy addressed a banquet of the Young Democrats, initiating many of his contacts in the state. After his narrow loss of the vice presidential nod to Estes Kefauver in 1956, he stumped in 26 states for the Stevenson-Kefauver ticket, including New Hampshire. In 1958 he was back to address yet another party banquet. If that wasn't sufficient, his aides made occasional forays to feel the public pulse and divine the political currents. All this personal touch was vital; New Hampshirites had come to expect it, but it also was needed to complement the organizational work necessary to turn the New Hampshire Democratic Party into a viable entity.

In October of 1956 Bernard Boutin was in Washington attending a meeting of the Democratic National Committee. As the Kefauver state chairman, he had been selected by the convention delegation to the national committeeman post.

Kennedy's assistant, Ted Sorensen, contacted Boutin, inviting him to meet with the senator for half an hour in his office.

Kennedy told Boutin he was considering running for president in 1960 and that he would appreciate Boutin's help, particularly in preparing for the next New Hampshire primary. Over the next few years the two men met frequently in Boston and Washington. Invariably the conversation turned to the development of the New Hampshire Democratic Party and how it could assist Kennedy's presidential ambitions.

In analyzing the status quo, Boutin knew first-hand that the party was similar to "the tail at the end of a dog." Part of the problem, according to Boutin, was that some of its leaders were busy "looking for handouts from the Republican Party, minority appointments to commissions and other goodies of recognition." Then there was the wing that was owned by Bill Loeb (called the John Shaw faction after the losing gubernatorial nominee in 1954 and 1956). Both men knew the vigor and posture of the party would have an effect on Kennedy's aspirations, and Boutin believed that "what the New Hampshire Democratic Party stood for was the exact antithesis of what Kennedy stood for...we were at the time to the right of the Democratic Party of Mississippi."

A reconditioning job was necessary—new leadership recruited, fresh resources tapped, grassroots workers devoid of the fatigue and fratricidal tendencies of the old hands cultivated. New ideas needed to be tested and put into action.

With Kennedy's support, advice, and financial assistance ($2,500 of the $16,500 campaign cost), Boutin ran for governor in 1958. He beat Shaw for the nomination but, even though he lost to Wesley Powell in the finale, a beachhead had been secured. From that point the State Committee, the next target, was turned into what was essentially a subsidiary of the Kennedy presidential campaign. On a periodic basis aides such as Larry O'Brien, Ken O'Donnell or Ted Sorensen would come in to check over the trouble spots and confirm all the good news Boutin and his cohorts were passing down to Boston and Washington.

The Kennedy operation never missed a move. In mid-March of 1959, Ted Sorensen wrote to Boutin that a reporter from the *Chicago Daily News* was polling all 1956 national delegates with respect to their preference for 1960. Sorensen alerted his New Hampshire chief: "Naturally, the results will make quite an impression on the delegations getting ready for 1960 and we would like to make sure that all friendly delegates in your state return their ballot. Would you be willing to contact them accordingly?" He also stated, "It is, of course, of the utmost importance that the initiative in this matter appear to be originating from you and I am sure that you will proceed accordingly."

It was clear that they had accomplished much of their task when Hubert Humphrey proved unwilling to take the same risk as Kennedy was taking: challenging Humphrey in the Wisconsin primary while Humphrey was unwilling to enter the New Hampshire test. Kennedy was in for a free ride, but there were problems on the horizon: William Loeb, Wesley Powell, and Paul Fisher would all guarantee that.

By 1960 the major-domo of the Eisenhower administration—Sherman Adams—had retreated to his red house in the White Mountains to write his memoirs and resume life as a private citizen. In the early summer of 1958 a storm had erupted about Adams's granite-like facade; after the first barrage it subsided for a time, only to return in September with a fury that swept him out of the White House and political power forever.

As a congressman, Adams was in the habit of aiding constituents with requests for information from government agencies on various matters. In the White House, Adams continued the practice. To avoid misunderstandings that might occur if the calls were made by lower-echelon aides, Adams made many of the calls himself. He would later admit in his book *Firsthand Report*:

> As I look back, I was not sufficiently aware of the added importance that I might be giving to these inquiries by handling them myself. A call or inquiry from the assistant to the president was much more liable to cause suspicion of interference than a call from a less prominent White House staff executive, but I was not alert to the fact at the time. If I had been, I might have saved myself later embarrassment.

In 1957 the House Commerce Committee studied the operation of six large regulatory agencies. Investigators discovered some evidence that business concerns were sometimes manipulating the regulatory bodies. Some cases pointed toward the White House, but the committee decided to stop the inquiry. By the following year a disgruntled committee staffer told columnist Drew Pearson that Adams had interfered with some of the agencies to aid his friend Bernard Goldfine, a textile mill owner who was under investigation by the Federal Trade Commission and the Securities and Exchange Commission.

After Pearson's revelations hit the nation's newspapers and airwaves, the House Special Subcommittee on Legislative Oversight began to examine the Goldfine matter. It was discovered that Adams had received the following largesse from the businessman: $3,096.56 for Boston and New York hotel bills, two suits, a vicuna coat (the press reports said it was worth $700, Adams said $69), and the loan of an oriental rug valued at $2,400. Goldfine had written off some of the expenditures on his federal income tax.

The Federal Trade Commission also issued complaints against Goldfine's textile mills charging false labeling practices. Adams asked the FTC chairman, Edward Howrey—a man he had helped to select—to send him a report on the matter. In revealing to Goldfine the information the FTC passed on to him, Adams violated FTC regulations; he later defended his role in the controversy, stating, "At no time in my communications with the chairman of the Federal Trade Commission did I ask any favor or special consideration for Goldfine. I only asked for factual information about the labeling ruling."

Goldfine's woes with the SEC were based on eight years of violations concerning his failure to file required annual reports for his Boston real estate company. In 1956 Goldfine complained to Adams about the way the SEC was treating him. Adams asked Gerald Morgan, special counsel to the president, to look into the case. Adams claimed: "Again, in this instance, neither Morgan nor myself made any effort to influence the SEC's action against Goldfine one way or another." Yet the SEC, which had already obtained a civil-contempt conviction against Goldfine, called off its criminal contempt proceedings after Morgan's contact.

When this information began to surface in the 1958 subcommittee hearings, Adams cut short a fishing trip to return to Washington to testify before the subcommittee. This in itself was news; when previously asked by congressional committees to testify on other matters, he had refused to do so, citing executive privilege.

On June 17th, in a jammed hearing room, Adams asked the subcommittee: "Did Sherman Adams seek to secure any favor or benefits for Bernard Goldfine because of his friendship? The answer is...no. I have never permitted any personal relationship to affect in any way any actions of mine in matters relating to the conduct of my office." He did concede that any errors on his part in the controversy were of judgment and not intent. An admission of imprudence sent the mass of reporters off with their story lead.

The following day at a press conference President Eisenhower stood foursquare behind his beleaguered chief of staff. He also proclaimed, much to the later regret of those supporting Adams, "I need him," an admission of weakness from a man in one of the most powerful leadership posts in the world.

The campaign theme that the Republicans had used with such impact for so long—"clean up the mess in Washington," the very thing that had stirred General Eisenhower on that morning in August 1951 when Robert Burroughs met with him in Paris—was now shattered. Even though Adams had dismissed other administration officials for much smaller transgressions, Eisenhower refused to cut him loose. Adams was not merely an aide; he was a system of government.

Two international crises, the first in Lebanon and the second in the Quemoy Islands gave Adams a respite of sorts. However, as the mid-term elections approached, Adam's days were numbered. Eisenhower came to depend on him less and less, and party leaders and candidates despaired of the controversy's effects on their political hopes in the fall. All that was left was a public note of disapproval to push him over the edge. The Maine state election, held as it was then in early September, provided just that.

In 1958, for the final time, Maine conducted its general election two months ahead of the rest of the nation. The cliche, "As Maine goes, so goes the nation," was amended that year to "As Maine goes, so goes Sherman Adams."

The Republicans had enough trouble that year with a recessionary economy, racial troubles brewing in the South and the loss of international prestige with the launching of the Soviet spaceship Sputnik. The Maine returns were a clear sign that the party faced a debacle in November. The incumbent GOP senator, Frederick G. Payne (a Goldfine associate and recipient of a $3,500 loan to help purchase a Washington, D.C., home), was upset by the young, two-term Democratic Governor Edmund Muskie. The Republicans also lost the governorship and the two congressional seats. The cry for Adams's scalp soon reached a fever pitch.

The month before, Vice President Nixon had reported to Eisenhower that virtually every one of the 36 Republican candidates for the United States Senate, as well as most House candidates, wanted to see Adams given the boot. Many Republican National Committee members felt the same way. The party fat cats were galvanized by the Maine returns to close their wallets until the "Adams mess" was cleared up.

On September 22nd Adams flew to Newport, Rhode Island, where the president was vacationing, and tendered his resignation. He also delivered a brief speech on television that same evening: "A campaign of vilification by those who seek personal advantage by my removal from public life has continued up to this very moment. These efforts, it is now clear, have been intended to destroy me and, so doing, to embarrass the administration and the president of the United States."

Years later the script of the Adams firing would continue to generate controversy. In July of 1974, as the House Judiciary Committee released previously suppressed transcripts of White House conversations concerning the Watergate break-in, Nixon created the "smoking gun" that ensured his downfall. Nixon said he did not want his staff injured in the Watergate affair the way Adams was in the Eisenhower administration:

> I think he made a mistake, but he [Adams] shouldn't have been sacked. I don't give a shit what happens. I want you to stonewall it, let them plead the Fifth Amendment, cover-up, or anything else, if it'll save it, save the plan.

In spite of Adams's fall from the heights of power, the lesson of his ascension starting with a New Hampshire primary was not lost on the man who now occupied the post Adams held eight years previously—the first-term governor, Wesley Powell.

At the age of 24, in 1940, Powell became the administrative assistant to Senator Bridges, one of the youngest top Senate aides at the time. For the next ten years he held the post, excluding military service, until 1950, when he decided on a bold gamble. Although he had no experience in running for political office, he decided to challenge 12-year incumbent Senator Charles Tobey for the GOP nomination. In a bitter fight he was narrowly defeated.

In 1954 Powell was back on the stump, only to lose the senatorial primary to Norris Cotton. In 1956 he was unsuccessful in unseating the incumbent governor, Lane Dwinell. Finally in 1958 he succeeded. With the vigorous editorial support of the *Manchester Union Leader*, something he had enjoyed in all his early campaigns, he won the governorship, defeating Boutin by 6,800 votes.

With Powell in such a prominent position, much of the 1960 primary news revolved around him, for he was never averse to the public limelight. The main question in that primary was not "Who will win?" but "What will Wesley do next?" Early on he tried to launch a favorite-son candidacy for Styles Bridges, but this violated the populist and progressive intent of the primary, and the idea died on the vine.

In early October of 1959, at the height of the fall foliage season, Vice President Nixon ventured into the state to dedicate a flood control project. Powell's reputation for eccentric behavior was enhanced when he refused to allow the vice president to ride in the lead car of the procession. Nixon was relegated to the second car along with Senators Bridges and Cotton.[1]

Publisher Loeb was quite disturbed about the manner in which the Nixon people were treating him and Powell. On October 13th, shortly after the Nixon visit, he wrote to Herb

---

[1] Senator Cotton enjoys relating what Nixon thought of his reception that day. The vice president had recently received a tumultous welcome in Poland where, as a sign of the crowd's affection, many a rose was tossed at the Nixon motorcade. Cotton: "It was early in the morning, about 8 o'clock as we were going through the streets of Concord to the dam dedication. There were a few people lining the streets, but not a great number by any means. They would wave at the car and say 'Good morning, Mr. Vice President.' The vice president turned to me and said, 'They aren't too demonstrative are they—you New Englanders are a little reserved.' I said, 'Let me tell you, when a New Hampshire Yankee gets up at 8 o'clock and says 'Good morning, Mr. Vice President,' why that's much finer than thousands of roses in Warsaw.'"

Klein, a Nixon press aide: "You have been told a great deal of hooey about Powell and myself being highly controversial. Well, somewhat over 50 percent of the citizenry supported us in the last election." Harping on his kingmaking prowess, he continued, "We took an unknown man, Wesley Powell, in 1950 and we came within 1,200 votes of beating Senator Tobey. We kept right behind him until we helped him get in the governor's chair nine years later." In concluding the very bleak picture, Loeb warned Klein, "Right now you haven't got a snowball's chance in hell of carrying New Hampshire. You are behind now, before the Rockefeller millions and the Dartmouth boys have even gotten out of first gear."

Powell, never to be deterred, next commenced a flirtation with the supporters of New York Governor Nelson Rockefeller, a move destined to fail but nevertheless bothersome to the Nixon people. Because the vice president was trying to project a more somber and serious mien than in the days when he wandered about the nation blistering the Democrats, the Nixon camp wanted to steer clear of the controversial and conservative Powell—but not clear enough to force him into the Rockefeller camp.

In mid-December Powell executed a bold move that resulted in his appointment as the chairman of the Nixon primary candidacy in the Granite State. The Powell power play left the powerful Bridges in the role of back-up man to his former aide. Powell called the vice president in Washington and listed the three conditions that had to be met to win his support:

- —he would have veto power in the direction of the primary campaign;
- —all funds for the campaign would be channeled through him; and
- —the vice president would write a letter to Powell soliciting his support, a letter that Powell would make public.

Nixon rejected the demands. Intermediaries next tried to appease Powell and his opponents at the same time by giving him an honorary chairmanship. He could have the title but no real control over Nixon's fortunes. Then a small group of party heavyweights gathered in Concord in mid-December to try to smooth things out. Besides Powell, the group consisted of Senators Bridges and Cotton and the former GOP National

Committeeman and fundraiser, Frank Sulloway. They were hit with another of Powell's bombshells. He had been offered an "important" post in the national Rockefeller campaign, and would accept unless he were handed the Nixon chairmanship by 4:00 p.m. that very day. A lengthy phone call to the Nixon headquarters at the Sheraton-Park Hotel in Washington followed. Nixon's top aides, Len Hall and Robert Finch, received the news, and by the end of the day word was sent back that Powell would become Nixon's chairman. He had forced what the party moderates called a "complete capitulation."

In the end, Powell had little to do with the day-to-day operation of the Nixon effort. He was busy being governor, and had little relish for the nitty-gritty work of getting out the vote. In addition, to the surprise of many, by the end of December Nelson Rockefeller dropped the bombshell that he would not be challenging the vice president for the nomination after all. Dick Nixon had a free ride to the nomination.

Between October and December Rockefeller had embarked on two elaborate trips around the nation to test the waters for his presidential prospects. The news he brought back to New York was disheartening. The party professionals, especially those who would fill up the chairs at the national conclave in Chicago in August, wanted one thing—Richard Nixon as the standard-bearer.

Rockefeller would have been forced to wage an expensive and exhaustive fight for the nomination. Even if he toppled Nixon, the victory would have been virtually worthless after such an intra-party fracas. Even with Rockefeller's robust ability on the stump, it would require a superhuman effort to simultaneously serve as the chief executive of the nation's largest state and to campaign in the primaries. The final straw was the polling news from New Hampshire, critical to launching the Rockefeller momentum and to slowing Nixon's. The polls indicated that the vice president had an insurmountable lead–75%-15%. On December 29th, Rockefeller pulled out of the race.

It was a move without precedent. In September—before the presidential campaign year commenced—the New Hampshire Democratic State Committee unanimously endorsed the candidacy of John Kennedy. This move formalized what had become increasingly obvious: for once the state's Democrats had ceased their in-fighting, bickering, and back-stabbing to unite in a common cause—supporting the presidential drive of their neighbor from the Bay State. In another first, the Kennedy organization authorized the State Committee to select the slate of delegates pledged to his candidacy. Also, for the first time, all the delegates were to be selected from either one of the two congressional districts; there would be no at-large seats as in the past, diluting the impact of the Manchester vote.

Even with an unknown opponent of little consequence, Kennedy scheduled two trips to New Hampshire. Boutin was so buoyed by the crowds' response to Kennedy that he predicted the candidate would double the vote Kefauver had received four years previously, something Kennedy found difficult to believe.

All was not smooth sailing, however. In a year that, some contend, hinged on the outcome of the first in the series of Kennedy-Nixon debates, a not-so-great "debate" created one of the more interesting stories as the primary wound down to its final hours.

On his last day of stumping, Kennedy and his entourage wound their way through a series of engagements in the seacoast area. In the afternoon he addressed a crowd of 1,700 at the University of New Hampshire in Durham. His opponent, Paul Fisher, had been trying without success to arrange a speech at the school. He was tipped off by *New Hampshire Sunday News* editor, Bernard McQuaid, that Kennedy would appear on Monday, March 7th, at 2:30 p.m. Upon hearing this, Fisher wired the vice president and provost, Dr. Edward Eddy, Jr., that he was being discriminated against in not being invited. He informed Dr. Eddy of his intention to "appear in New Hampshire Hall next Monday at 2:30 p.m. and walk to your stage to demand my rights as a presidential candidate to equal time at your university-sponsored convocation. I warn you in advance not to cancel this convocation and not to deny me an equal opportunity to be heard, or your officials will convict themselves of an effort to rig the New Hampshire primary election."

The provost wired in response that he was unaware Fisher wanted to address a campus meeting and invited him to do so— on Monday at 4:00 p.m. Fisher realized that such a time would leave him out of focus of the publicity machine whirling about the senator, so he turned down the invitation, calling it a "separate and not equal" meeting. He further advised the UNH official that he would be arriving at 2:30 and "Senator Kennedy could speak either immediately before or immediately after me, whichever he preferred."

By the time the "debate" began, it had become one of the hot news items in a lackluster election. Fisher carried out his promise to appear, and two university people showed him to a seat in the front of the hall. He refused to be seated there; instead he climbed over a row of press tables and placed himself on the stage. Once there, he refused appeals to leave. Fisher invited the officials to throw him off the stage, which they would not do.

By this time Kennedy was waiting in the wings; the decision on eviction of the intruder was left to him. He said no, came out onto the stage, was introduced, and delivered a talk on disarmament. After the ovation at the end of his address, Dr. Eddy came to the podium and declared the meeting adjourned, had the curtain pulled, and the public address system disconnected. Fisher by then was standing at the podium feeling "alone, disappointed, and with anger and frustration slowly rising up within me." However, hearing the chant, "We want Fisher, we want Fisher," he stepped through the curtain, faced the audience and cracked a joke. By this time the hall was in an uproar, with cheering and jeering, and the university officials knew they had been licked by the stubborn and persistent pen manufacturer. They pulled the stage curtain open, replugged the public address and invited Fisher to sit down while he was properly introduced. Kennedy decided to stay and listen. The speech itself was anti-climactic; Fisher refrained from attacking his opponent or the school officials. Instead, he seriously discussed his campaign platform, particularly the provision calling for the abolition of all taxes on incomes of less than $10,000.

Fisher finished the primary with 13.5% of the Democratic primary vote (6,853 Democrats and 2,388 GOP write-ins). Little was ever heard from him again, aside from his return in 1968 to contest yet another New Hampshire primary.

The size of Joseph Kennedy's fortune and his willingness to use it in his son's behalf would be an issue throughout the primary season, thanks in large part to Hubert Humphrey. The first primary was no exception. Publisher Loeb was hurling charges that the elder Kennedy was trying to buy his son the White House, and the issue of campaign spending was a sensitive one for the Kennedy camp. They were eager to develop as much volunteer support as possible, saving their resources for the more expensive tests further down the road.

The desire to keep spending below $30,000 in the initial primary conflicted with some party pols' desire to see a portion of the Kennedy fortune spread around the state into traditional Democratic cities to aid in the get-out-the-vote drive. For instance, the former party state chairman, attorney Fred Catalfo of Dover, contacted Kennedy and requested that $10,000 be spent in addition to the regular budget for the election-day drive. The money would go to regular party workers and he wrote, "I concur that volunteer workers are fine, but to depend on them alone is to allow your campaign here in New Hampshire to chance." Boutin, who was opposed to the outlay, lobbied against it, and the money request was turned down. According to Boutin the Kennedy campaign adhered to its $27,000 primary budget.

Since Richard Nixon was unencumbered with any primary combat, he was presented with the opportunity to mold and redefine the Newest Nixon—a moderate, widely traveled and seasoned back-up man, ready and mature enough to follow in the footsteps of the great Dwight D. Eisenhower.

In the 1960 primary, Wesley Powell saw a once-in-a-lifetime opportunity to step into the national spotlight. He decided to borrow a page out of the Dick Nixon textbook on how to rise in national prominence by engaging in some rock 'em-sock 'em smear charges in the final hours.

On the busy Monday just before the voting, Governor Powell held his monthly press conference in the State House, charging Kennedy with a "demonstrated softness toward Communism which the people of our state would not want to see exhibited in the White House."

After his UNH speech Kennedy called a press conference and proclaimed he was "disgusted that Governor Powell should attempt a smear of those proportions out of political pique." He called upon the vice president to repudiate his state chairman for the remark, which Nixon did.

Eager to get a final word in, Powell purchased time on the Manchester television station to discuss his position in the controversy and to read a telegram he had sent off to his candidate. It read in part:

> The senator you defend now has straddled the Communist issue since the days of the McCarthy trial. If

you and the Republican Party expect to win, you had
better be on the attack lest the unjust attacks by
Kennedy upon the Eisenhower administration leave the
Republicans holding the bag. This Republican governor
did not attack Kennedy's loyalty. I did attack his soft,
straddling record in his approach to the Communist
menace, and I shall continue to do so.[2]

The Powell antics resulted in loads of publicity for him—
some of it extending from outside the borders of the first primary
state. The day after the vote, the avidly Republican *New York
Herald Tribune* commented on the Powell behavior in its lead editorial:

> Before the first vote was cast in New Hampshire's pri-
> mary yesterday the name of the biggest loser was clearly
> established. It was Wesley Powell, sharp-tongued politi-
> cian who is governor of his state and campaign manager
> there for Vice President Nixon.
>   His election eve accusation that Democratic
> Senator John Kennedy is soft-headed on the Communist
> issue was not only amazingly maladroit in view of the oc-
> casion, but irresponsible, damaging to the Republican
> Party and, unhappily, perfectly in tune with the Powell
> pattern of unfair play. Furthermore, it cost him stature as
> a party strategist.

The *New Republic* endeavored to tie the present Powell
behavior to the manner in which Nixon had conducted himself in
the past:

[2] Powell's tirade was not without an ulterior motive; at the same press
conference he let it be known that he would accept the vice presidential
nomination of his party if it were offered to him. A write-in drive with
that goal had sprung up, endorsed by Loeb, and a telephone blitz was under
way to drum up support. It netted only 9,620 Republican and 1,127
Democratic votes, far behind the benchmark Nixon had established in
1956 and not significantly more than the surprising 6,567 tallies cast by
Republicans for the ambassador to the United Nations, Henry Cabot
Lodge. Vice presidential, and even presidential, dreams continued to
pound in the breast of Governor Powell, but his 1962 defeat for renomination for a third term ended forever his unlikely prospects for national
office.

It is grossly unfair to criticize Governor Powell. He was only using the play the coach taught him, and all of a sudden he finds himself thumbed to the bench for subordination, or something. First Murray Chotiner and now Wes Powell. One wonders where Mr. Nixon can recruit people to do the work he finds it tactically inadvisable to do himself, if willing servants are so summarily dealt with.

William Loeb was not to be denied his shots in the vilification campaign being waged against the young senator. In a front-page election day editorial entitled "You Are Voting For Your Life," Loeb attacked:

> We would consider Kennedy's nomination to be extremely dangerous to the safety of the United States....Kennedy does not understand the Communist menace....His entire record proves that Senator Kennedy is not capable of dealing with Khruschev and his fellow Russians. It is for that reason this newspaper would consider Kennedy's nomination and election a national disaster which might cost us our very lives....If we elect charm in the form of Kennedy to the White House, in the solemn opinion of this newspaper we are just about through as a nation.

Kennedy's victory was no surprise, but the total vote was. Boutin's prediction was almost fulfilled: Kennedy gathered in 43,372 votes, nearly doubling Kefauver's last total. This win provided new material for the Kennedy propaganda machine on how one candidate was beginning to create an enthusiasm that no one else could match. Formidable challenges lay ahead; yet Boutin, perhaps overstating the case, would reflect years later, "If he hadn't done well in New Hampshire, I think that the West Virginia victory and the victory in Wisconsin would have been impossible."

For an election without meaningful competition on either side, the 1960 primary turnout was nothing short of astounding. It came within a whisker of topping the total for the intense 1952 fray (136,179-135,109). The vote was testimony to the unified backing Nixon and Kennedy both enjoyed in their respective parties and to the elaborate organizations they constructed to turn the event into a public relations bonanza. Nixon's 65,204

beat Eisenhower's 1956 total by almost 10,000 votes and set a
GOP record that would stand until 1968. Kennedy made news
not only for his doubling of the last Kefauver vote, but for cutting
the traditional Republican margin in New Hampshire, thus
adding one more ingredient to his publicity barrage. Even at that
early date, once the returns were known the speculation started
that the stop-Kennedy drive was losing its momentum. Only
one state had been heard from, but already many pundits were
talking of a November showdown between Kennedy and Nixon.

In light of what happened to another New Englander 12
years later, John Kennedy's next-to-last campaign appearance in
the general election is worth recounting. On the final day of traveling in five of the New England states, Kennedy was greeted with
massive, enthusiastic crowds at every stop.

Bill Dunfey, coordinating the states of Maine, New
Hampshire and Vermont, met the entourage that last day in
Burlington and flew with the candidate to Manchester. There
Kennedy was to address an early evening outdoor rally, and
conduct a half-hour nationwide telecast from Manchester. Then
he would proceed to Boston for the last speech of the campaign.

On the flight to the Queen City, Dunfey provided the
candidate with copies of the latest editions of the *Manchester
Union Leader* for his perusal. Dunfey, turned on by the crowds
and the intense level of activity, was confident he would see his
three states fall into the Kennedy column the next day.
Kennedy was of a different mind. He said they would do all right
in the southern part of the region, but he felt that the religious
issue was killing them in more rural, Protestant northern New
England.

Dunfey, disturbed by how depressed the candidate
sounded, remembers him saying: "I can almost feel the thing
slipping away from me. We had it a week or 10 days ago. Now
I feel it slipping away by the hour." Kennedy wanted to know
what ideas Dunfey had for his speech and asked him, "Why is it
every time I come into this state I've got to prove I'm an
American."

The crowd that gathered that frigid night was one of the
largest in the state's history for a political event. Ironically, the
gathering was held within easy shouting distance of the fortress-
like *Union Leader* building. Ted Sorensen, who had traveled with
Kennedy as much as anyone, considered the speech "a rare
show of public irritability and incaution in blasting one local

publisher for saying once again that Kennedy was a Communist sympathizer."

Dunfey, who made an effort not to steer Kennedy away from confronting Loeb and admits to egging him on, reflected later:

> John Kennedy did the same thing and fell into the same trap that Ed Muskie did. Only he was lucky—it was the night before the election. Some of those who'd followed the nominee for months couldn't believe that somebody could get under his skin that much. He'd always had the ability to rise above the heat of the battle and not let things get the best of his emotions, but not this time.

In the speech Kennedy wanted to know why, every time he visited New Hampshire, "I have to again deny that I am a member of the Communist Party." In calling for the defeat of the state's Republican ticket, he proclaimed, "It's time to bring an end to the Know-Nothing movement" that had controlled the state's politics for so many years.

In *Who the Hell Is William Loeb?*, author Kevin Cash recounted more of the speech:

> He told the crowd that he felt that inasmuch as his campaign had begun in Manchester, it would be only fitting that it end there. Then, "I would like to have the *Union Leader* print in a headline that we carried New Hampshire." Kennedy received a deafening roar of applause for an answer. Apparently pleased with that trial balloon, Kennedy intoned: "I believe there is probably a more irresponsible newspaper than that one right over there somewhere in the United States, but I've been through forty states and I haven't found it yet." The crowd's roar seemed to echo off the *Union Leader* building itself and lasted for what seemed almost a minute. Kennedy continued: "I believe that there is a publisher who has less regard for the truth than William Loeb, but I can't think of his name." And the applause this time put the previous two outbursts to shame.

The attack came so late that Loeb missed the opportunity to place one of his famed front-page rebuttals in the election day morning edition. He did manage to fire off some salvos in a news story: "Kennedy's tirade indicates that Kennedy is lacking in the basic dignity expected of a president of the United States." He was called a "liar and a spoiled brat....his childish ranting last night shows that he is completely lacking the necessary stature to be president of the United States."[3]

But Loeb hit back with too little, too late. Election day had arrived and the all-night vigil to reveal the winner soon followed. New Hampshire had helped to launch John Kennedy on the road to the White House. It would never have the opportunity to help keep him there in 1964.

[3] The previous high vote for a Democratic candidate was Franklin Roosevelt's 125,262 against Willkie in 1940. Kennedy topped that with 137,772, but unlike FDR he lost the state—Nixon received 157,989.

1962
An Interlude

To determine the strength of the GOP's grip on the first primary state in the early sixties, one must pull out the record book. A Democrat had not won the First Congressional District since 1936. The last senator elected by the Democrats was in 1932, the last governor in 1922; only once in this century had they secured the Second District seat in 1912.

Republican Styles Bridges, once the boy wonder of New Hampshire politics, was for decades the major lynchpin in its political structure. It was not an exaggeration to say that nothing moved until he gave the nod. Never an inspiring orator, lacking authorship of any major piece of legislation during his 24 years in the Senate, he was a consummate backroom pol: a masterful negotiator who accumulated enormous power while building the Republican Party organization.

Yet beneath the firm grip he held on patronage appointments, the surface unity and the easy, almost laughable wins over the downtrodden Democrats every biennium, tension and conflict—even hatred—stirred among the tribal chiefs and their followers.

Bridges's career paralleled that of Charles Tobey. In 1934, Bridges was elected governor, the youngest man ever to hold the post up to that time, and the only Republican to win a State House race that year. In 1936 he continued to buck the Democratic tide as he won a seat in the Senate. His arrival in the Senate two years prior to Tobey, who was 18 years his senior, never failed to grate on the older man.

Bridges saw his colleague as a sanctimonious opportunist who ditched his isolationist sentiments with an eye on the next election. A few days before the attack on Pearl Harbor Tobey told an audience in Nashua that Japan would "never dare attack the United States." (Shortly afterward the senator was left dazed outside his hometown post office and general store after an irate female interventionist weighing 150 pounds launched a powerful right hook as her commentary on the senator's foresight.)

The feud between the two men was kept out of the electoral arena until 1950, when Bridges's former administrative assistant, Wesley Powell, took on Tobey in the Republican primary. Tobey won despite severe attacks on his voting record.

Three years later Tobey was dead. To indicate the harshness of emotions the Tobey family held toward the senior senator, his widow let it be known that Bridges was not invited to the funeral. Vice President Nixon, who was to represent the Eisenhower administration at the services, found that his friend was not going to be there. He passed the word to Mrs. Tobey that if that were the case, not only would he not be in attendance, but he'd guarantee that no one from the Senate delegation would be there either. She finally relented.

The ritualistic bloodletting that was building included a Bridges-Adams rift. The state simply was not large enough for two men with such enormous power and influence. Bridges coveted the presidency, and it galled him that a non-politician such as Dwight Eisenhower had achieved it so easily. To make matters worse, Bridges's arch-rival, Sherman Adams, sat at the president's right hand.

Some contend that with a few well-placed phone calls Bridges could have averted the 1958 Adams catastrophe. For years he had been able to stop investigations into his own questionable dealings largely because of the gumshoe operation he ran out of his office—a system that collected embarrassing information on the mistakes, bad habits and peccadilloes of the powerful and prominent. Bridges had leverage everywhere, but he never exercised a bit of it to help save Sherman Adams.

Adams's demise was quickly followed by Eisenhower's mandatory retirement and Nixon's failure to succeed him in the presidency. The removal of these three men from the public limelight had important ramifications; when the next tragedy befell the New Hampshire Republicans, no one individual would be in a position to prevent the consequences.

In September, 1961, at the age of 63, Styles Bridges suffered a mild heart attack. He was believed to be on the road to recovery when he was stricken again. The senator died at his East Concord home in the early morning hours of November 26th.

With Bridges's quiet, coalescing presence gone, the complexion of the body politic was certain to change. The explosion to follow might have been averted if someone other than the colorful and charismatic Wesley Powell had been in the governor's chair.

Powell had deeply hungered for a Senate seat, but he refused to appoint himself, as he had the power to do. He said he
wanted to go to the Senate but he wouldn't do it over Bridges's
body.

Even before Bridges had been buried, publisher Loeb had
begun to raise the cry for the appointment of the senator's
widow, Doloris. Powell decided instead to fill the remaining year
of Bridges's term by appointing his former aide, a 34-year-old
unknown named Maurice Murphy.

Immediately the scorned Loeb shifted his editorial fire-
power to the man he had supported for 11 years. Mrs. Bridges
and Murphy both began running for the Republican primary the
following September, as did both congressmen: Perkins Bass,
son of former governor Robert Bass, serving his fourth term in
the Second District; and Chester Merrow, a liberal, labor-union-
backed former schoolteacher who tossed away 20 years' senior-
ity for the high-risk Senate gamble.

As 1962 progressed, the primary fight became as bitter
and divisive as any waged this century. Bridges's widow and
Bass became the frontrunners. Mrs. Bridges was a one-time
government secretary who campaigned as her husband's clone—
a militant conservative who lashed out repeatedly at Kennedy
administration policies. She stressed her desire to follow her
husband: "If they can't have him, they would like to have me.
I'm a Styles Bridges Republican and everybody knows what that
is."

Bass was the moderate who brought the stronger organization to the fray. He hoped his middle-of-the-road status
would appeal to Republicans. He often questioned Mrs.
Bridges's right to the Senate seat by inheritance with the
observation: "How many of us, if our doctor died, would go to
his widow for treatment?"

The vote was close—Bass won by 1,692 out of some
100,000 cast. Bridges demanded and received a recount. She
lost 10 votes. The fight went on. Instead of the traditional
kissing and making up at the State Convention, the feuding
spilled over onto new fronts. Mrs. Bridges had the nominee
served with a summons to disqualify him, charging that he had
exceeded the $25,000 spending limit. Her charge was subse-
quently dismissed by the state Supreme Court.

The situation became even more confused and bitter for the Republicans. Governor Powell, regarded as a cinch for renomination and re-election to a third two-year term, hoped to widen his quest for power. A lengthy article in *Time*'s "Politics" section of May 4th, 1962 discussed Powell's future plans. After his re-election, he was going "to start barnstorming nationally in 1963, then to enter New Hampshire's presidential primary, the first of the year, in March of 1964. He will gleefully invite other Republican national aspirants to contest him in that primary." After a rousing start, he planned to sweep on to the important Wisconsin test and then to the GOP nomination.

Powell's scenario for the taking of the White House would face one last hurdle—John Kennedy. *Time*: "Powell says he has already figured out how to handle Kennedy. Beginning next January, Powell plans to take a 'potshot a week' at the president. And if he wins the Republican nomination, Powell will really set out after Kennedy: 'I'll just build up every brick, brick by brick, in that wall around Berlin. I'll ask every day, "Why did not you put those planes over the Bay of Pigs?"'

Powell's dreams for a national role were shattered—he was upset in the September primary by a state legislator from Manchester who ran with the tacit blessing of the *Union Leader*. Out of anger Powell then endorsed the Democratic candidate for governor, John King. The Republican knives that had been held in check were now slashing out all over the state.

Republican disarry was almost complete. As a last-gasp attempt to unify the warring factions in the final weeks, the party called upon the inspirational presence of former President Eisenhower. At a mid-October rally in front of Manchester City Hall, those who failed to show attracted as much attention as those who appeared. Merrow and Mrs. Bridges both stayed away, and Governor Powell, furious at the routine nature of the invitation sent to him, also declined to appear.

The Republican debacle following the election would have seemed impossible a few months before. Democrat John King swept into the State House by more than 40,000 votes, and Tom McIntyre bested Bass for the Bridges Senate seat by 10,000. The Styles Bridges era came to a sudden end.

1964
A Yankee Surprise

1964: A YEAR TO REMEMBER. By then New Hampshire was not quite so rural, so Yankee and so isolated as legend held it to be. The myth was never accurate to begin with. The state was not chock full of wizened old-timers sitting around pot-bellied stoves musing over the weather and awaiting the arrival of the next carload of city folks to fleece. One of the most industrialized states, it was strongly affected—as was the entire nation—by changes wrought in the sixties.

A bit more than half the state's population lived within a 60-mile radius of Boston. The arrival of the slick expensive four-lane interstates thrusting through the verdant forests tightened the bond between the growing southern portion of the state and the Boston metropolitan region. (The population in the decade from 1950 to 1960 increased by a hefty 13.8%, from 533,000 to 606,000.)

New Hampshire would not miss out on the economic boom of the new decade. The diversification efforts following the collapse of the mill economy in the thirties and forties guaranteed that. The electronic, computer and aerospace firms springing up around the Route 128 industrial complex encircling Boston would find their way north. As government contracts poured out of Washington and sent start-up company income levels soaring, the old mills would give way to plush new offices scattered about the pine, maple and birch forests.

Yet in spite of its similarities to the rest of the country, the 1964 edition of the first-in-the-nation primary provided a result so startling and unprecedented in American political history that the belief in the Yankee traits of independence and inscrutability were revitalized. By the time the Republican voters concluded winding their way through the poster-sized March 10th ballot (a foot and a half in length, with five names listed on the beauty contest and 125 delegate hopefuls for the 14 seats), the already colorful, controversial record of the primary opened a new and provocative chapter.

A New Hampshire winter is almost without exception harsh and long, with bitter cold, piling snow, treacherous ice storms and short days. It gives way finally, but only to the accompaniment of blustery winds far into the spring. The winter of 1963-64 would be particularly harsh, bringing with it bleak sorrow over the murder of President Kennedy.

The assassination left few with a relish for primary politics; the pain was too immediate and cut too deep. But once the 30-day moratorium on politics was over, the inevitable was at hand. It was time for another quadrennial frolic in the snow.

The new president, Lyndon Johnson, undertaking the task of transition, found no need or desire to hit the hustings. He had more important things to contend with as he endeavored to place his own imprint on the federal governing system.

Pugnacious, rabble-rousing segregationist George Corley Wallace, the governor of Alabama, would stir up trouble for Johnson in the later primaries (particularly Maryland and Indiana), but cold and distant New Hampshire was not one of his targets that year.

The shaken figure of Attorney General Robert Kennedy would be of much more concern to Johnson as he tried to shape his administration. A vice presidential write-in drive for Kennedy swept New Hampshire, but, unlike Eisenhower in 1956 (when moves by Nixon forced him to keep him on the ticket), Johnson was much more adept at handling other politicians. When it came time to announce his running mate, Johnson would not have his hand forced by Bobby Kennedy or 25,094 New Hampshire Democrats.

For the first time since 1952 a real head-to-head clash of serious contenders occurred in the premier primary. The announced contestants were fighting not just for the Republican presidential nomination, but, they believed, for the heart, soul and future of their Grand Old Party.

Senator Barry "Mr. Conservative" Goldwater of Arizona and New York Governor Nelson Rockefeller both cared enough to come—in fact, Goldwater devoted 21 days to the primary and Rockefeller seven more. Both men spent well in excess of $100,000 wooing voters. Thousands of hours were spent elaborately constructing organizations to try to persuade the expected 100,000 Republican voters. Both men had ample opportunity to expound on their views of the issues at hand; or, as Goldwater aptly put it at the end of one kaffeeklatsch, "It gave me a chance to find out what's on your mind and you to find out whether I have one."[1]

However, by the primary's conclusion, the two candidates discovered that neither one had any real appeal to a broad cross-section of the party. Goldwater's neanderthal view of the world did him in; Rockefeller's well-publicized remarriage was his kiss of death.

As in 1952, the voters' lot was cast with a man thousands of miles away who never lifted a finger in his own behalf or articulated a word about any issue—a man who had not won an election since 1946 and who had turned off party professionals with his alleged lackadaisical effort as Nixon's 1960 running mate. The write-in victory for the American ambassador to the war-torn country of South Vietnam, Henry Cabot Lodge, would shake the candidates and the Republican Party to the core.

With the floundering of Goldwater and Rockefeller becoming more apparent in the late fall of 1963, Boston lawyer David Goldberg and business executive Paul Grindle began looking for "something fun and exciting to do." Following the Kennedy assassination, their plans crystallized around the idea of running Henry Cabot Lodge for the Republican presidential nod—or more aptly, drafting him for the job.

Grindle, a former reporter and promoter who knew how to create as well as write copy, helped open the Boston campaign office in January with a public relations flourish. But the first "Draft Lodge" physical plant lasted only a day. Massachusetts Secretary of State Kevin White allowed it only that brief life span because it lacked Lodge's authorization.

---

[1] In 1955 the state legislature passed a law limiting the expenditure of money in a presidential primary to $25,000 per candidate. The law was loophole-ridden and eventually repealed. No state statutes exist controlling the expenditure of funds for the election—only federal rules.

Their attention began to shift more and more to the north, where the much more flexible and wide-open New Hampshire primary was about to begin. No authorization was necessary for a headquarters, only a check to pay the rent. Absolutely anybody, if so inclined, could stroll along the portraits of the past governors lining the State House walls and file as a Lodge delegate. Lodge could do nothing to stop it. Most important of all, in a state virtually devoid of voting machines, a write-in campaign could catch fire off paper ballots and pencils. The draft campaign had found fertile territory to take root.

The news from Dwight Eisenhower in early December that Lodge should return from his South Vietnam post to be available for the Republican nomination was not an endorsement, but it had the same effect. Grindle and Goldberg then picked up the pace, scouting out the terrain in New Hampshire. They touched base with people disillusioned with Goldwater and Rockefeller, and with those who believed that the ambassador could restore the mantle of leadership that had fallen from Eisenhower's shoulders with his retirement.

Goldberg and Grindle, or the G-men, as they became known, resolved that they needed some signal from Lodge that they could go full-bore without being disavowed—not necessarily a yes to the draft, but an indication that Lodge would not say no.

Halfway around the world in Saigon, Lodge was effectively out of touch with stateside politics. Enterprising reporters tried to reach him by telephone, but connections were poor and the resulting news stories were often garbled. Lodge's son George, for whom the G-men had been campaign managers in his 1962 bid for the Senate, thought his father was particularly vulnerable to this type of news reporting. George viewed his father as an isolated figure in a beleaguered city, absorbed by the military and diplomatic demands of his mission. He knew that as the presidential primaries began, the public focused on any presidential prospect. He worried that the most casual remark could become distorted on its way from Saigon to Walter Cronkite's evening news. George thought it was vital that someone talk with his father face to face—someone experienced in politics, learned in the technical requirements of New Hampshire primary laws and with no ax to grind. He needed a man of probity and prudence who was absolutely trustworthy.

Through family connections, George had known William Treat, a Hampton attorney, probate judge, and the state Republican National Committeeman. A former Republican state chairman (1954-1958), Treat was approached by Lodge. Treat immediately pointed out that he was a neutral in the primary contest and intended to remain so until the convention. As the National Committeeman, he had maintained relations with both the Rockefeller and Goldwater camps. The other leaders in both campaigns had been his close allies in politics for the past ten years. After carefully spelling out his requirements, Treat accepted the Saigon assignment.

The short vacation Lodge had planned for himself and Mrs. Lodge between Christmas and New Year's had been abruptly canceled following an escalation of military activities in Vietnam. Therefore the planned rendezvous with Treat in Hong Kong had to be scrubbed. Treat was left with the choice of either returning home, assignment incomplete, or to fly on to Saigon. He decided to complete his mission. As the amabassador was to comment, Saigon was a beleaguered city, with travel in and out of the Saigon Airport a risky business. Communist troops often lay at the ends of runways, firing on the incoming and departing planes. Treat's plane landed without incident, however. After checking into his hotel, he called the ambassador's residence. A man answered the phone, brusquely saying that the ambassador was not in. When Treat identified himself, the tone of voice changed abruptly, "Oh, hello, Bill, this is Cabot. How are you and how was your trip?" Eager to fulfill his mission and return to the United States, Treat allowed that he was fine and would like to see the ambassador as soon as possible. Lodge urged him to get a good night's sleep and said he would pick him up in his limousine the next day for lunch.

Lodge arrived promptly for the appointment. After a ride through the city, the two arrived at the ambassador's residence. As with any politician, Lodge loved to talk politics and they immediately fell into a spirited dialogue. What was the latest word about his old friends, Bob Burroughs and Sinclair Weeks? He had entered the Senate in 1936 with Styles Bridges, two young men in their mid-thirties with only 15 Republican colleagues in the Senate during that nadir of Republicanism under FDR.

Treat spoke bluntly to Lodge about the criticism of his alleged shirking of campaign duties during the 1960 race when he was Nixon's running mate. Lodge hooted at these accusations.

He claimed that the campaign schedulers had completely under-estimated the value of TV. In his judgment, it was far more important to be fresh and rested for a TV appearance on a typical campaign day than to try and make every last campaign stop. Treat recalled Nixon's worn appearance, especially on his first TV debate with Kennedy, and wondered if perhaps the campaign would not have gone differently if Nixon, too, had husbanded his strength.

The conversation shifted to the New Hampshire election. Lodge was told there was considerable movement in his behalf. His reaction: "Well, you know there's nothing I can do." He recited the provision that precluded any political activity while in the Foreign Service, saying "I keep a copy of this in my desk just to remind people who call me up that I can't engage in anything political."

Lodge believed that, in order to win an election, you had to be there. At that point a wide smile crossed his face as he said, "I can imagine that those other guys must be gnashing their teeth realizing that I don't have to take a position on anything."

As with any national politician, Lodge would have enjoyed being president. However, at 61 the fires of political ambition were dimming. Yet, a lifetime of public service and an instinctive sense of *noblesse oblige* made a firm declination inconceivable. He was just going to keep silent and let things run their course. If called upon to serve his party as their presidential nominee, he would do so, but he would not hustle and scramble for the job.

The prospects for a successful write-in were indeed remote as the new year began; yet, by not shutting the door, Lodge's "positive inaction" was the signal which Goldberg and Grindle needed to proceed.

Within a week, the trio of Goldberg, Grindle and George Lodge arrived at Treat's home for a briefing. They were full of questions regarding the ambassador's health, his state of mind, interest in his new position, and how Mrs. Lodge was. But the most significant question of all was: Would he stamp out the life in the budding draft movement? With the "he didn't say yes, he didn't say no" information in hand, the way was clear to move forward.

With just two months until the election, they had much to do. They had to locate and fill out a slate of favorable hopefuls, open up a headquarters, raise some money and blitz the electorate with information on the distinguished career of Ambassador Lodge.   By the time they were done, Barry Goldwater and Nelson Rockefeller would no longer consider this lark very humorous at all.

Early sampling in the state revealed that Senator Barry Goldwater held a substantial lead over Rockefeller; the figures ranged from 3-1 to 4-1.   Goldwater also held a virtual monopoly on the party establishment.   His Senate colleague, Norris Cotton, was his state chairman.   The state Senate president and the speaker of the House also supported Goldwater.   The former governor, Lane Dwinell, arduously courted by the Rockefeller camp, came out for Goldwater, too.   Numerous party func-tionaries in the legislature, county and town offices climbed on board, all set to give the straight-talking, silver-haired, bespecta-cled westerner a firm send-off down the road to the nomination.

Rockefeller was quite dismayed that Cotton decided to head up Goldwater's campaign.   Back in 1954, when Cotton first ran for the Senate, he had difficulty raising funds.   His fiscal agent and main fundraiser, a prominent Concord attorney named Dudley Orr, was a Dartmouth alumnus who knew Rockefeller well.   Orr went to New York City and returned with $4,500, $1,500 of it from Rockefeller.   The contribution was not listed on the contributor report in the State Archives, nor did Orr tell Cotton about it.   In 1964, Rockefeller told people he could have understood Cotton's neutrality, but he felt betrayed after the help he had given in the past.   It turned out that Cotton knew nothing of the mysterious contribution until years later.

Senator Goldwater enjoyed one other considerable bless-ing.   He gave publisher William Loeb the chance to shift from his usual editorial opposition to liberal or moderate candidates and ideas to preach the wonders of the conservative gospel according to Barry Goldwater.   The publicity and propaganda barrage re-leased that year by New Hampshire's only statewide daily news-paper has rarely, if ever, been matched.   Barry Goldwater was everywhere—on the front page, on the back page, and endlessly in between.

Loeb was also occupied with heaping verbal abuse on the "Wife Swapper" and "Home Wrecker" Rockefeller, regardless of the fact that Loeb himself had divorced not once, but twice.

In spite of these same advantages Nixon had parlayed into a state lock-up in 1960, Goldwater's candidacy saw many a discouraging and tumultuous day. Little planning was initiated for the election, and it showed. Senator Cotton, successful practitioner of old-time politics, very much ran his own campaigns. He wanted to do the same thing for his good friend Barry, even though this was a different ball game and he had his Senate duties to attend to. However, a campaign manager was finally selected: House Speaker Stewart Lamprey, a rising star in the GOP.

Cotton and Lamprey came into immediate and prolonged conflict. Lamprey was hired to run the campaign and he intended to do so, no matter how much Cotton wanted to interfere. They fought constantly. Cotton believed that Lamprey's plans for a "new politics"-style endeavor with computer voter identification, door-to-door canvassing and a mass media blitz was too alien and elaborate for his land of taciturn Yankees. He much preferred the quiet cultivation of party leaders and important families, combined with some stumping, media coverage and a last-minute phone campaign to get out the vote.

The problems were compounded, for little direction emanated from Goldwater national headquarters. The conflict between Cotton and Lamprey would escalate to a point where either threatened to quit the campaign and Goldwater aide Richard Kleindienst (later to be one of Richard Nixon's attorneys general) or Goldwater himself would be called upon to calm emotions and smooth ruffled feathers.

The most grievous mistake in the campaign—aside from the candidate's shoot-from-the-hip comments and his decision to enter the primary in the first place—was the use of the candidate. Lamprey laid out a rugged 21-day ordeal with as many as 18 stops a day in the cold and harsh climate. It was a regimen that even Estes Kefauver would have found challenging.

The Arizonan was ill-suited for the ordeal. He was hampered at first by a cast on his right foot, after an operation to remove a calcium spur on his heel. Comfortable with wandering throughout the land preaching his monologue of conservatism to large, receptive audiences, he was ill-prepared for the running debate a candidate must endure with querulous citizens, questions planted by opponents, snide college and high school students eager to get their digs in, and the ever-present news media.

Goldwater was a disaster during his first sustained and intimate contact with the national press corps. They kept printing what he said, not what he really meant to say. These stories and subsequent clarifications of his remarks saw every verbal blunder turned to Nelson Rockefeller's advantage; Goldwater's lead quickly dissipated.

The Goldwaterisms that filled the press accounts—on Social Security, Cuba, the state of the nation's military preparedness, civil rights, Vietnam, the role of the federal government—soon convinced the populace that this fellow was a conservative all right, but of the wild western variety, not the mature and sagacious eastern species. In p.r. jargon, Lamprey bemoaned, "It reached a point where it became impossible to sell the product."

Nelson Rockefeller was as tailor-made for the rigors of the New Hampshire test as his chief declared opponent was ill-suited. His gregarious "Hi, how are ya fella" style that had captivated the voters of the Empire State in 1958 and 1962 was ideal for the Kefauver-style campaign he needed to wage. It was not only vital for the voters to meet him face to face and to hear his views (a technique approaching the status of ritual for the primary), but also to break down the barrier of suspicion and distrust in which his great wealth encased him. Those perceptions of his aloofness, manipulativeness and lack of feeling for the common man's plight all had to dissolve into a feeling of affection—that "Nelse" was really just another guy, with a bit more money than most, but still a regular fellow.

To begin with, Rockefeller had a much finer sense of the state and the region. He had been born in Bar Harbor, Maine, and he frequently summered there. He attended Dartmouth College, graduating in 1930 with a degree in economics. For a decade he served as a college trustee, and he governed a state separated only by Vermont. The old boy network of Dartmouth grads provided a base for the Rockefeller organization, albeit not as solid as Goldwater's party pols.

Goldwater perceived from the beginning that New Hampshire was not critical to his nomination aspirations. The winner-take-all California match was the only primary essential for his nomination. It turned out that his perception was correct. Rockefeller approached New Hampshire from the opposite direction, and thus had stronger psychological motivations to do well. It was vital for him to badly bruise Goldwater. If he failed, it would doom him in the eyes of politicians and the press, constituencies that had already given him a nine-count due to his marital complications.

With his prospects so bleak, Rockefeller turned to two state political figures to guide his fortunes, although both men had little clout at the time: former Governor Hugh Gregg (1953-1955) and his right-hand man, Bert Teague, an unsuccessful congressional candidate in 1954 and 1962 and once an aide to Senator Bridges. As a condition of their backing, the duo demanded and received full control for the primary. The New York governor's national operatives were relegated to a rear seat in a contest that could make or break their boss's nomination hopes.

In spite of differing backgrounds (Gregg's well-to-do and Teague's working class) the two worked well together and experienced little of the conflict Cotton and Lamprey underwent. But they did spend considerable time fighting off the high-powered, high-finance plans of the New Yorkers. The two men considered their state a unique political environment; only they knew how to divine its currents, pitfalls, and nuances.

The accent would be on the candidate's Dartmouth background, his warm personal style (on occasion he would treat a gang of kids to ice cream cones), and his maturity and considerable government experience. He was a proven leader with a list of accomplishments as chief executive of his state.

A slick direct mail campaign, expensive television blitz, or other components of the new age of mass-appeal electronic electioneering would not fly in New Hampshire. Gregg and Teague held out against these plans as long as they could. By February Rockefeller began to beam political ads into the state from out-of-state television stations. Cotton attacked this practice until he learned to his embarrassment that the ad agency preparing Goldwater's television spots would do the same thing.

With his substantial expenditure of time and money, Rockefeller began to hack away at the Goldwater lead. He made particular headway attacking Goldwater's comments on the Social Security program. Goldwater's ideas threatened the financial security of the elderly in a state with the fourth highest percentage of people over the age of 65 (11%). In addition, Goldwater's foreign policy view—militant concern over the spread of Communism without an accompanying commitment to alleviate the underlying economic and political causes of Third World unrest—provided Rockefeller with the opportunity to convert much more of the electorate than anyone originally thought.

But Rocky could never make the necessary breakthrough. As he began to pull even with Goldwater in the polls, an interesting phenomenon occurred. The undecideds were increasing, not decreasing, as is the normal pattern with an approaching election. The Republican voters had started with Goldwater, been repelled, moved on to consider Rockefeller, and, after giving him a hearing, finally nestled in the undecided column.

The most damaging element for Rockefeller was his remarriage. It was not the remarriage itself; it was the fact that his new wife, the former Margaretta Fitler Murphy, had to give up legal custody of her four children to her husband, a doctor who worked for the Rockefellers, to secure her divorce. As she toured the state with her husband, "Happy," as she was nicknamed, was the target of some verbal abuse. "Hello, Mrs. Murphy, did you bring the good doctor with you today?" was one of the more common comments.

Theodore White, in his best seller *The Making of the President 1960*, recounted one Rockefeller stop:

> I followed Rockefeller in the last week of campaigning, and in the town of Hollis, New Hampshire, on the Saturday before primary day, I preceded him to a mid-morning rally....He arrived with Mrs. Rockefeller and, since she was heavy with child, someone hastily brought a little folding chair upon which she might sit. The TV crew quickly rearranged its lights, and their glare flooded her. Her husband stood beside her; she sat—the only seated person in the hall—as if in a witness chair; the townspeople gathered in a semicircle somewhat apart from the candidate and the seated woman, as if they were a jury. And then, as he spoke—excellently that day on the subject of leadership and responsibility in a world at war—I watched the audience. Whether or not they were listening to him I cannot say, but their eyes were all staring unnervingly at the handsome woman with bowed head and curled legs who sat in the spot of light. They might have been a gathering of Puritans come to examine the accused. They had made up their minds. Hollis was to vote: for Henry Cabot Lodge, 238; for Rockefeller, 120; for Goldwater, 85.

The "Puritans" had other names to pause at and mull over. Senator Margaret Chase Smith of neighboring Maine stumped the state a bit, yet she was not taken seriously, as was the case with the ever-present Harold Stassen.

Another figure out of the past and still to be reckoned with was Richard Nixon. He was now in self-imposed exile in New York City, practicing law, after his humiliating defeat by the colorless incumbent Pat Brown for the California governorship in 1962.

In the first post-assassination Gallup Poll of Republican voters throughout the country, the top choice for president was Nixon with 29%, Goldwater 27%, Lodge 16% and Rockefeller 13%. In January Nixon rented a suite at the Waldorf Tower in New York City and invited 15 of his political associates to mull over his role that year. He was of the mind that neither Goldwater nor Rockefeller would win the nomination, and he wanted to know what strategy would place him as the compromise choice. Nixon, eager to see which way the winds were beginning to blow and if they contained sufficient velocity to resurrect his fortunes, made the same decision regarding the first primary as Lodge and Robert Kennedy—he didn't say yes, he didn't say no, he just let it go to see what would happen. The write-in was directed by the volatile Wesley Powell. It proved to be a healthy vote, but Nixon's hopes of a startling upset victory went unfulfilled.

That honor would befall the man he had picked as his running mate in 1960. The voters were in search of something tried and true, yet at the same time fresh and different. They were in search of a seasoned leader not given to the rantings of a Goldwater; a man of good reputation not embroiled in the personal scandal devastating Rockefeller. They were in search of a man willing to serve—not a Nixon hungering and maneuvering to do so.

As decision day approached, increasing attention focused on the distinguished, aristocratic figure of Boston Brahmin Henry Cabot Lodge.

The tasteful brochure was part of the phenomenon. On the front flap was the impeccably groomed non-candidate, straight-arrow behind a podium, looking every inch a president of the United States.

The brochure's flashbacks on Henry Cabot Lodge's career started with a photograph of a young, serious Lodge, dressed in military garb, poised beside an anti-aircraft gun. He was the first senator since the Civil War to resign from the United States Senate to serve the nation's military in a time of war. He concluded active duty at the rank of major general, and held an abundance of battle stars and honors. And it was noted, "This military service now stands him well in Saigon, where on some days he can hear Communist gunfire through his embassy office windows and where American soldiers have been shot only eight miles away."

Lodge's relationship with Eisenhower was not bypassed. It was described as being "intimate, cherished and enduring." His role in helping to create the 1952 campaign and the transition of the government was recalled. The caption concluded, "It was natural that this relationship should culminate in President Eisenhower's recent request that Ambassador Lodge return to the United States and seek the Republican nomination for president."

In a not-so-subtle dig at Goldwater's inexperience in foreign affairs, a weary Lodge was pictured huddling with the ambassadors of Belgium and France on the floor of the Security Council during the explosive Congo crisis. This service "demanded the full maturity of the United States delegate as the leader of the Western World."

For the common-man touch, Lodge the outdoorsman was pictured puttering around with the motor of his 19 foot boat at his seaside home in Beverly, Massachusetts. Finally Lodge was shown towering over an equally joyful Vietnamese woman on the streets of Saigon. On why he accepted the difficult post, the reader was informed, "President Kennedy needed an experienced diplomat, a tough negotiator, a trained soldier who was fluent in French, the language of the area. Henry Cabot Lodge was approached, and he accepted."

The brochure sent to 97,000 households from a list sold by the Republican State Committee urged New Hampshirites to write in Lodge on March 10th. The significance of the action was clear: "New Hampshire can lead the nation in drafting Lodge, in demanding that he return to the United States to even greater responsibility and become the Republican candidate for president. Don't be satisfied with the available. Select the best."

Along with the brochure came a pledge card, a simple device to fill out and send to Concord to be forwarded to the ambassador in Saigon. The idea behind this was to establish a continuing relationship with the contact–a standard direct-mail technique–and to gauge the public's response. By the end of the campaign, almost 10,000 of the cards had been signed. As they piled up in the office they provided tangible evidence that this write-in lark was full of promise. With no candidate, the G-men were free to focus in on the media and on organizing aspects. There would be no need to engage in the complicated procedure of scheduling the candidate, since there was no candidate. There was no need to move him about speaking to groups, or to bundle up and trudge through the freezing New Hampshire morning to greet equally grumpy factory workers arriving for another monotonous day on the job.

George Lodge, every bit as tall, handsome and immaculately groomed as his father, would have made an ideal surrogate to stump the state. When asked why he did not, he replied, "I can't recall it ever being discussed. It would have gone against the grain of the draft and it would have been like sending Milton Eisenhower to New Hampshire in 1952. It wouldn't have been appropriate for me to be campaigning there. A stand-in wasn't necessary. My father was well known. The nature of the effort was such it would have been confusing for me to be there."

Simple in its execution, the Lodge campaign was complex in other ways, especially in its assessment of the electorate. Grindle talked later about the approach:

> Within two weeks of our arrival we really thought we could beat both Goldwater and Rockefeller with a write-in. The typical thing that is done wrong in the New Hampshire primary, year after year after year, is that everybody underestimates the intelligence of the New Hampshire voter. They play it way, way down. It's just abysmal. You can't believe that they do it so badly. Nelson Rockefeller was just unbelievably condescending, and so was Goldwater. We became quite confident that something that really challenged them intellectually would be very attractive. So we never tried to simplify the campaign.

The second tactic—another public relations stroke also engineered by Grindle—was a five-minute film on Lodge that was shown 39 times the last few weeks on the Manchester television station, Channel 9. (Unlike the well-endowed Rockefeller and Goldwater treasuries, the Lodge write-in had inadequate funds for the more expensive Boston television that permeates much of the Granite State.)

How Grindle came to secure the film is a matter of dispute. Gene Wyckoff, a New York-based public relations man, had worked on films, radio and television and had written and produced political media as well, particularly for the 1960 Nixon-Lodge campaign and for Nelson Rockefeller. Wyckoff claims that Grindle came to see him in New York that January, wanting to look at some of the 1960 Lodge material for ideas on how to promote him in the New Hampshire primary. A still-picture, impressionistic treatment of Lodge turned Grindle on. Backing up the shots of Lodge in dramatic action at the United Nations was the unmistakable voice of Dwight D. Eisenhower praising him to the heavens. Grindle told Wyckoff he was going to show the film "to a few friends."

Grindle had the film edited for $750, inserting a new introduction that described the origin of the film so as to avoid charges of misrepresentation (which were leveled anyway). The presence of Eisenhower was clear and powerful—"I want him"—and, in closing, it showed how to mark the ballot for the Lodge delegate group and how to write in the name Henry Cabot Lodge.

Grindle contradicts Wyckoff's story on how he secured the film: "We didn't pirate it at all. Wyckoff called me one day and said that he had this film and I went down to New York to look at it and get a copy. He called me out of the blue and volunteered it. He simply gave me a print and said I could have it. That's the last time I ever saw him."

Goldwater was so livid over the use of Eisenhower for the narration that he flew to Gettysburg to try to talk the former president into stopping its use. The G-men, tipped off about the trip, were relieved at Eisenhower's reaction. He thought it was quite amusing and would do nothing to stop its use.

The mailer, film, delegate slate, headquarters and media play all were effective. The Lodge campaign was a refreshing, creative and challenging experiment. Yet only an image had been created. The reality of casting one's ballot for Goldwater or Rockefeller was quite unappealing (two-thirds of those polled were opposed to both candidates), but the problem still persisted: Would the write-in step be taken?

The doubts about Lodge's intentions was the final obstacle to overcome. The completion of a third track (Lodge returning home as a candidate) would be vital. With enough words, newspaper headlines, insinuations and speculation, the sparkling figure of Lodge, brought to life by Grindle's public relations touch, needed the *fait accompli*. It had to appear that Lodge was throwing his hat into the ring while he remained in Saigon, silent, aloof and distant, never saying a word.

The finishing touch to this portrait of a true patriot ready and willing to serve his country if called upon was left to Robert Mullen, a Washington-based public relations man who had been active in the 1952 Eisenhower campaign. One week prior to the vote he left his Washington office (which also happened to be the national headquarters for the Draft Lodge movement) for the final days of the primary.

To lay the groundwork for his eventual sleight of hand, Mullen had sent to the media a series of "backgrounders," releases not intended for direct attribution, on Lodge's intentions.

The first one on January 16th stated: "I personally have no question but that, given any sort of respite in South Vietnam and given a clear signal that he has a fighting chance for the nomination, Cabot will make the race." In the next backgrounder (dated February 11th) Mullen admitted that he did not have any hint of when, if ever, the ambassador would return, but, "We know that if the clear call is sounded, he will report for duty and he will report with the full elan of a good soldier full of fight and spirit and with the smell of victory in the air. His own commitment to an all-out campaign is the least of our worries."

The final one (February 29th) reviewed the progress of the New Hampshire campaign and, "If we give him a clear indication that he is a serious contender, he will come back and put on the most spirited and effective campaign ever seen in U.S. history."

As Mullen arrived in New Hampshire, he realized that the tempo had to be increased, the strands pulled together in harmony to complete the illusion. A calculating mind, good timing and finesse were required. On the Saturday just before the voting, Mullen conducted a press conference in Manchester. He offered the observation that Lodge would allow his name to remain on the Oregon ballot. In that primary state, the secretary of state placed on the ballot all prominently mentioned candidates, declared or otherwise. If one was named and wished to have the name removed, one had to notify the Oregon official by

Monday, March 9th, at 5:00 p.m. Pacific time—just hours before the opening of the polls in New Hampshire.

If this news regarding Oregon were true, Lodge would be close to crossing that fine line between draftable and actual candidacy. Mullen cited George Lodge as his source of information. Reporters scurried to call the ambassador's son, who denied that his father had said he would not remove his name from the Oregon ballot. Then, in effect, he confirmed Mullen's statement as he proclaimed, "It is my firm belief that he will not take his name off the Oregon ballot." Ambassador Lodge, as usual was stonefaced in reacting to the developments.

The Mullen gamble, designed to make the headlines, succeeded. The Sunday papers, particularly the Boston ones, played it as important front-page news. *The Boston Herald*: "It's Official: Lodge in Race," and *The Boston Globe*: "Lodge a Candidate, Stays in Oregon Test."

The next evening, primary eve, a sigh of relief went up in the Lodge headquarters as the Oregon deadline passed and Lodge's name did indeed stay there. Mullen had forced the matter into the media while it still had time to register an impact. After another 24 hours had passed, the impact was quite clear.

The Rockefeller hopes were high near the end. The latest Gallup Poll results were encouraging, indicating a 6-point climb for the governor and a 13% fall-off for Goldwater. The trend was similar in New Hampshire, yet the undecided bloc remained substantial.

The response on the street was heartening. Goldwater would belittle Rockefeller's proficiency by saying, "I'm not one of these baby-kissing, handshaking, blintz-eating candidates...thinking that a whack on the back can get you a vote."

Hand to hand and man to man, Rockefeller at a distance of a few feet was the most effective Republican politician of his era. New Hampshire's postage-stamp size seemed made to order for his ebullient, jouncing, winking, clasping and clutching— all triggered after the release of the rip cord of his famous grin. He was obviously having a very good time. The *Saturday Evening Post* wrote, "He went through Dover (pop. 19,131) like a small boy set free from school." In the neighboring city of Rochester he shinnied up a firehouse pole. While pressing the flesh in the downtown business district, he wound up behind the counter of a local bank (the president of which informed him that was illegal). Former Republican Party Chairman and National

Committeeman Richard Cooper, a local attorney, accompanied Rockefeller and told the bank officer, "You know the governor and his family could gobble up this little bank by tomorrow afternoon if they wanted to," whereupon the candidate was allowed to roam at will.

Yet in the town halls, the civic clubs and the campaign rallies the magic rays did not reach the customers as easily as they did on the streets. As the campaign wound down, the candidate had little remaining enthusiasm to repeat what he had said so many times before.

The Rockefeller camp's evaluation of the Lodge write-in had altered radically since January. No longer considered a mere nuisance, it had become a move that would divide the moderate and liberal vote and guarantee Goldwater's success in the well-publicized first primary. On two occasions Rockefeller tried to get a message to the ambassador to call off his backers—once by contacting George Lodge and once through a trans-oceanic telephone call to Saigon—but Lodge would not issue orders for withdrawal.

Some observers contend the February call Rockefeller made to Lodge in Saigon was a critical turning point. Thaddeus Seymour, then the dean at Dartmouth, was a Rockefeller supporter and traveled with the entourage on the North Country campaign. Seymour:

> I believe that he (Rockefeller) was beginning to pick up support during the last month of the campaign and that we would have won it except for an accident which gave the Lodge people their opportunity. I was there when it happened, and I believe that it is one of the unrecorded events in the history of that campaign.
>
> The incident occurred at Franconia College. Rockefeller was resting at the president's house before lunch. As the party walked from the house to the dining hall, the president's wife said, "Mr. Rockefeller, if your Saigon call comes through, you can take it in my husband's office."...The press was very interested to learn whether Rockefeller had had any contact with Lodge. An alert reporter overheard this comment and the next day the press corps was buzzing about the phone call....The press characterized his call as telling Lodge to "put up or shut up." The Lodge forces immediately began to issue

press releases which characterized Lodge as the hard-working patriot in Saigon and suggested that he was being abused and exploited by Rockefeller on the campaign trail. Lodge, who had hardly been mentioned in the press up to that point, suddenly became front-page news and dominated the coverage of the campaign during the final weeks.

Since Lodge had privately told Rockefeller he would support him the previous summer, the governor now felt double-crossed. Rockefeller's aides took the G-men aside on occasion to persuade them to call their lark off; they claimed it was jeopardizing the future of the GOP's modern wing.

Alexander (Sandy) Lankler, a dapper Washington attorney who had worked in Rockefeller's previous gubernatorial election, was in the state to keep an eye on the interests of the candidate and the national staff. Grindle recounts how Lankler tried to pound some sense into their thick skulls:

> Lankler would corner us and try and tell us the whole world was going to fall apart if we continued with this thing—and ruin the Republican Party's chances. We'd sort of laugh and say, "For Christ sakes, how many people have you got?" They had sixty or so. We'd ask what their budget was (it was astronomical) and that sort of thing. There were just four of us on a shoestring. We told him, "If you can't trounce us with all the resources at your command, the sooner you know it, the better."

In spite of the precipitous drop in support in the national and state polls, the panic in the Goldwater camp gave way to quiet confidence in the last days of the primary campaign. The crowds that greeted him were large by New Hampshire standards, the scheduling improved and the devastating comments declined, since Goldwater now paused and reflected for a moment prior to responding to a query. Hundreds of dedicated volunteers trudged about the state, survey sheets and propaganda nestled against their chests in the bitter cold. (Lamprey estimated that 60% of the households in the state were canvassed in pushing Goldwater's gospel; he found the workers in that campaign to be the most dedicated he had ever seen.)

Senator Cotton was quite apprehensive about what was happening to his colleague. He felt two weeks of North Country campaigning on his part was necessary to "disabuse their minds of some of the impressions that they had of Goldwater." He considered the effort "one of the most discouraging experiences of my life. Friends of mine came out and would come up to me before I had a chance to talk and say, 'Norris, I know what you're trying to do and we understand—but *no* Goldwater.'" When informed that there was a discrepancy between his recollections years later and the encouraging comments he made to the press after the trip, he answered: "If I did, it was a piece of political hypocrisy and I freely confess to it."

Goldwater, bouyed by his last round of politicking, predicted that he would probably receive 40% of the vote, saying, "If you don't have it made by Saturday night, you are not going to make it—and I have it made." Goldwater should have stuck around for another day or two.

Pollster Louis Harris revealed some startling information in the March 9th issue of *Newsweek*: If all the candidates running or being drafted in the primary were listed on the ballot, Lodge would win handily, 31% to Nixon's 24%; Goldwater had 18% and Rockefeller 12%.

However, the experts were skeptical about the write-in. It was not a common practice; voters feared misspelling the name, thus discounting the vote. The "if he won't put his name on the ballot, how much does he want the job?" argument had to be contended with also. In surveying the sample regarding the ballot as it was, and allowing write-ins, Harris came up with a different response: Goldwater and Rockefeller were tied at 24%, Lodge had 16%, Nixon 15% and Senator Smith 7%. (All this polling had been done before Mullen captured the headlines with his "Lodge is Running" news.) The mood of uncertainty at the end was perhaps best expressed by a tall, stiff-spined farmer, 70-year-old Jesse L. Ambrose, who told a reporter from *Time*, "I've had so much information from so many candidates about what I should do, that my bucolic mind is utterly confused."

A snowfall measuring 10-14 inches greeted voters on primary day. The Lodge headquarters, using a multiplier of three for every pledge card returned, predicted a vote of 27,000 for their man. They underestimated a bit, for the voters did what many said they would not do—they wrote in the famous and easy name to spell with a relish. Within 18 minutes of the close of the polls, the CBS computer predicted a Lodge landslide. And landslide it was. Lodge received 33,007 (36%), Goldwater

20,692 (22%), Rockefeller 19,504 (21%), and the Nixon write-in 15,587 (17%). Senator Smith gathered 2,120 votes, but it turned out she was in the wrong race, as she received even more votes for vice president—3,163.

Upon hearing the bleak news from the north, Goldwater told a group of supporters gathered for a Washington victory celebration that he had "goofed up somewhere." Since the tally for the delegate slate would not be known for hours after the beauty contest, the Goldwater people kept their hopes high that some of their delegates would win. That was not to be—every one of the Lodge aspirants won, and a group of political novices were on their way to the July Republican National Convention in San Francisco.

Rockefeller, trying to conceal his anger and bitterness at the result and Lodge's refusal to call off the draft, called the result a victory if not for him, at least his wing of the party—"a victory for moderation." Rockefeller also considered the surprise vote a phenomenon of regionalism, since Lodge was virtually a favorite son, albeit an absent one.

That summer Grindle spent a weekend at the home of Pennsylvania Governor William Scranton. Rockefeller was there also. After a couple of drinks Grindle said Rockefeller asked him, "Paul, what would it have taken to get you the hell out of New Hampshire?"

Grindle responded, "We were sitting around, waiting for a bribe. If you had slipped me ten grand I'd have gotten out of there that same night."

Rockefeller had a look of astonishment on his face and said, "You're not serious?"

Grindle: "Absolutely I am. I've never been bribed to do anything in my life. I've always wanted to be bribed. I always expected you to do it. We'd have closed up shop for ten grand."[2]

Grindle says that he asked Rockefeller how much he had spent there—it was an astronomical sum. "[Rockefeller] couldn't

---

[2] Grindle may never have been bribed in his lifetime, but he certainly paid one. In 1949, while running a furniture factory in Framingham, Massachusetts, he told a *New York Herald Tribune* reporter that he had given $1,000 to a former Army officer who said he could influence the awarding of a federal contract. This revelation led to the uncovering of the "five percenter" scandal that rocked the Truman administration.

believe it—that we were just doing it for the hell of it at that point, before it got serious."

Oblivious to the hopelessness of his cause, Rockefeller pressed on, swearing never to support Lodge if he himself were unsuccessful and if Lodge did return to campaign. The defeat had extracted something else as well. The day after the vote the governor was campaigning in the San Francisco Bay area, preparing for the early June California primary. One account in *The New York Times* noted the toll that New Hampshire had taken: "The effects of the governor's arduous efforts in New Hampshire were apparent. He looked less vigorous than on his first campaign trip to this state late in January. He was pale, and the lines around his eyes and mouth seemed deeper." (He would press on until narrowly defeated in California by Goldwater: 1,120,000-1,052,000.)

Henry Cabot Lodge heard the first reports on the election while flying from Hue to Saigon. As the plane landed in Saigon, Lodge was the center of attention. A group of reporters had traveled out to the airport to record his reaction to the news from the political front back in the States. As Lodge walked down the plane ramp he was greeted with a shout, "Mr. Ambassador, you have been declared the winner in New Hampshire." Lodge, touching down by now, severely responded, "There will be a statement in New England about that. I am precluded by Foreign Service regulations from talking politics." He finally warmed up a bit and conceded that he had been accorded "a great honor and a great compliment." In response to how he would answer this call for political duty, Lodge proclaimed, "I do not plan to go to the United States. I do not plan to leave Saigon. I do not intend to resign."[3]

Lodge did return prior to the national conclave, yet well past the point when it mattered. Despite a commanding Lodge lead in the early Oregon polls, Rockefeller put on a spirited effort that won him the state. He pressed on to retain a voice in the nomination struggle, but California ended his role in the contest.

---

[3] Those who cast aspersions on the value of the New Hampshire kickoff test must examine what happened to Lodge in one national poll after his unexpected victory. In February Lodge polled just 12% of a Republican nationwide sample. In March, just prior to the New Hampshire returns, he stood at 16%. But by April Lodge had taken perhaps the most pronounced leap for a presidential possibility—he had skyrocketed to 42%.

Pennsylvania Governor William Scranton's last-minute attempt was a mere irritant to the Goldwater momentum. Goldwater's nomination represented the final passage of power from the eastern wing of the party based in New York, Massachusetts and Pennsylvania to the Sun Belt states. The Lodge victory in New Hampshire and the Rockefeller win in Oregon were the last gasp for the wing of the party that had dominated every convention since 1940.

What was Lyndon Johnson to do about New Hampshire? The irrepressible organizer, Bernard Boutin, now the head of the General Services Administration, was a long way from his real estate, insurance and variety store business in Laconia. In a December 1963 memo to the White House, Boutin laid out some ideas on approaching the opening primary. Unless another strong contender emerged (one did not), the pledged delegate slate that caused some controversy in 1960 would be forsaken. It should be a wide open delegate race, allowing anybody wishing to run favorable to Johnson. Boutin also wanted the president to place his name on the ballot. Before the assassination, he had given this idea some thought, with a goal of more votes for the winning Democrat in the primary than for the winning Republican, confirming that New Hampshire was finally maturing into a two-party state.

But the president, eager to mold and shape his "consensus," wanted little to do with partisan politics. He vetoed all Boutin's ideas. There would be no get out the vote drive, no name on the ballot, no visit, and, as far as the favorable delegate slate was concerned, he had no control over that anyway. The new president was occupied with being president; New Hampshire and its quadrennial frolic in the snow would have to take a back seat.

There was no direct threat to Johnson, but there was an indirect one: the so-called "Bobby Problem." In February a Manchester public relations man, Robert Shaine, and the Manchester City Democratic chairman, Joseph Myers, launched a vice presidential write-in drive for Attorney General Robert Kennedy. They wanted to force Johnson to put together what many party leaders perceived as the dream ticket: the unbeatable combination of Johnson and Kennedy. Never mind that there was a deep personality and power clash between the two men; if John Kennedy could run on the same ticket with the Texan, so could his brother.

Johnson, to put things mildly, saw things differently. He was livid over the write-in, perceiving it as a ploy to sandwich his presidency as a tiny footnote between the reigns of John and Robert Kennedy. White House aides were soon busy trying to put a damper on the write-ins, as Johnson slowly stewed.

It was a grass-roots uprising that nothing could contain. Party workers, still somewhat numb over the tragedy of November 22nd, stirred into action for the first time. To top things off, the press played it for all it was worth. If Shaine or Myers had called a press conference for a remote northern town such as Colebrook, they could not have found a hall large enough for all the press people who would have showed up. The Kennedy name was magic, and never more so than in early 1964.

To counteract the Kennedy drive, an Edmund Muskie vice presidential trial balloon was floated for the senator from Maine. He made a trip into the state in February, but his star was rather dim that year; he netted a grand total of 87 votes for the second spot.

From out of the blue Governor John King, the first Democratic governor elected in 40 years, endorsed the Kennedy drive. As for the attorney general's role, in spite of the contention by some that he disapproved of what was transpiring, he did the same thing Lodge did—he never stamped the life out of the effort. A lukewarm statement came through an aide a few days before the vote: Kennedy "wishes to discourage any efforts on his behalf in New Hampshire or elsewhere."

The drive, however, accomplished the opposite of what was intended: it pulled the nation's two most powerful Democrats further apart. The main cause for concern was that Lyndon Johnson was going to be embarrassed—worse, humiliated—in New Hampshire by having the Kennedy vote top his own. Aware of this danger, the final week before the primary was spent putting a brake on the Kennedy effort and making sure it did not run ahead of the Johnson tally.

The avoidance of humiliation just succeeded. LBJ gathered 29,317 write-in votes for the top spot, with Kennedy winning 25,094 vice presidential write-ins.

Some similar Kennedy efforts were attempted in other states, but they were futile. Johnson held all the cards; there was no way he would anoint Kennedy as his running mate. On July 29th Johnson invited the attorney general into the Oval Office for a chat, and informed him that he would not be his running mate. The honor later went to Minnesota Senator Hubert Humphrey.

Lyndon Johnson finally visited New Hampshire late September of 1964 on a campaign swing through the Northeast. He was received with a hero's welcome. A crowd of 25,000 people lined the streets of Manchester to greet him.

On the Johnson itinerary was an address before a banquet of the New Hampshire Weekly Newspaper Publishers Association at the Carpenter Hotel. Johnson, devoting his speech to foreign affairs, mentioned for the first time in the campaign his opponent, Barry Goldwater. He listed him along with Nixon, Rockefeller and Scranton as having suggested the possibility of "going north in Vietnam."

The words spoken that night would return to haunt the president and later be used against him the next time New Hampshire figured in his political career:

> And as far as I'm concerned, I want to be very cautious and careful and use it only as a last resort when I start dropping bombs around that are likely to involve American boys in a war in Asia with 700 million Chinese. ...So just for a moment I have not thought that we were ready, our American boys, to do the fighting for Asian boys. And what I've been trying to do with the situation that I found was to get the boys in Vietnam to do their own fighting with our advice and our equipment, and that's the course we're following. So we're not going north and drop bombs at this stage of the game....

1968
Johnson's Retreat-
Nixon's Resurrection

ALL WOULD NOT BE smooth and easy sailing for Lyndon Johnson in 1968. The portents had commenced in New Hampshire as much as a year in advance.

In March of 1967 Bill Dunfey, the state Democratic chairman, went to Washington for a conference of the party chieftains. Much of the conclave consisted of a stream of briefings from top administration officials in a downtown hotel. One after another they unloaded, in their bureaucratic jargon, progress reports on the War on Poverty, the vitality of the national economy and rosy reports on the Vietnam War. If there were any doubts harbored deep in the party leaders' minds as to who ran the party as well as the country, they were dispelled at the luncheon on the last day of the conference. Vice President Hubert Humphrey was billed as the featured speaker, but suddenly four television sets were rolled in; the group instead watched one of the president's live press conferences, most of it devoted to defending his increasingly controversial Vietnam policies. The loquacious Humphrey had little time left to pontificate on the wonders of the Great Society, the Democratic Party and Lyndon Johnson.

By late afternoon the chairmen moved to the White House for an audience with the president. Dunfey had increasing reservations about the Vietnam War, but that day his concern shifted to the president's behavior. Once the chairmen were seated, Johnson went off on a harangue on the war and against his opposition. Marvin Watson, one of Johnson's top assistants, sat silently in the back of the room, never informing the president that the party officials had heard the same tirade a few hours before.

The last item on the agenda that day was a social one, a formal dinner at the Statler-Hilton Hotel for the chairmen and their wives, with the Johnsons as the honored guests. The president was called upon to make some remarks, and in spite of the social nature of the occasion he let loose with yet another of his Vietnam diatribes. His obsession with the war was total. The indirect references to his opponents as traitors continued unabated. As he went on and on, the discomfort in the room grew. Finally Johnson remarked that he could tell by the look on Lady Bird's face that it was time to "wind it up." He had already been speaking for 40 minutes; he would go on for another 15.

After this final performance Dunfey had smoke coming out of his ears. Over the previous decade he had played a prominent role in building the state's modern Democratic Party. With his impressive track record, the hotel owner was being touted by Bernard Boutin and others as the man to handle Lyndon Johnson's fortunes in the first primary in 1968. It was not to be.

As Dunfey left the Statler-Hilton with his wife Ruth, George Mitchell, the state chairman of Maine, told him he shared his discomfort. He asked Dunfey what he was going to do. The response: "I'm done, I'm quitting, that's it. What he said in there tonight made up my mind. Somebody else is going to have to run the first primary. I'm not going to hurt him, I won't go off and raise hell, but there's no way that I'm going to run his campaign up there."

Dunfey soon followed through with his threat to resign. For months thereafter the chairman position remained vacant. Senator McIntyre and Governor King, the top party officeholders, were not consummate party men. They had run their campaigns, as was much the vogue in the sixties and seventies, as independents who happened to belong to the Democratic Party. They believed that such an approach was necessary in a state where they had to attract many Independent and Republican voters to achieve victory.

King and McIntyre were not knocking themselves out to fill the vacancy created by Dunfey's resignation. Some felt that they feared that an active chairman would be a threat to their own power bases. An active leader could siphon off workers and contributors and, by being too vocal, scare off Republicans. Even with the party's recent successes, it was a perilously weak structure; yet King and McIntyre resisted pressure to move quickly. Dunfey lobbied for the appointment of a woman, but that suggestion was ahead of its time. Finally, by the fall of 1967, a Manchester attorney, William Craig, was picked for the post—as fine a seatwarmer as could ever be found.

Bernard Boutin, who had followed his service in the General Services Administration with top positions in the Small Business Administration and the Office of Economic Opportunity, left the federal government in September of 1967 to return to his native state. He ultimately came to take command of Lyndon Johnson's fortunes in the first primary. He did not return to his real estate, insurance and variety store business, but instead ensconced himself as the director of corporate information at Sanders Associates, a growing Nashua-based electronics firm and the state's largest employer at the time, reaping $125 million of its $140 million gross income from defense contracts.

Joseph Grandmaison, then 25, was in the state's Young Democrats organization. Of French-Canadian ancestry, he had been reared in a working-class Nashua neighborhood. His father Oscar was active in Democratic politics and was a living testament to the upwardly mobile nature of American life. In the early forties the elder Grandmaison had been arrested for helping to organize the New Hampshire Shoeworkers Union; by the sixties he had been rewarded for his toil in the political vineyards with the appointment to the post of state director of the Selective Service System.

In October of 1967 the younger Grandmaison was helping to organize the Young Democrats' yearly convention. He was taken aback when Boutin, at the behest of presidential aide Marvin Watson, began to press for the convention's endorsement for the president's re-election. Grandmaison saw the move as a clear indication that Boutin had lost his perception of the state and was allowing himself to be pushed around by a "nitwit in the White House." He felt Boutin misjudged what an endorsement would mean—virtually nothing.

One Johnson loyalist who visited the state in January of 1968 was Spencer Oliver, then the chairman of the Young Democrats of America.[1] He was a guest at the Governor's Ball which honored the New Hampshire Young Democrats. He later wrote:

> I stood in the receiving line next to Governor King and Bernie Boutin as all of the Democratic precinct workers and ward chairmen came through the line. As each person came through Bernie would introduce them to the governor and tell him what a great job each of these people was doing on behalf of Lyndon Johnson....After the receiving line was over I meandered through the crowd and overheard numerous conversations among these so-called "Johnson Loyalists." What they were saying to each other in private conversation was markedly different from what they were telling Bernie Boutin and the governor. Most of their comments revealed that they resented Johnson for not directly entering the primary and thought that the write-in effort was ill-advised and would be unsuccessful. They also didn't seem to give a damn whether Johnson did well in the primary. In my travels through the state, I got the same story from a number of New Hampshire Democrats who were old personal friends of mine. I returned to Washington certain that Gene McCarthy was going to do one hell of a lot better in the New Hampshire primary than the people at the White House and the Democratic National Committee could imagine in their wildest nightmares.

But these matters went unnoticed; they were far from the public eye. If the press had troubled itself to ferret out these cracks in the president's popularity, they would have been evaluated as small impressions, nothing deep or consequential. Lyndon Johnson, the pundits told themselves and their audi-

---

[1] Years later Oliver would tumble inadvertently into the pages of history, for while serving as the executive director of the Association of State Democratic Chairmen, his phone was tapped along with that of Democratic National Chairman Larry O'Brien by the Watergate burglars.

ences, could have the nomination for the asking. No one was willing to challenge him. Senator Robert Kennedy of New York stood immobile, fearful that his candidacy would be construed as a personal vendetta instead of a debate on the issues of the war and the urban crisis. Such a brawl, Kennedy and many of his top advisors felt, would leave his party hopelessly divided, destroy his future in national politics and deliver the White House to the Republicans.

And there was the war. The war in Vietnam was killing not only Vietnamese and Americans by the thousands each month, but also Johnson's presidency. The war drained away precious attention and resources for his beloved Great Society, his passkey into history. It distorted the economy; the demand for goods outstripped the capacity to produce them, with defense requirements primarily causing the distortion. In addition it divided the country, exacerbated the growing tensions between black and white, and alienated many young people from the mainstream of American life.

The war and the subsequent anti-war demonstrations made Johnson a White House captive. Presidents can be divorced from reality, but the demonstrations completely sealed Johnson off. He managed to bypass the Congress and the courts to escalate the war, but it was inevitable that the constitutional process would exert itself as election time approached. The primaries acted as a referendum and a check on Johnson and his war, pushing it into reality, where the electorate would start to speak in a tongue the politician could understand—the language of votes.

One of the great ironies of the Vietnam War was that, in 1954, when the United States first considered sending aid to the battered French forces, then-Senator Lyndon Johnson, Democratic minority leader, had helped batter down the proposal. David Halberstam, who won a Pulitzer Prize for his dispatches to *The New York Times* from Vietnam in the early- and mid-sixties, later wrote a best-selling book on America's involvement in Vietnam, *The Best and the Brightest.* He recounted how Johnson once helped prevent the United States from expanding its commitment in the area.

In early April of 1954, at the behest of President Eisenhower, Secretary of State John Foster Dulles had held a meeting with top congressional leaders to determine support for aid to the French. The mood in Congress had already been made clear the previous February, when it was announced that the United States would send 40 B-26 fighter bombers and 200 American technicians. A hostile reaction on the Hill stopped the action.

At that time Johnson and his Democratic colleagues were still smarting from allegations by Senator Joseph McCarthy and Vice President Richard Nixon that their party had helped "lose" China to the Communists and that they had failed to achieve a settlement to the Korean War. However, they were pleased to be consulted in the important matter of French aid, for they shared the concern over the deteriorating situation.

At the meeting Admiral Arthur W. Radford, chairman of the Joint Chiefs of Staff, presented the case in favor of escalation. The administration was testing the sentiment for a congressional resolution to use American air and naval power in Indochina, including a massive air strike to relieve the garrison under attack at Dienbienphu.

When Radford was asked what the follow-up would be if the air strikes failed and whether ground troops would then be necessary, he gave no satisfactory response. When Dulles was asked by Johnson what other allies had been signed on (Truman was attacked during the Korean War for not gaining sufficient assistance of our allies), the secretary of state had to confess that he had not consulted with any other nation.

Johnson's thoughts at the time, according to Halberstam, were similar to those of his mentor, Senator Richard Russell of Georgia. They both saw American involvement as a giant trap, an overextension of American power in a country already drained, fatigued and embittered by the Korean experience.

The mood of Congress was fairly clear. Neither were all the top brass in the Pentagon behind the escalation drive. The final and perhaps decisive input Eisenhower received on the matter was a report compiled by the Army Chief of Staff General Matthew Ridgeway, who led the American troops in Korea after General Douglas MacArthur's dismissal by President Truman.

Ridgeway's figures on the projected cost of escalation made a deep impression on Eisenhower. The tally read in part: 500,000-1,000,000 ground troops to defeat the enemy; enormous construction costs for port facilities, airfields, roads, communications systems and other logistical support, due to Vietnam's physical underdevelopment; and draft calls of more than 100,000 men a month.

After the fall of Dienbienphu, and as the Geneva conference opened to conclude French involvement in Indochina, Ridgeway took his assessment to the president. Eisenhower knew the nation was not ready for such a move following so closely on the heels of Korea, and a major commitment was shelved.

The piecemeal secretive approach for entering Vietnam in the sixties varied substantially from the debate and wide-ranging input of the fifties. By then President Johnson faced no Korea as a block to escalation; that war was only a dim memory brought back to life by movies or television. Johnson faced no complete and dramatic collapse of a European power to draw headlines or to remind people that the region was a quagmire for modern Western armies. Furthermore, no check and balance was provided by Congress; President Johnson had learned to manipulate this body from the White House just as well as he had controlled the Senate from the majority leader's post.

With costs and dissent escalating in 1967, the only way to open a full-scale debate on the purpose, means and objectives of the nation's commitment was to drag the matter into the electoral arena. But as 1967 wound down, the problem still remained—who would step forward to challenge the president?

There could be no campaign without a candidate and since no one stepped forward, a candidate would have to be recruited. Two men served as the prime igniters of the "Dump Johnson" movement: Allard Lowenstein, a freelance liberal activist and occasional lawyer who headed up the National Student Association in the early fifties, and Curtis Gans, a lean, youthful New Yorker then serving on the staff of the Americans for Democratic Action.

The pool of possible candidates was small, with Kennedy its most powerful prospect. Harvard professor and economist John Kenneth Galbraith considered running, but his Canadian parentage made him ineligible. Senators Frank Church of Idaho, George McGovern of South Dakota and Lee Metcalf of Montana were all approached by Lowenstein. McGovern, an early critic of the war, was the most intrigued by the idea of running but he had his hands tied. He had won election by a mere 500 votes in 1962; in 1968 he faced a tough fight to maintain his Senate seat. A presidential race in the same year would be impossible. He suggested that Lowenstein approach Minnesota Senator Eugene McCarthy.

McCarthy, of ample intelligence and cutting wit, was one of the more aloof, enigmatic figures in the upper chamber. He felt that Kennedy should challenge Johnson. Since Kennedy would not, McCarthy continued to meet with Lowenstein. The thrust of the discussions changed from why do it to how and when and where to do it. Finally, on November 30th McCarthy announced his decision to take on the president.

The initial blueprint of the McCarthy challenge called for entering the primaries in Massachusetts, Wisconsin, Nebraska, Oregon and California. New Hampshire was not on the initial list. Gene McCarthy was more than willing to forego trudging about the snows and cold of the Granite State in the winter of 1967-68. It could come and go with nary an effort on his part— or so he first thought.

McCarthy's avoidance of New Hampshire was not difficult to understand. It was considered territory too hawkish and conservative for his dovish crusade. In addition, the state was as dependent, economically speaking, on the Defense Department as Nebraska is on corn, Texas on oil or cattle, and Florida on citrus and tourists. The Portsmouth Naval Shipyard, the Pease Air Base near Portsmouth and Sanders Associates pumped tens of millions of dollars into the New Hampshire economy. Any anti-Vietnam crusade could be construed by many of the state's workers as a threat to job security.

Then there was the Democratic Party to contend with. In an example of high-handed Texas-style politics, the Democratic State Committee—in a controversial move—endorsed the re-election of the president on November 19th, even before McCarthy announced his candidacy. This step was handled in a vastly different manner from the careful, cautious planning the Kennedy forces had engaged in eight years previously. Those attuned to the party's inner workings also knew that a number of prominent Democrats were refusing to sign on board with Johnson. In the furor over the endorsement and the role of the party organization, the lesson of Kefauver's thrashing of the party pols in 1952 and 1956 was forgotten.

The experts badly misread the New Hampshire story in 1968 (as they had in 1952) due to their overblown calculations of the clout of the Democratic Party "machine." One source compares the role played by the titular head of the party at the time, Governor John King, to that of "a latter day rotten borough politician. John King's main interest was his own perpetuation in office. He was the titular head but he wasn't ready or willing to lead."

Not only was the governor unwilling to lead and expand upon hard-won recent successes, he saw new ideas and new leaders as threats to his hegemony. If something were proposed it had to be King's idea or he would oppose it—and thus kill it. Senator McIntyre was more willing to help in the development of the party apparatus, but he was far removed from the scene and not assertive enough to challenge King. When the crunch came King simply said no—and nothing was achieved.

McCarthy paid a visit in mid-December to deliver a lecture on civil rights and to meet with a group of liberal Democrats in a suburban Manchester home. The meeting and speech were arranged by David Hoeh, who, along with his energetic wife Sandy, had been involved in past Democratic campaigns.

McCarthy lit few bonfires during his brief talk and gave no sign that he was about to change his position on staying out of the first primary. But the Hoehs persisted and with Gerry Studds,[2] a history teacher at the prestigious St. Paul's prep school in Concord, they created a memo listing reasons the senator should change his mind.

They believed that, since the Johnson leaders were predicting that a challenge such as McCarthy's would achieve no more than 10% of the vote in such a conservative state, anything above that would be interpreted as a victory of sorts. His entry would reaffirm the seriousness of his intentions; a victory (which they thought possible) would ignite his candidacy and "have major national repercussions."

[2] In 1969 Studds left New Hampshire to take up residence in Massachusetts. He planned to manage the 1970 campaign for the Democratic aspirant in the 12th Congressional District, which stretches from the southern portion of the Boston suburbs to the tip of Cape Cod. When no candidate stepped forward, Studds ran himself, losing by 1,520 votes to the six-term incumbent, Hastings Keith. However, Studds won the seat in 1972 by 1,100 votes out of more than a quarter of a million cast. In July of 1983 he was censured by the House of Representatives after admitting to having a sexual relationship with a 17-year-old male congressional page a decade earlier.

The primary was budgeted at $55,000. (Costs went far beyond that figure, however.) Since McCarthy was already committed to running in Massachusetts, the memo pointed out, the two states could be treated as one media package, as they were adjacent geographically and the primaries were only a month apart.

The Hoeh-Studds memo closed with a proposed 12-day schedule of personal campaigning and an assessment of the grassroots work being undertaken. All they needed was for McCarthy to give the okay.

Another advocate for his entry in the first primary was the McCarthy national campaign manager, Blair Clark, a former CBS news executive and Harvard classmate of John Kennedy. Clark had a good feel for the state; he had spent two years in the late forties publishing the *New Hampshire Sunday News.* He believed—an assessment that proved to be correct—that McCarthy's low-voltage, individualistic style, not to mention his Catholicism and Irish name, would be well-received in a place attuned to low-voltage, individualistic campaigns.

On the evening of January 2nd Hoeh and his wife Sandy met with Gerry Studds and Blair Clark in a room at Bedford's Wayfarer Inn. While they chatted, Senator McCarthy called and talked with Clark and Hoeh. Clark told them McCarthy planned to make a decision on entering the New Hampshire primary within 24 hours. The group went to the dining room; while there, Hoeh was called to the phone to talk with the senator again. Studds recalled:

> David came back to the table looking like he just swallowed a canary. That was nothing to the way Blair Clark looked when David said, "That was the senator and he is coming to New Hampshire." Blair's chin sort of fell into his soup, and I dropped everything, and I thought Sandy was going to faint.

George Romney, serving his third term as governor of Michigan, would display no such hesitation, reluctance or tardiness in coming to New Hampshire in search of a launching pad toward the Republican presidential nomination. In such a topsy-turvy year few could have predicted that a rather lackadaisical, inadequately financed, disorganized campaign (McCarthy's) would ignite and take a firm hold on the body politic, whereas the heavily funded, highly programmed, organized effort of another upper midwesterner (Romney) would prove a total dud. Such an outcome disproved the belief that planning, money and exertion alone create bona fide contenders. It took some other ingredients as well, particularly the ability to perceive the mood of the public over a sensitive issue like the war and the ability to survive the scrutiny and harassment to which the ever-present media entourage subjected the aspirants.

Regarding New Hampshire, George Romney would have been better off if he had stayed home and dismissed the entire quadrennial frolic from his mind. He invested almost $200,000, devoted weeks to campaigning, opened 450 home headquarters, and compiled the most sophisticated computer list ever of the state's Republicans. It was all for naught.

Romney could have saved himself considerable agony and humiliation if he had bothered to listen to the first advice he was proffered about the kickoff primary. In the fall of 1966 a Dartmouth alumnus, John Martin, the Republican National Committeeman and Romney partisan from Michigan, was in Hanover attending a football game and class reunion. On his visit he met with William Johnson, another college alumnus who had stayed in Hanover to practice law and teach at the college's business school.

Just a few weeks before, in a 1966 race for the Senate, William Johnson had engaged in one of the classic cases of Loeb-baiting to try to win the GOP nomination for the United States Senate seat held by Democrat Tom McIntyre. He had used the *Union Leader*'s opposition to solidify the support of the party's liberal wing and to exclude any other candidates who shared his political philosophy. With Loeb's editorial opposition, it was not a difficult chore to gain support from much of the anti-Loeb press (or the "pipsqueak press," as Loeb called it). The attacks in the state's largest daily were prominent (albeit negative) mention as Loeb blistered Johnson repeatedly.

When Martin collared Johnson in Hanover, the memory of the hard and bitter fight (he had finished third in the primary) was still fresh in Johnson's mind. He told Martin to advise Romney to forget running in the New Hampshire primary. Martin urged Johnson to put his thoughts down on paper and send them to Romney in Michigan.

In what has to go down in the annals as the longest treatise ever written on why someone should not enter an election, Johnson sent a 127-page analysis on why Romney should stay away. Johnson's main thrust was that Romney must avoid "the chewing-up effect." Romney was bracketed in the party's moderate-to-liberal wing and he had refused to back Barry Goldwater in 1964. Both of these facts would work against him with the conservatives who still controlled the party. And Romney's lack of support for Goldwater was particularly galling to publisher Loeb, who, upon Romney's first foray, began to swing his editorial ax in Romney's direction with a relish.

Johnson informed Romney that he would not have far to go in concocting an excuse as to why he had to skip New Hampshire. The Michigan Legislature would be in session at least during the months of January, February and March, the months the primary unfolded; diligent George Romney could claim to be tied to his duties in Lansing. Once New Hampshire was over, Romney's schedule could suddenly open up and allow time for him to compete with Richard Nixon in the more approximate (in both geography and ideology) Wisconsin primary.

To Johnson's considerable chagrin, Romney rejected his advice. He recalls that Romney "wouldn't avoid a challenge. There was no problem he felt he couldn't lick. He had absolute faith in himself."

What Romney failed to calculate was that the not-quite-so-irresistible force (his presidential candidacy) would collide head-on with the immovable object (the esteem New Hampshire Republicans, both leaders and rank-and-file, still held for Richard Nixon). It would proceed to be the mismatch of the century.

In his years of exile Richard Nixon had not forsaken New Hampshire, and as he again started on the road to the presidency, it would not forget him. In 1964, as the leaders of the Republican eastern establishment ran for cover from the Goldwater-Miller debacle, Nixon came to its aid, including a stop in the Granite State. The conservatives did not forget his help, nor the failure of others to do the same.

In the 1966 mid-term elections, the Republican Party picked up 47 seats in the House of Representatives. Much of the credit for this accrued to Nixon, who had stumped vigorously for many of the candidates. Once again that year he kept his lines open to the first primary state with another visit.

Following the mid-term victory Nixon had to be careful. He was too well-known, too intensely disliked in some quarters (the so-called liberal news media in particular), and, with years spent seeking national power and never winning the presidency, dangerously close to becoming regarded as another Harold Stassen.

His attempt to win the GOP presidential nod in 1968 had to be a carefully and perfectly executed coup. Staff could be hired, support secured, world travels undertaken; but Nixon's reappearance on the presidential campaign circuit had to be severely limited to avoid overexposure and any pratfalls.

Overeager George Romney, his inexperience matched only by his naivete, served as the perfect foil for Nixon. The more Romney traveled and talked, the less was written about Nixon. The more Romney tried to dodge the press corps' questions on issues such as Vietnam, the more his fortunes sank, leaving Nixon standing alone for the party leaders to rally around.

In the early spring of 1967 Nixon conducted an intensive poll of 500 New Hampshire Republicans, a high sample for such a small state. The remarks were tape recorded and soon became carefully read transcripts in the Nixon New York City headquarters.

The poll inquired about the significant issues of the day, yet its real purpose was to probe the attitudes voters held toward the former vice president. There was favorable commentary: he was regarded as experienced, intelligent, candid and able to handle world issues. The real material for perusal, however, was the negative commentary, which boiled down to the theme that Nixon was a loser. He was regarded as a perennial candidate who could not win what he had desired for so long, who had tried before and failed, yet could not face that failure and call it quits.

Before Nixon's positive attributes could be clearly projected, the loser image had to be erased. This made the 1968 first-in-the-nation primary critical for the resurrection of Richard Nixon. He had not won a contested election in his own right since 1950, when he beat Helen Gahagan Douglas for the United States Senate in California. New Hampshire would either make or break him. If he won, the crucial momentum would be secured to win other primaries, and the party leaders controlling non-primary delegations would be forced to climb aboard. If he lost, it would take a miracle for him to recover—something George Romney, Nelson Rockefeller and former movie-actor-turned-California-governor, Ronald Reagan, would arduously try to prevent. Nixon had to roll out of New Hampshire on Wednesday morning, March 13th, with "winner" all over him.

Handling "cranky" New Hampshire would be a delicate operation. Being present infrequently would leave him susceptible to the charge, "he didn't care enough to come." If he campaigned too much, he risked overexposure, boring the electorate.

Nixon aide Patrick Buchanan's game plan called for Nixon to only "flash" his credentials while Romney would expose his own at great length. The thrust for Nixon would not be gladhanding and backslapping from Coos to the sea, for his personal appearances would be quite limited.[3]   Television would be the tool. Buchanan, in a memo reprinted in Joe McGinniss's *The Selling of the President 1968* wrote:

> Then to hammer the loser thing (at the same time we dispel the myths of RN being tough and mean and political and intense), we use the TV to show everyone in New Hampshire that RN is enjoying the hell out of this campaign. He is smiling, confident, easy-going (no cornball stuff), comes off well in "feature" settings, with kids, with folks, etc. In short, while RN talks like the president-in-exile, he is a good democrat (with a small d) who believes that communicating with the people is one of the great joys of seeking the presidency.

With the accent so strong on television, other forms of advertising and the use of surrogates to carry the Nixon message, the candidate held back, doing only what was considered essential. If Romney were to move up in the polls, Nixon would be unleashed more than planned. If not, Buchanan advocated, "While RN has a schedule perhaps half that of Romney, our people ought to have the line out that RN has determined to do whatever is necessary to get his message across to the people of N.H., to go into the towns if need be and the city halls, etc. We will consider it an all-out campaign. That might well be the line."

So George Romney was allotted the first curtain call, to reveal his limitations and inadequacies. Nixon, the seasoned

---

[3] From "Coos to the sea" is an expression defining the geographic sweep of the state: from its northernmost county, Coos, a heavily forested, sparsely populated area bordering Quebec, down to the heavily populated, rapidly growing 18-mile coastline, a summer tourist mecca sandwiched between Maine and Massachusetts.

professional, would make relaxed jaunts around the country and prepare for his formal announcement on February 2nd. For a campaign in virtual hiding, its eventual emergence was quite impressive. As Nixon flew to the Granite State to announce, a mailing of 150,000 pieces to 85% of the state's households was dispatched in secret, yet it was simultaneously revealed to the news media as they arrived in the mails.

The mailing, addressed to the citizens of New Hampshire, contained in the lead paragraph the personal touch the state's voters had learned to expect from Nixon:

> I hardly need to remind you of the importance of the New Hampshire presidential primary—both to the candidates and the country. This importance stems from more than the fact of its being first. It stems also from the spirit in which New Hampshire's voters approach the election, keenly aware of their special responsibility, of the broad influence of their votes.

In the letter, Nixon called for "new leadership." He then pointed out that he was not quite so new after all: "During fourteen years in Washington, I learned the awesome nature of the great decisions a president faces." He next made a virtue of the fact that he had been out of office since 1960: "During the past eight years I have had a chance to reflect on the lesson of public office, the measure of the nation's tasks and its problems from a fresh perspective."

In closing, Nixon reiterated the significance of New Hampshire: "I have visited New Hampshire often—as a candidate, as a public official, as a private citizen. I appreciate the many courtesies you have paid me. I am deeply grateful for your support in past elections. But in asking your support now, I ask it not on the basis of old friendships. We have entered a new age. And I ask you to join me in helping make this an age of greatness for our people and our nation."

On the night of February 1st, accompanied by a few aides, Nixon flew from New York to Boston and drove up to New Hampshire. In keeping with the secretive nature of the operation, the inn-keepers of the Nashua hotel where Nixon stayed were unaware of their guest's identity until he arrived. The next afternoon, he traveled to Manchester to formally announce he would seek the presidency once again.

Nixon's opening line was a master stroke that portrayed a more mature, relaxed man: "Ladies and gentlemen, as we start this campaign, there is one thing we should say at the outset. This is not my last press conference." From the time of his famous "You won't have Nixon to kick around any more" remarks following his 1962 defeat for governor of California, he had conducted 300 press conferences; but his remark in Manchester finally put it all behind him.

Nixon's reception on that first tour was all he could have hoped for. He and Mrs. Nixon, their daughters Tricia and Julie and prospective son-in-law David Eisenhower were received, not with wildly cheering throngs but with a courtesy and respect and as much enthusiasm as New Hampshirites deem appropriate.

Everywhere Nixon and his entourage wandered on his leisurely 20-day procession, he was greeted with fine turnouts. Nixon had managed to pass beyond the realm of politician; he was now an elder statesman of the Grand Old Party. There was an aura about him of maturity and knowledge backed up by the cool professionalism of his entire operation. The campaign never lacked resources, due to the efforts of fundraisers Maurice Stans and Peter Flanigan in New York City.

When Romney tried to bait Nixon into a debate, he was nonchalantly brushed off. Nixon, ever the party unifier, dismissed the debate as an exercise in unneeded intramural warfare; the debate could only hurt the party; ammunition must be saved for the main target—Lyndon Johnson.

The New Hampshire Republicans respected Nixon. They respected his anti-Communism. They respected the rapport he had enjoyed with the late Styles Bridges and the editorial support of the *Manchester Union Leader*. They revered the fact that President Eisenhower had picked him not once but twice to be his running mate. His modest family background and financial means worked to his advantage, and his persistence and struggle to achieve were the stuff of American success stories. He was not too flashy or flamboyant, but was the type of politician New Hampshire Republicans seem to like the most: aloof and distant, yet efficient, diligent, moderate-to-conservative, and Republican. Nixon had it in the bag.

Every time George Romney returned to the state William Johnson noticed how much more worn and tired he looked. The strain of the long 16-hour campaign days and attendance to his gubernatorial duties took its toll, even on the physical fitness afi- cionado who neither drank, smoked or campaigned on Sundays.

All the exertion was useless. Romney was finished before he entered the primary. His campaign, though well-organized and amply funded was all over even before the kickoff on a 15-below-zero January morning at the Sanders plant gate in Nashua. The aura of respectability that encased Nixon never came near Romney. William Johnson soon sensed that "It reached a point where people literally wouldn't cross the street to meet him."

Johnson pulled together a spirited, although not massive campaign team. There were the people who had helped him in 1966, some college students, young men and women just beginning to work their way up the party organizational ranks, and many a Mormon who traveled in to assist their fellow Mormon.

Romney also had the assistance (at $300 a day) of a new group called Campaign Consultants Inc. (CCI), whose president, David Goldberg, was the Boston lawyer and veteran of the Draft Lodge campaign in 1964. Another leading light in the group was John Deardourff, a confidant of Nelson Rockefeller, and one who would help run the Ford Presidential campaign in 1976. (One of CCI's lasting contributions to 20th-century American politics was the handling of the gubernatorial candidacy of one Spiro T. Agnew, who defeated segregationist Democrat George Mahoney in Maryland in 1966.)

Romney's Herculean exertions and messianic pro- nouncements for restoring morality in America and for cleaning up the "mess in Washington" made little headway. To separate himself from the deteriorating American position in Vietnam, he broke with the Johnson policy (or the Johnson-Nixon policy, as he referred to it) and took a more dovish stance. That shift did him little good.

The Michigan governor was forced to run against the possibility of a Nelson Rockefeller candidacy as much as he challenged Richard Nixon. In early January, with a growing "Draft Rocky" movement building in New Hampshire, Johnson invited Rockefeller to come to New Hampshire in an attempt to head off the drive and convert it toward Romney's candidacy.

The Rockefeller visit was visible proof that Romney was going to find it very difficult to shake off all the speculation. The leader of the remnants of the Rockefeller organization, former Governor Hugh Gregg, failed to show at a closed-door session aimed at convincing Rockefeller's supporters to back Romney.

At a press conference another visiting governor, Rhode Island's John Chaffee, a Rockefeller man supporting Romney, committed the gaffe, "I pledge my whole-hearted support for Governor Rockefeller...uh...Governor Romney." Rockefeller's own performance before his 1964 backers and at the press conference only reaffirmed the belief held by many that he, not Romney, had the personality and experience to hold forth the moderate-to-liberal banner.

With three weeks to go before the first primary vote, Romney's seed money was near exhaustion. He had spent a million dollars nationally, including almost $200,000 in New Hampshire. Another $150,000 was budgeted, mostly for the media blitz. But more discouraging than the financial picture was the one provided by the polls, something Romney had watched fervently throughout his political career. It would take Romney months to get the message, and, when he finally did, the polls were the messengers.

The word from his own polling guru, Fred Currier, foretold disaster in New Hampshire: Nixon 70%, Romney 11% and Rockefeller 8% and gaining. The Rockefeller write-in threatened to place him in a humiliating third-place showing. The Harris Poll told the same story, and *Time*'s Roper Poll indicated Nixon at 65%, Rockefeller at 13%, Romney at 9%, with the remaining 13% undecided or casting their lot elsewhere.

Observing his man running like a dry creek, Johnson was the first to suggest withdrawal even before the voting, the so-called "first technical knockout" in American political history. Discouraged at the lack of response and the polls, Johnson called Len Hall, the national Romney chairman, and suggested that Romney drop out. Hall called some of the key Michigan aides, asking them to join him, Romney and Johnson for a meeting in a Boston-area hotel. A few weeks earlier, the Romney hierarchy had been surprised when the idea of dropping out was first tossed around and the tenacious Romney failed to explode at its very mention. At the final meeting, the small group looked at the latest polling results, assessed the picture in New Hampshire and Wisconsin, and examined the bleak financial outlook. Romney said he would sleep on the idea of quitting.

The arguments for such a move were persuasive. It would save him the humiliation certain in New Hampshire and soon to be repeated in Wisconsin. The withdrawal would deprive Nixon of what he needed most—a clear victory over active competition, thus leaving the field open for another challenger to stop him in the later primaries. Romney could also retain some semblance of a voice in party affairs, for he would still be leading the large Michigan delegation to the national convention. His announcement, in the form of a report to the nation's Republican governors assembling in Washington, would allow them the opportunity of unifying around another candidate, possibly Rockefeller.

Romney awoke the next morning with his mind made up. Gathering up the various drafts of his last campaign speech, he called his wife with the news that he was quitting.

The next morning, Romney flew to Washington to appear before the governors and announce his decision. That day Nixon was traveling in southern New Hampshire, being greeted by good crowds at every stop. In the mid-afternoon he concluded a speech to 300 people at the Knights of Columbus Hall in Milford, a town of 6,000 on the Souhegan River in the western part of Hillsborough County. Before the press could reach him for reaction to the rumors that Romney would call it quits, two aides pulled the candidate into a restroom for a hurried conference. When told of the rumors by reporters after the impromptu meeting, Nixon feigned surprise and said, "I don't believe it...I don't comment on rumors."

The entourage proceeded on schedule, stopping to open a headquarters in Merrimack and to speak to 200 people at the Bedford Town Hall. By late afternoon the Nixon group arrived at their headquarters in the sprawling Highway Hotel in Concord to await the Romney announcement from Washington. Then, according to Jules Witcover, author of the book *The Resurrection of Richard Nixon*, a curious thing happened. Nixon decided not to watch Romney on television. He wanted to avoid emotional involvement in what was about to occur. In his stead, he dispatched aides to watch the live broadcast and report to him.

An hour after the announcement, a bland statement was issued to the press corps hungering for a reaction from the Nixon camp. The Nixon staff was soon burning up the telephone lines around the country, assessing the ramifications of the Romney decision trying to discern whether it was part of a plot to see Nelson Rockefeller entered in the later primaries.

No such Rockefeller drive was under way, although the New York governor made it clear that he would respond to a draft call from the party. The write-in for him had an expanded opportunity with Romney out, and many Romneyites signed up. Hugh Gregg pumped $15,000 of his own money into the movement. Gregg targeted 15% of the expected 100,000 Republican voters as his benchmark for "success." Nixon upped the ante: he said it would take a 30% showing for Rockefeller to prove his popularity.

Nixon, trying to maintain Republican interest, began to promote the possibility of a contest between himself and President Johnson. The mass of reporters wandering into the state for the final 10 days of the electoral frolic failed to take the bait. Nixon was on the ballot, running against an unauthorized write-in for a man who had failed in the state in 1964. Johnson was a write-in facing a stiff and now well-financed effort for Eugene McCarthy. There was one more reason the press disregarded Nixon's interpretation of the returns: the reporters were given expense accounts not just to drink it up, trade stories and joke with their colleagues, but to divine what it all meant. It was their job, not Nixon's, to decide what votes meant what to whom.

But what was not obvious until the end of the primary was how the scene had suddenly shifted. It was as if, a few moments before curtain time, the leading man in the play had been suddenly taken ill, possibly a psychosomatic reaction to having to face the audience and critics on opening night. But Eugene McCarthy was waiting in the wings, a stand-in who now took his lengthy strides onto the stage and immediately began to win the hearts of the audience with his poise, clear resonance, handsome looks and mastery of the script.

By then the bloodiest convulsion of the war had transpired—the Communist Tet offensive unleashed during the truce over the Vietnamese New Year holiday in late January of 1968. One Viet Cong suicide squad attacked the American Embassy in Saigon and held out for six and a half hours. American military commander General William Westmoreland was forced to take refuge in a windowless bunker outside Saigon, and Ambassador Ellsworth Bunker was taken away to a secret hide-out.

In one bold offensive the Communist forces changed the nature of the war. It moved overnight from the villages and rice paddies to the cities. The Communists terrorized 26 provincial capitals and, for a time, large sections of the former imperial capital of Hue.

As the nature of the war shifted, so too did the American public's perception of it. The newfound skepticism and dismay was reinforced by comments made by President Johnson and General William Westmoreland that the Tet offensive was actually defeat for the enemy. The public had seen the war with their own eyes via television, and realized that much of what Johnson and top officials said about it were lies.

For the first time Vietnam seemed like a World War II type of war, not an invisible guerrilla action. This realization carried a devastating psychological impact, confirming the doubts and complaints of the war's critics that there was no light at the end of the tunnel. The pro-war advocates were angered that the combined might of the American forces had been made to look as impotent as a beached whale.

To add to Johnson's woes, there was the timing of the offensive, just six weeks away from the first electoral test of his war and his leadership since 1964.

McCarthy was the only Democratic candidate to register a direct challenge to the president. With his small core of Granite State backers, McCarthy traveled around New Hampshire to drum up audiences. By the beginning of February a small stream of out-of-state college students began to filter in, mostly on the weekends. Then the Tet offensive unleashed a torrent of students, the "Clean for Gene" army.

President Johnson had a decision to make—what to do about the New Hampshire ballot. Should he place his name on the preference poll and thus become, in effect, a declared candidate early in the election year? Or should he allow someone to stand in for him, such as Governor King or Senator McIntyre? Or should he keep his name off the ballot and let his lieutenants wage a write-in on his behalf, as was done in 1964?

The stand-in idea took many hours to resolve. The Johnson camp was suspicious of a suggestion by Bill Dunfey that Senator McIntyre run as the stand-in. They imagined the idea was a trap to create a contest between McIntyre and Dunfey's crony—Robert Kennedy—which would tear McIntyre to shreds. Dunfey believes that the Johnson camp's response to his idea was similar to the Nixon campaign's reaction to Romney's withdrawal: "They saw a grand plot in everything even when there wasn't." In fact, Dunfey was opposed to Kennedy challenging Johnson in the state and had told him so. He believed that the state was too hawkish, the president too strong and the abuse to be suffered from the *Union Leader* (Loeb intensely disliked Kennedy) not worth the effort.

It was finally resolved that Lyndon Johnson would be a write-in candidate. That decision made a once-easy election difficult. A public education campaign would have to be waged to show voters where to write in the president's name. And with his name absent from the ballot, Johnson lost control of his delegate slate. Any Democrat could now file as "favorable" to the president. Had he been on the ballot, he could have hand-picked a pledged slate to match the 24 contested convention seats. But instead, a wide-ranging group of 45 people signed on, making a scattering of the delegate vote inevitable.

Lyndon Johnson was a consummate politician when dealing with his native Texas or the United States Senate. However, when it came to the great game of national politics—particularly running for the presidency—he was out of his element, and the way he approached the New Hampshire fray proved that flaw. No good politician ever gives up control, and that is just what Johnson started to do. He would lose control in other areas as well before the New Hampshire primary was over.

The necessity of a write-in education program gave the irrepressible Bernard Boutin an idea. It might be feasible, he thought, to combine that chore with the rebuilding of the Democratic State Committee master card file, which had fallen into disrepair. So, the famous "pledge cards" soon appeared.

A perforated, three-part card, individually numbered at the top of each section, was printed and distributed. The recipient kept one section consisting of a pledge to support the president by writing in his name on March 12th. Another part, the "headquarters copy," was deposited with the State Committee to be used for the get-out-the-vote drive on election day and in subsequent elections.

The center of the card was the explosive device. Proclaimed the "White House copy," it read, "President Johnson, I pledge my support to you and will WRITE IN your name on my ballot in the March 12th New Hampshire presidential preference primary." The voter was requested to print plainly his name, address, telephone number and indicate whether or not he was a Democrat or Independent. (Independents could vote in either primary, but if they did so, they would lose their independent status permanently. This law was later changed to allow them to regain their independent status at a later date.) The card closed with this: "As an expression of your support, this card will be forwarded to President Johnson at the White House in Washington, D.C." Boutin envisioned using the personal touch so cherished in the state by having the president occasionally call a few of the pledge card signers to thank them for their support.

Boutin's hope of trying to find a vehicle to rebuild a viable Democratic Party was not to be fulfilled. With all the bad news pouring forth from Vietnam, when party regulars started circulating the cards, the timing could not have been worse. The pledge cards gave McCarthy his first chance to move beyond the war issue.

To McCarthy, the existence of the numbered cards smacked of big brotherism, and he proceeded to raise hell about it. McCarthy called the device a "Texas-style branding party" and an "intrusion into a free democratic process not altogether inconsistent with the way the Johnson administration is operating." His campaign copied the card onto a flyer and queried independent New Hampshirites, "What ever happened to the secret ballot?" The allegation of bossism was reinforced when Governor King proclaimed, "Now is the time for Democrats to stand up and be counted—or be counted out."

As criticism of the project mounted, more than 20,000 of the signed cards were gathered up and shipped to the White House. The White House, wishing the whole matter would go away, said they never received them; the phone calls to registrants never came about.

Boutin feels, somewhat justifiably, that the pledge card issue was blown out of proportion. He claims the cards kept by the State Committee after the primary were used by the McCarthy people in subsequent campaigns. Lyndon Johnson, Boutin asserts, had more things on his mind than keeping a ledger of everyone who had signed up. Yet even if it were a phony issue, it was an effective one. It epitomized the type of loyalty-conscious presidency that Johnson conducted. The door had been opened for McCarthy a bit more.

In late January and early February a trickle of students from Massachusetts and Connecticut college campuses arrived to help McCarthy. The locals needed the assistance. The in state group was composed mostly of professional people, whose first responsibility was to their professions. They lacked the time and, in many cases, the political experience to contribute more than some money, offer their homes for a kaffeeklatsch, or, if they had a spare bedroom, shelter a student or two.

The students were surprised when they arrived to see just how little substance the campaign had and the depth of the state's slumber over the election. Ben Stavis, a Columbia University student who spent the election year assisting McCarthy, wrote a book on his experience, *We Were the Campaign—New Hampshire to Chicago for McCarthy*. His first assessment of the New Hampshire scene:

> I was depressed at first by this lack of local involvement but gradually realized that in New Hampshire presidential politics is a spectator sport, not a participant sport. The people are amused every four years to see presidential aspirants coming to their small mountainous state to seek support. They observed McCarthy with the same detachment and could not perceive the campaign as their own, in which they should work. This general feeling was· strengthened by the nature of the McCarthy candidacy. It dealt with fundamental, controversial issues. In the small towns, where everyone knew, watched and gossiped about everyone else, not many people wanted to make a public commitment to work in the campaign.

Another hindrance to the development of the campaign was that the students knew very little about McCarthy. When the Amherst College students supporting McCarthy held their initial meeting in late November, the first order of business was to form a committee to find out details about this man from Minnesota and his record in public office. But he had begun to "project," slowly percolating to the surface.

Some people felt they already knew enough about McCarthy. These negative feelings provided the fuel that turned a sluggish and dull contest into a no-holds-barred donnybrook by its conclusion. Boutin's opinion is a prime example:

> I have to say I've never liked Gene McCarthy....In 1960 he was supposed to give one of the nominating speeches...for Kennedy. He got out there [Los Angeles] and nominated Adlai Stevenson. In the Senate some of his statements sounded very good, very scholarly, but the fact of the matter is I never saw him at a hearing that started before noon. His reputation was that he was a

hell of a lazy guy, who didn't work hard at a great public trust. So I never admired Gene McCarthy. I thought Gene was an opportunist and could never make up his mind on anything. A guy who preferred the sack to really getting out and working.

The McCarthy campaign took on more sinew and shape after Tet. The gathering strength, coupled with Robert Kennedy's continued refusal to enter the primaries, caused former Kennedy and Johnson speechwriter Richard Goodwin to throw his typewriter into the back of his car and drive from Boston to Manchester to assist McCarthy. In addition, Curtis Gans was brought in from Washington to take charge of the first primary, and Sam Brown, a Harvard graduate student, came in to guide the Youth for McCarthy recruitment drive.

The New Hampshire people were desperate for some full-time, professional help, as Gerry Studds told an interviewer for the McCarthy Historical Project in January of 1969:

> We pleaded as of the second week of January for Curtis Gans, who was the only person we knew at that point on the national staff, to get up here. And to our astonishment were told that Curt couldn't come here because he was in charge of non-primary states. And we said, "Well, as we figure it arithmetically, that's 35 or 36 states. What the hell is one person doing in charge of all that?" We thought that was pretty breathtaking for a presidential campaign. And we subsequently learned, of course, that when Curtis finally sprung to come to New Hampshire, his wife, Genie, took over the non-primary states. We tried to tell him that if New Hampshire went badly, they could forget the non-primary in every other state. It didn't make a damn bit of difference, they had better get some people up here. We never could accustom ourselves to the fact there was no real national—we learned gradually, in fact—that there was no real national staff, no national organization, no advance staff, no nothing.

The Tet offensive destroyed the belief that the war was going well, also unleashing a dramatic cash flow into the McCarthy treasury. The $40,000 media budget was reset at three times that amount as the money poured in.

In the final three weeks, the critical problems for the campaign were finding effective use for the thousands of students pouring in to help and constructing and delivering a well-executed and professional media blitz. The relations between McCarthy and the national press corps were cool. He had a disdain for them, and they failed to take him seriously. Romney's withdrawal freed reporters to cover McCarthy more intensely; the 30- or 60-second television reports on him were lengthened to two or three times that; subsequently, the impression he made was that much deeper.

At first, the New Hampshire press painted McCarthy as a tiny diversion from the real contest between Nixon and Romney. With Romney out of the race McCarthy gained more exposure, but not enough to increase his recognition factor substantially. It is impossible to use the medium of television in New Hampshire to increase a candidate's recognition level. The stations that do not have the expensive rates of the Boston stations—a Manchester station and a few Maine channels—never reach an adequate audience.

Much of the agenda for in-state news coverage is set by the *Union Leader*. The other dailies have a tendency to follow the *Union Leader*; the wire services quite often feed the dailies winnowed-down news accounts that provide little depth. The weekly press—small operations with tiny reportorial resources to draw upon—is even worse. It takes a cataclysmic event to force a national or international news story on a weekly's front page, and then the thrust is still the local angle ("Somersworth Reacts to the End of World War II" or "Wolfeboro Residents Mourn the Death of President Kennedy"). The papers sometime cover the candidates when they come into the circulation area, but provide no running account of the candidates.

The means for a candidate to build his recognition via the in-state media is quite limited, unless one is in the editorial good graces of the *Union Leader*. Even that is not a guaranteed path to success. Gene McCarthy had to fashion, to a great extent, his own way to reach the public with his message. The print and electronic media would only go so far; it was up to public relations to do the rest.

Throughout the fifties Merv Weston built up a public relations firm in Manchester. By 1960 he had decided to handle only Democratic accounts, the more liberal the better. He was hired to handle the McCarthy account; it would soon be transformed, according to Weston, into "the wildest, fastest, most intensive promotional campaign ever produced in northern New England."

The budget for the last three weeks of the blitz was $123,000—newspaper ads $31,000; radio spots $36,000 (the 7,200 spots set a record); $20,000 for television time in Maine, New Hampshire and Boston; the production and print bill came to $36,000, with 1.5 million pieces of literature produced.

The low-voltage yet wide-dispersal message was a clear contrast to the hard-sell waged by the Johnsonites. McCarthy's theme boiled down to the Stevensonian ideal of talking sense to the American people, while the Johnson camp overacted and screamed simplistic nonsense.

Whatever the form of delivery, McCarthy discoursed calmly and rationally, calling upon past military leaders (even General Douglas MacArthur popped up on one McCarthy flyer: "Anybody who commits the land power of the United States on the continent of Asia ought to have his head examined") to indicate that others shared his reservations about the war in Southeast Asia.

The financial cost of the war was brought home to the fiscally conservative state with McCarthy's newspaper advertisement capturing a photo of the gold-domed State House with the copy: "In the next 72 hours more money will be spent in Vietnam than the state of New Hampshire spends all year." The same ad harked back to the good old days of another election year: "In 1952 General Eisenhower promised peace with honor in Korea. He was elected and he delivered. Senator McCarthy can do the same. An honorable man can bring an honorable peace."

A secondary battle raged below the main one: who could inherit the John Kennedy legacy? A McCarthy flyer contrasted the records of achievement in the three years of the Kennedy presidency with the years of failure by his successor: "There is one candidate who can get this country moving again and carry on the traditions John Kennedy began. That man is Gene McCarthy."

In retaliation, the Johnson people took out full-page newspaper ads retorting "Today Senator Eugene McCarthy compares himself to President John F. Kennedy. It should be remembered it was Eugene McCarthy who was not only against the policies of our late president, but who also led the bitter fight against President Kennedy's nomination in 1960."

The finishing touch for McCarthy was the reprinting and wide distribution of Johnson's 1964 statement in Manchester about letting Asian boys fight an Asian war. Besides contending with an increasingly robust rival, Johnson now had to run against an earlier version of himself. The money and the thousands of canvassers starting to pour into the McCarthy camp, coupled with the host of celebrities stumping for Gene (one worker complained, "They had every actor but Lassie up here"), were of increasing concern to the trio of King, McIntyre and Boutin. They had begun to hedge their previous bets that McCarthy would receive around 10% of the vote, upping their predictions to 20-30%.

The McCarthy campaign produced one flyer of questionable taste. If given wide distribution, the flyer may have caused an uproar equal to the pledge card furor. It was an attempt to use statements of religious leaders calling for a halt to the Vietnam War as a part of the McCarthy propaganda arsenal. On one side of the flyer, a photo of Pope Paul VI appeared with the headline, "We Cry in God's Name *STOP*. . . ." On the reverse side the Pope, Cardinal Cushing of Boston and Bishop Fulton J. Sheen were quoted calling for an end to the conflict. Below these were a photo of Senator McCarthy, a list of the religious organizations to which he belonged and the address of the McCarthy for President state headquarters.

The senator and his wife Abigail, always careful to separate the political from the religious, discovered the literature before it had gone into distribution.[4] Abigail regarded it as an un-

---

[4] Mrs. McCarthy's autobiography (*Private Places/Public Faces*, Doubleday and Company, 1972) goes into some detail of her experiences in the northern mill city of Berlin, a largely Franco-American Democratic bastion and a "machine stronghold" that McCarthy carried by 112 votes. At a reception for women who had been helping McCarthy in Berlin a high school girl approached Mrs. McCarthy:

"Mrs. McCarthy, Mama wants to meet you. I told her about you when I came home from school this afternoon and she said she'd like to talk to you." I turned to the mother, I think with the public manner one acquires after years of receptions and said, "I'm so happy to meet you, is there anything I can do?" Her answer stunned me. She said, "Yes, ma'am, my son was killed a month ago in Vietnam and I've been wondering and wondering what I could do so that other boys wouldn't

subtle and unsuitable attempt to appeal to the Catholic vote and personally destroyed many of the flyers that had been printed without the senator's knowledge. It would never be circulated to the public.

Lyndon Johnson was a difficult product to sell in the winter of 1968. After he had become president in 1963, the first Gallup Poll said that eight out of 10 people approved the way he was handling his new job. But with each passing year his public support had dissipated. By 1967 only four out of 10 people approved of his performance, a fallout of one in 10 persons for each year he was in office.

In the 1968 premier primary, Johnson could not call upon past personal contact to halt the drift of eroding fortunes. He had never spent a winter's morning standing outside the Brown Paper Company in Berlin greeting workers arriving for their shift. Nor had he ever strolled up and down a main street greeting shoppers or merchants. He had never ambled into a town hall to open himself up for questions from the citizenry, lingering to press the flesh and engage in small talk. He had never built up, due to the way he achieved the presidency, that reservoir of friendship that a Kefauver, Kennedy or Nixon had. Very few New Hampshire folks (Boutin, King, and McIntyre and a few others being the exceptions) had ever been called to the Oval Office for the famed one-on-one LBJ treatment. The towering presence, the masterful storyteller, the subtle probing for each visitor's weak spot could not be put to use for the March 12th voting. There was no way the Oval Office could be shipped up north for the president to hold court. He was at the mercy of his surrogates, a captive of his post.

While Johnson pulled the strings through aide Marvin Watson, the cutting edge was in the hands of the trio of King, McIntyre and Boutin. As more and more college students poured in for McCarthy, the concern in the Johnson headquarters mounted. The students were not what some had envisioned—long-haired, stoned, socialistic freaks—but rather a committed, diligent, well-dressed, articulate group concerned for

---

have to die like that. When my daughter came home this afternoon, I thought maybe there's something I can do to help Senator McCarthy win, maybe Mrs. McCarthy can tell me, maybe if he wins, other sons won't die."

the future of their country. The reserved and aloof New Hampshirites were impressed by the sincerity of these young people who were so willing to trudge through the snows and cold for what they believed in.

The Johnson reaction in the final two weeks was loud, harsh and controversial. As the Democratic in-fighting grew to a continuous roar, the once-dominant Republican test was forgotten. The signs were clear that the Democrats were in for a long, divisive and confusing brawl for the nomination.

What was left of a very short fuse between the McCarthy and Johnson camps was fired by Governor King when he addressed the Berlin City Democratic Committee on Sunday, March 3rd. The red-baiting that dominated the last nine days of the primary campaign was launched.

King informed his audience that the "freedom of mankind has been under continuous attack since 1945," an assault met by Truman in Berlin and Korea, by Eisenhower in Lebanon and Quemoy, and by Kennedy in Cuba. "And President Johnson continues to meet this challenge in Vietnam. Because of our determination and steadfast response to these challenges, the enemy has learned that he cannot break the will of our forces on the battlefield. As a result he has adopted a typical Communist tactic—to destroy the support of the people at home for the boys on the firing line by sowing the seeds of mistrust in our government."

A few days later King continued in the same vein during a press conference, where he said a significant vote for McCarthy would be "greeted with great cheers in Hanoi." McCarthy's solution for Vietnam was to "pack up and quit."

McCarthy, addressing a service club in the town of Derry, responded to King's charges, saying he did not believe those Americans opposing the Johnson war policies were doing so as a result of a subtle Communist propaganda drive. He said, "I hate to give them [the Communists] that kind of credit for subtlety and wisdom and this power to intrude into American life and to influence American opinion."

The Johnson camp was not finished, however. For weeks they had received polling data from the New York firm of Quayle Associates. Support for McCarthy was rising, yet the data also indicated few people comprehended his position on Vietnam. Thus, the "cheering in Hanoi" theme was put on full blast.

Newspaper ads touting Johnson as "A Strong Man in a Tough Job" gave way to the patriotism motif. One full-page ad harangued: "We Urge You Support Our Fighting Men. We know the Communists are watching the New Hampshire primary to see if we at home have the same determination as our soldiers in Vietnam. To vote for weakness and indecision would not be in the best interests of our nation."

Senator McIntyre took to the radio airwaves to accuse McCarthy of asking for "laws which would allow American draft dodgers, men who have fled to Canada or Sweden to avoid fighting in Vietnam, to return home scot-free without punishment. This is a cruel affront to those who have answered their country's call to duty. To honor draft dodgers and deserters will destroy the very fabric of our national devotion. This is fuzzy thinking about principles that have made our nation great."

An irritated McCarthy, motivated by his colleague's attack, released the text of remarks he had made at Dartmouth College about the draft. He desired a revision in the selective service law to allow for "selective conscientious objection," which, if extended to those who went to Canada, "could use it as a way of coming back and assuming citizenship in this country again. It's a kind of modified amnesty which I think we ought to consider."

McCarthy called upon McIntyre to come to his headquarters and show how his statement at Dartmouth "supports the cruel and false attack he has made. If he refuses, then at least let him have the courage and decency to withdraw this latest lie from the air waves."

The onslaught (including King's observation that McCarthy was "a champion of appeasement and surrender") drew criticism beyond the opposition camp. The *Concord Monitor*, bored by the absence of a Republican match, decided to break with tradition by acknowledging the existence of the Democrats. An editorial on the Johnson message stated, "Their actions and statements are a disservice to their candidate, President Johnson, an insult to the state's Democratic voters and a violation of the democratic process. Their activities hark back to the darkest days of American politics—big-city bossism and the era of the smear and innuendo characterized by the late Senator Joseph McCarthy (R-Wisc.)."

Five Johnson delegate candidates and one alternate from the Upper Valley also criticized the tactics. Joseph Myers, who had served as the Manchester Democratic City Committee chairman from 1954 to 1965, was a delegate candidate favorable to Johnson until he issued a statement at 5:00 p.m. on March 11th, the day before the vote, which read in part: "After the most serious soul-searching in my lifetime as a loyal American, and as a loyal Democrat for 45 years....I owe it to my country to set aside all partisan consideration, and wholeheartedly support Senator Eugene McCarthy for president."

One reason Myers gave for bolting the Johnson camp: "I cannot and will not remain silent when I hear, at the last minute, the desperate, unfair, unscrupulous personal attacks made against the character of Senator McCarthy, an honorable and courageous American...." Myers called for the Democratic voters "to join me tomorrow in rejecting any attempt to dictate to us how we vote, based on threats about pleasing or displeasing Communists in Hanoi. We can decide for ourselves, as Americans, how each of us vote."

Even Richard Nixon chimed in his view of the controversy. He thought it was unfortunate that the Democratic primary had degenerated into a personality clash rather than a discussion of the issues at hand. The New Nixon added for good measure: "If we disagree [with other candidates], let us do it without attacking their patriotism and love of country."

The gray skies on election day gave way to snow by late afternoon, the type of weather ideal for McCarthy—many of his committed voters would hurdle snowbanks for the opportunity to vote against LBJ. Lukewarm LBJ supporters would not do the same in his favor, and so their cause had one more strike against it.

Over the final weekend more news broke that increased the demoralization in the Johnson camp. A story leaked out of Washington that General Westmoreland had requested 206,000 more men to try to regain the initiative in Vietnam. The request touched off a heated debate in the top echelon of the administration. The price tag for this 40% increase in manpower would be $4 billion. To pay the price, the administration needed to ask for an increase above the 10% tax surcharge already requested but bogged down in Congress, reduce non-defense spending, or a combination of the two schemes.

The great numbers game continued like an endless poker game, with the stakes constantly being raised for the new man at the table. Boutin said near the end, "It would be a disgrace if

McCarthy gets less than 40% of the vote." The strategy now was to overestimate the vote of the opposition; if they failed to achieve that, encouragement could be drawn. *The New York Times*, in their election-eve edition, declared both Johnson and Nixon "prohibitive favorites." *Time* published a Roper Poll that called the election a landslide–Johnson with 62%, McCarthy only

For McCarthy, encamped at the sprawling Wayfarer Inn in Bedford, the very first return was good news. In every election a few tiny hamlets get a jump by conducting a midnight voting session as the election day arrives. This time one of the first to report was Waterville Valley: eight for McCarthy, two write-ins for Robert Kennedy and zero for LBJ.

The wait was on until shortly before 7:00 p.m. The city of Portsmouth was the fastest to reveal its tally because it was equipped with voting machines. McCarthy received more good news: with only one precinct missing, he garnered 52% (the final count was actually much higher).

Shortly after 9:00 p.m., McCarthy greeted the crowd in the hotel convention center. The mood was buoyant; the networks were projecting McCarthy with 35% of the vote. The candidate called the situation "encouraging," and returned to his private quarters to wait for more good news. They had passed their own benchmark; Boutin's would be the next to tumble.

By midnight McCarthy returned to greet his now-ecstatic boosters. The 40% barrier had fallen. The happy candidate proclaimed, "We're prepared to negotiate a surrender if we can find a neutral ship in the harbor of Chicago," and, "If we come to Chicago with this strength, there will be no riots or demonstrations, but a great victory celebration." With 87% of the vote tabulated, McCarthy held 41% of the vote.

The news made front-page headlines in the American and European press the next day. If the Republican votes were included in the tally, McCarthy had come within a few hundred votes of defeating the president. The Minnesotan had also collared 20 out of 24 convention seats. Only King, McIntyre, Boutin and state chairman Craig were going to the convention favorable to the president.

On the surface the White House reaction was calm. Under the public relations veneer, however, there was consternation over the result and depression at the prospects further down the road, particularly the next primary in Wisconsin.

The following night Boutin was in his home when the president called. "He just said, 'Bernie, I want to thank you for all the hard work and everything you did.' He said the fact it didn't come out better 'was our fault–you didn't get any help.'"[5]

Another interested party, Robert Kennedy, watched the returns from his apartment in New York City and called McCarthy after midnight to congratulate him. For months New Hampshire had been on his mind. In February Kennedy had made a secret trip to New Hampshire to do some skiing at Waterville Valley. While there he met with Bill Dunfey and informed him he was moving closer to running. The New Hampshire primary results broke the bonds restraining Kennedy.

He regarded McCarthy's win as a "brilliant job," but rationalized that the results showed the way was now clear for him to enter the fray. The returns, Kennedy observed, "demonstrated that there is a deep division within the Democratic Party. One of the major reasons I didn't want to become involved earlier was because I thought that I might be the instrument of dividing either the country in a way that would be difficult to put back together [or] dividing the Democratic Party in a very damaging way."

McCarthy's opportunity to bask in the glory of his "win" was short-lived. Everywhere he turned in subsequent days the talk was of Bobby Kennedy. By Saturday, March 16th, Kennedy strolled into the chandeliered Senate Caucus Room, where his brother had first announced his candidacy for president in 1960, and became one more challenger to Johnson's renomination. He failed to heed McCarthy's suggestion that the primaries be

[5] In his book, *The Vantage Point* (Holt, Rinehart and Winston, 1971), Lyndon Johnson showed his penchant for rewriting history in his evaluation of the New Hampshire returns: "I must admit that the results of the New Hampshire primary surprised me. I was not expecting a landslide, I had not spent a single day campaigning in New Hampshire and my name was not even on the ballot. And the fact that I received more votes as a write-in candidate, than Senator McCarthy—49.5 percent as against 42.4 percent—seems to have been overlooked or forgotten. Still, I think most people were surprised that Senator McCarthy rolled up the vote he did. I was much less surprised when Bobby Kennedy announced his candidacy four days later. I had been expecting it."

left to him. Faced with this competition, Johnson announced his retirement by March 31st.

Mostly lost in the uproar–the Democratic fracas, the surprising McCarthy showing, Kennedy's entry, Johnson's withdrawal, the assassination of Martin Luther King, and Vice President Hubert Humphrey's entry–was the fact that Richard Nixon was sailing unopposed through the primary calendar. New Hampshire had provided him with a nice send-off: his smashing victory of 80,666 votes trounced the write-in for Rockefeller (11,241, just under 11% and below the 15% his people had hoped for). Rockefeller regarded the return not "particularly significant," but it proved otherwise. Nixon managed to dismiss Romney even before the vote, clobbered a Rockefeller write-in and gained such momentum that he could sail with a full head of steam toward the nomination. After declaring he would not run, Rockefeller switched his stance after Johnson dropped out and tried an unsuccessful multi-million dollar public relations blitz in hopes of persuading uncommitted delegates he had the appeal to win in November, bringing in other Republican officeholders on his coattails.

Nixon's nomination and ultimate election would have been impossible without the launching pad New Hampshire gave him. A stumble at the beginning of the presidential year could have proved fatal to his resurrection. That stumble did not occur; thus, one more man who took the oath on January 20th on the steps of the Capitol had made his first advances to the White House in the premier primary.

President Harry Truman greets General Dwight Eisenhower in 1951.
National Archives

Tennessee Senator Estes Kefauver is interviewed during the 1952 primary.
National Archives

Massachusetts Senator Henry Cabot Lodge addresses a rally for General Eisenhower prior to the 1952 primary. National Archives

Main Street, Nashua, 1952 primary. National Archives

California Senator and Republican vice presidential nominee Richard Nixon speaks at Hampton Beach, August 20, 1952. Photo by E. Harold Young

President Dwight Eisenhower, accompanied by Senator Styles Bridges, arrives at the State House plaza, Concord, June 23, 1955. Photo by William Finney

Former President Harry Truman at the 1956 Democratic National Convention in Chicago with the presidential nominee, former Illinois Governor Adlai Stevenson and his running mate, Tennessee Senator Estes Kefauver. National Archives

Vice President Richard Nixon and Sherman Adams, assistant to the president, 1956. National Archives

Massachusetts Senator John Kennedy speaking at the University of New Hampshire on March 7, 1960.

New York Governor Nelson Rockefeller campaigning in the North Country town of Groveton on February 21, 1964.

President Kennedy meets with Henry Cabot Lodge, who was appointed ambassador to South Vietnam in June 1963. National Archives

Michigan Governor George Romney campaigning. Romney withdrew from the Republican nomination race on February 28, 1968.
© Washington Post/D.C. Library

Former Vice President Richard Nixon, accompanied by his wife Pat, campaigns at St. Anselm College on February 3, 1968. National Archives

Minnesota Senator Eugene McCarthy conducts a press conference in Bedford on March 13, 1968, the morning after his narrow loss to President Lyndon Johnson.

Maine Senator Edmund Muskie in Manchester on February 26, 1972. Courtesy of the Union Leader Corporation.

Former Georgia Governor Jimmy Carter campaigns in Manchester on August 3, 1976, shortly after winning the Democratic presidential nomination. © *Bob LaPree*

President Gerald Ford along with wife Betty and daughter Susan arrive at the Manchester airport on February 7, 1976. © *Bob LaPree*

Former California Governor Ronald Reagan and Nancy Reagan campaigning in Manchester on November 14, 1979. © *Bob LaPree*

Massachusetts Senator Edward Kennedy launches his 1980 primary effort with a speech in Manchester on November 7, 1979. © *Bob LaPree*

Former Texas Congressman George Bush in Concord in October of 1979. © *Bob LaPree*

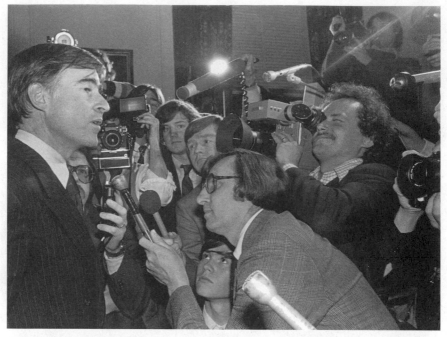

California Governor Edmund Brown Jr., meets with reporters in the State House on April 2, 1979. © Bob LaPree

The eight Democratic presidential hopefuls prepare to debate at Dartmouth College on January 15, 1984. © Stuart Bratesman/Dartmouth College

Former Vice President Walter Mondale in Concord on November 28, 1983.
© *Bob LaPree*

The Reverend Jesse Jackson campaigns in Nashua on February 17, 1984.
© *Bob LaPree*

Colorado Senator Gary Hart on Mount Washington, August 7, 1983.

1972
Nixon's Final Campaign

NEW HAMPSHIRE IS A POLITICAL junkie's dream. Countless federal, state, county and local offices are up for grabs along with the presidential quest. New Hampshire keeps the political juices flowing.

In 1972, New Hampshire was destined to be first in the nation once again and another well-covered news story. For two decades, the state had basked in its kickoff of the primary season. However, this sixth quadrennial fray required something like the tenacity of a northern New England wizened farmer trying to eke out a living in rocky soil and harsh climate to stay in its unique pole position.

New Hampshire, as some were quick to point out, had considerable drawbacks to its status as powerful kingmaker. The state was too small, too rural, too conservative and dominated by one party. Also, one statewide newspaper had far too much power in setting the agenda. The voters, some believed, looked upon the event with indifference or bemusement, not with the seriousness that was required for such an important task. The national news media was given much of the blame for the Granite State's prominence by reporting the primary out of proportion to the number of people involved, in contrast to more populous states, simply because it was first.

In 1972 the primary as a nominating instrument would be very much in vogue. By that year, the number of primaries had increased from 15 in 1968 to 21. Some states laid plans in 1971 to change the date of their primaries or revive defunct ones.

Florida and Vermont were two such states. Both looked enviously at New Hampshire's unique position and considered trying to cut in on the action, to share in the cornucopia of publicity, ego-massaging and economic pump-priming.

Vermont and Rhode Island considered holding their primaries the same day as New Hampshire. The Vermont Legislature failed to approve the idea and held to its caucus/convention format. Rhode Island settled for an April date, and in 1976 moved the date to June, feeling that the voters and politicians might have more interest once the field of contenders had thinned out.

The Alaska Legislature approved a bill to hold a primary in late February. However, Alaska Governor William Egan, feeling that the last thing the state needed was to have a pack of cold, dour journalists meandering about the frozen state following presidential dreamers, vetoed the bill. He believed such an ill-conceived idea would not help the state attract new industry and residents. Publicity is not always a desired commodity, at least not in Alaska in February.

That summer of 1971, California Congressman Paul McCloskey, beginning his long-shot crusade to deny President Nixon re-nomination, charged the Alaskan governor with having an ulterior motive in vetoing the bill. He claimed the action was a result of White House influence and fear of an additional election (February 26th) before the March 10th filing deadline for the California primary. If Nixon were bloodied in either Alaska or New Hampshire before this date, McCloskey reasoned, the chances of California Governor Ronald Reagan entering the primary against the president in his own state would increase. Governor Egan's office denied acting under White House pressure. But in an editorial the *Anchorage Times* suggested the governor could not afford to court trouble with the administration; its approval was necessary to start construction of the Alaskan pipeline to the North Slope oil fields.

In moving its primary from late May to the second Tuesday in March, Florida provided the Granite State with its toughest competition. The speaker of the New Hampshire House, portly Republican Marshall Cobleigh, had a pipeline into the Florida Legislature and monitored its every move. In a rare display of swiftness, the 424-member New Hampshire Legislature rushed through a revision of the primary in June of 1971, moving it up one week once Florida had committed itself.

Even with the seven-day difference, New Hampshire's sanctity was seriously threatened. Florida held a much richer delegate lode, 40 Republicans to New Hampshire's 14, and 81 Democrats to New Hampshire's 18. Experts evaluated Florida as a more representative microcosm of the national electorate. In addition, the Sunshine State had a new gloss to it, which appealed to the media in its endless quest for freshness. To top it all off, what journalist in his right mind would not prefer spending March in the Sunshine State rather than in snowbound New Hampshire?

Competition from Florida had one other consequence as well. It ended the three-week hiatus between the first primary and the one in Wisconsin, and established a new pattern: the primaries began to fall one right after another, week after week, for months on end. With so many primaries on tap, the traditional crucial ones such as New Hampshire, Massachusetts, Wisconsin, Oregon and California were joined by others of equal and sometimes greater significance. The watershed tests had gone from a handful in years past to a bushel.

The dream of the populists and progressives—"let the people rule"—was now fulfilled. Millions of Americans would stride to the polls to select the people, who would select the nominees, who would finally be decided upon in early November.[1] Yet the tough, exhausting agenda that was laid out would prove a dream to some men and a nightmare for others.

A Democratic Party leader, bemoaning the sheer length and exhaustion of the initial primary, once complained, "Every year somebody ups the ante. Where will it all end?" In 1952 Estes Kefauver did not show up until early February, just a month and a half before the voting. That same year, Robert Taft held off showing his face until the final week. In 1960 John Kennedy cut the ice in January, and in 1964 Nelson Rockefeller began in November, five months before the tally. In 1964 George Romney declared in November but began his soundings

---

[1] A total of 12,008,620 voters participated in the 1968 primaries across the country. In 1972 that figure almost doubled to 22,182,246. The New Hampshire turnout, aided by an infusion of first-time voters thanks to the new 18-year-old-voter law, jumped from 1968's 168,792 to 217,268, its greatest increase.

during the summer months. Each year it started sooner, and none started earlier than Senator George McGovern in 1971.

McGovern, who had led the building of a modern two-party system in South Dakota, first entered the Senate in 1962 with a narrow 597-vote win over Lieutenant Governor Joseph Bottum. In 1968 he won another term, defeating Archie Gubbard by 38,010 votes. On January 18, 1971, he announced his decision to contest for the Democratic presidential nomination, and within a month he arrived in the North Country for his first foray—more than a year before the voters would make their decision.

As an unknown, McGovern believed that the early start was vital. Having little in the way of a treasury, he had to construct a volunteer-oriented grassroots organization; as in his own state, he knew that the best way to get New Hampshire votes was to shake the voter's hand, answer questions and make himself available through small, informal gatherings. Just like many others who would see New Hampshire boost their stock on the national political market, McGovern visited the state early to get a "feel" for it and to initiate a network of contacts and supporters.

After a brief, unsuccessful attempt at the nomination in 1968 following Robert Kennedy's assassination, McGovern and his wife Eleanor spent some time vacationing in the state. In October of 1969 he returned, this time at the invitation of Senator McIntyre, to keynote a meeting of Young Democrats at a Nashua motel on a neon-cluttered highway near the Massachusetts border.

By June of 1970, during the college commencement season, he returned once more, this time to receive an honorary degree at Dartmouth and to brainstorm with a small group of party leaders about his presidential prospects. For that trip to the Upper Valley, McGovern, who had already begun to hire staff for his presidential bid, brought along Gary Hart, a Denver lawyer who had worked for Robert Kennedy in 1968 and who had signed on to assist McGovern in the western states. To his dismay, Hart discovered that no national campaign structure existed. He was invited north to talk the problem over with the senator and to listen once more to McGovern's urgings that he pack his bags and move from Denver to Washington to pull the campaign's very loose ends together. Hart wrote in his memoir on the McGovern candidacy[2] about the not-so-auspicious trip to Hanover:

> We were met at the West Lebanon, New Hampshire, airport by a lone student and driven the several miles to Hanover in an ancient, semi-enclosed jeep with the next presidential nominee of the Democratic Party in the front seat and his future campaign manager rattling around on top of the luggage. Somehow this did not conform to my preconception of a presidential campaign; where were the jubilant crowds, the banners and balloons, the eager supporters pressing to get closer to the great man? And most of all, where were the limousines?

One who dreams of the presidency—unless holding mass popularity or seizing on an issue to arouse the country—frequently proceeds toward the post on his talents and the talents of those he gathers around him. Finding good people is a difficult task. The burnout rate for campaign organizers is high; someone effective in 1968 can be tired and distracted by 1972. Others can learn the ropes and make contacts that enable them to move on to a comfortable job in Washington, the state capital, a newspaper or a public relations firm.

However, talented organizational types can be found. According to Hart:

> In each state these people exist. They are rare. But if one knows what to look for, they can be found. The characteristics of a good political organizer are universal: efficient, low-key, persistent, methodical, durable (mentally and physically), orderly to the point of compulsion. Since there are so few people with all these characteristics, capable organizers are sought for all sorts of projects and causes.

Since the New Hampshire primary is significant, so too are the people one gathers up. Given the resources and enough elbow room from the Washington "heavies," a good crew of full-time staffers can provide energy, recruit people to complete the

---

2 *Right from the Start: A Chronicle of the McGovern Campaign*, Gary Warren Hart. Quadrangle/The New York Times Book Company, 1973.

organizational structure and circulate the candidate for maximum exposure. A good staff is crucial in keeping the lid on conflicts that plague every campaign and occasionally leak out to the news media—stories that can cut off the flow of contributions and additional volunteers.

In making his decision to join McGovern's team, Joseph Grandmaison drew upon his contact with Maine Senator Edmund Muskie and McGovern the previous summer. In late May and the first weeks of June of 1970, Grandmaison drove the Maine senator and frontrunner for the nomination from Boston to the seacoast one weekend and around the Merrimack Valley another. Muskie delivered orations to graduating classes at the University of New Hampshire in Durham and at St. Anselm College in Manchester. After these visits Grandmaison found himself as impressed with the warmth, personality and genuine nature of the South Dakotan as he was unimpressed with the coldness, aloofness and distance of the "Man from Maine."

Today Grandmaison admits, "My politics at the time would have led everyone to believe I would have been for Muskie....I think it was strictly a personal thing. Some people have suggested I saw a great opportunity with McGovern. Well, I really didn't at that point." He discovered Muskie's staff was incredibly inept. Months before driving him about he had received "bullshit phone calls" inquiring: where he planned to have the senator have dinner and other nitpicking details.

Grandmaison also recounts: "I remember driving Muskie from Boston to Durham with four of us in the car, Eliot Cutler, a really superb fellow who worked for him; Muskie was in the front seat and Cutler was in the back seat with Bob Craig, a UNH political science professor. The whole time up, all Muskie would do would be to read jokes from a Farmers' Almanac type thing, and the only two people laughing in the car would be Muskie and Cutler." On Muskie's second trip, as he disembarked from his plane at the Manchester airport into the waiting car, Grandmaison overheard him ask, who this fellow was driving him. That "someone" had driven him around a few weeks before, a gaffe McGovern never would have committed.

George McGovern laid out his plans to visit New Hampshire as the one and only announced candidate from Thursday, February 25th, to Saturday the 27th, 1971. The candidate came in spite of reservations that it was too early, expressed by his eventual state chairman, Charles Officer, a retired millionaire in his early forties who had run for Congress in 1964.

The logistics for the February trip were handled by Grandmaison, then employed as the assistant to the president of a Nashua food corporation. Grandmaison and McGovern had seen each other on a number of occasions in New Hampshire or Washington, McGovern was impressed with his work, understanding of the state, energy and drive. On several occasions during that first campaign trip, McGovern asked Grandmaison to join him as a full-time paid staffer for New England.

Grandmaison tried to avoid any commitment as McGovern pressed him to sign on. "I tried to explain to him I didn't want to give up my political virginity, for the moment you start taking a salary you lose all this great independence you've had. But I told him I'd *help* him if he needed something done. Finally by the end of spending three days with him I cared so deeply for him and the warm, genuine person that he is, I signed on board."

By late April of 1971 the first McGovern for President headquarters was opened on the fifth floor of the Carpenter Hotel in downtown Manchester. Charles Officer and Dartmouth history professor James Wright worked up a proposal to recruit a number of college students to travel over the state and establish an "infrastructure" for McGovern's candidacy. The project was then proposed to Hart in Washington. The petulant Officer stormed out of the meeting when he learned that the $20,000 he wanted to carry out the project was not available. Wright pulled the project together even without adequate funding, a necessity in the lean McGovern operation.

The goal was to "establish the fact that the McGovern candidacy is visible, genuine and relevant to the voters' concerns, assist in the establishment of McGovern organizations in as many areas as possible working down from priority areas, identify new voters and see that they are registered."

Another McGovern objective was construction of a "dynamic, open organization" by recruiting people who were new, and fresh and brimming with vitality, not the "tired organizational types." It was critical to stress McGovern as a positive alternative to Muskie, who garnered much of his backing only because he looked like someone who could defeat the number one negative: Richard Nixon. The plan included a target of registering 20,000 new voters. Since this was the first primary that permitted 18-year-old voters, potential existed for as many as 70,000 new voters in the 18-24 category. This group had never participated before, and unless registered would not do so in 1972 either.

The young McGovern recruits were broken down into teams of two, briefed on the area they were to cover and let loose for a week or two (depending on the area's size and Democratic strength). Each team began by calling on the local party chieftains to let the party establishment, which was heavily inclined toward Muskie, know the competition had arrived. The teams secured the cadre for an organization, gathered the names of McGovern partisans or leaners and sent them off to Manchester, where they would help compose the statewide mailing list. After making a contact the volunteers sent off a thank-you note (shades of Estes Kefauver); at the end of the summer a worker took charge of an area to sign up as many new voters as possible before school began.

None of this strategy generated any press in *The New York Times*, *The Washington Post*, network television or even in the state press. However, it brought results that would become apparent as McGovern's momentum grew. Edmund Muskie was indeed the frontrunner in the polls, in press coverage and in the support of the party leadership. But as the New England summer gave way to the fall, the frontrunner began to trail the long-shot liberal from South Dakota in one critical area—organization.

Muskie held many other clear advantages—so many in fact, that one Concord Democrat and high-priced lobbyist, argued that Muskie should stay out. He had really nothing to gain and could only be cut up and bruised. That suggestion was not given much consideration. What the Muskie organization did consider was that New Hampshire could be the first in a string of smashing wins that would carry the Man from Maine all the way to his party's nomination in Miami in July and ultimately to his election over Richard Nixon in November. Muskie had every expectation that New Hampshire would do for him what it did for another Catholic Democratic senator from New England: provide the presidential launching pad as it had done for John Kennedy just over a decade before.

Muskie was born and reared in the mill town of Rumford, not far from the New Hampshire border. His rise to power was well-reported all over New England. In the previous 17 years he had visited New Hampshire 10 times to help its candidates and help fill its coffers. When Senator McIntyre, then the most popular politician in the state and the sole major officeholder for the party, unveiled his Muskie endorsement in mid-December, he said, in "many lean, thankless years, many times before there could have been any political advantage to him, Ed Muskie labored in our state unselfishly to help build a Democratic Party all New Hampshire could be proud of."

Poll upon poll confirmed Muskie's strength. In October the Public Television Network sampled 2,000 voters; among Democrats Muskie held 44%, Ted Kennedy 20%, Hubert Humphrey 10% and George McGovern a scant 9%.

Kennedy and Humphrey were not running, however. As the warm-up year concluded and Muskie prepared to announce his candidacy formally, the kickoff event in the 47th presidential election shaped up as a one-on-one struggle between the persistent, insurgent, liberal McGovern and the frontrunning, establishment, middle-of-the-road Maine senator. Washington Senator Henry "Scoop" Jackson all but decided to enter the race but backed off once a poll showed him with a severe recognition handicap. (He chose instead to prospect for the nomination in Florida.) Senators Harold Hughes of Iowa, Fred Harris of Oklahoma, William Proxmire of Wisconsin and New York City Mayor John Lindsay—who had recently shifted parties—all tested the water and for a variety of reasons failed to take the plunge. The absence of Jackson warmed the hearts of the Muskieites, for the Washington senator would have competed for the allegiance of those at the center or right of the spectrum; the absence of the others placed smiles on the faces of the McGovern troops, as it avoided any attack on the left flank.

With the circulation of nominating petitions to qualify for the ballot the finishing project for the year, the picture came into focus: Muskie faced a direct challenge from McGovern; Indiana Senator Vance Hartke and Los Angeles Mayor Sam Yorty were the wild cards in the deck. Arkansas Congressman Wilbur Mills also fell into the latter category once his well-financed write-in was unveiled.

To his consternation, Muskie would find that life in the 10 weeks before the March 7th balloting would be harsh and difficult. New Hampshire took on a significance for his White House plans far different from what the state had meant for John F. Kennedy.

Edmund Muskie brought his "New Beginning" to Concord on Thursday, January 6th, 1972, officially kicking off his primary drive. He performed the ritual of strolling into the secretary of state's office, handing in the petitions that qualified him for a spot on the ballot. (Five hundred names from each of the two congressional districts were needed; Muskie played it safe and handed in 4,000.) He paid the $500 filing fee and joked that he had mulled over the possibility of putting the money down on the state's lottery, but had decided to bet on himself instead.

Throughout that day's activities, Muskie was wired for sound and filmed for a half-hour television commercial which was aired in the state that night. Muskie was shown being showered with adulation in front of the State House; giving his calm, thoughtful—if not particularly concise—responses to reporters' questions in the Executive Council chambers; and playing the calm, cool Yankee leader addressing his neighbors, asking them to do for him what they had done for John Kennedy years earlier.

It was an impressive beginning—saturation campaigning that, if maintained, could devastate his opposition on March 7th. But it was pure media politics. Behind the mirage, Muskie's assumed strength was like the facade erected to try to enhance it.

Having the senator greet people on the State House plaza was indicative of the bad planning of the Muskie operation, and its insensitivity to New Hampshire's particular and peculiar populace. Muskie came out onto the front steps and, rather than pausing to say a few words at the top of the granite steps, he immediately walked into the cheering group of a few hundred people and started pressing the flesh. For the next 40 minutes, Muskie engaged in what a distant observer would have perceived as a mass freak-out. There the New Lincoln stood, shaking hands, while all about him swirled a screaming, jumping mob comprised mostly of Catholic high school students who had been let out of class to greet the Catholic candidate for president.

The Muskie staff had promised, supposedly at the demand of the candidate, to appear only where he could "have an opportunity for some sort of substantive exchange." What transpired that day in Concord was something quite different. The event was used as a filler for the half-hour broadcast, to show some "Kennedyesque" excitement and to add some zest to the "instant" documentary.

The author remembers watching Muskie being moved through the crowd that day. At one point near the conclusion of the improvised wrestling match Muskie inadvertently pushed an elderly woman into a snowbank near a small replica of the Liberty Bell. A pained look appeared on his face (did he have visions of wiping out the senior citizen vote with this one shove, as Goldwater had with his comment on Social Security?), a look that gave way to a sigh of relief as the woman was pulled up, brushed the snow off her black coat, and let out a hearty laugh.

After the mob scene, some press people stood around and, as they are wont to do at a political or sporting event, analyzed what they had just seen. Steve Nevis, a reporter for Channel 4 in Boston, began to compare notes with Michael Brewer, the McCloskey campaign manager who had wandered over from the nearby McCloskey state headquarters to see the Man from Maine and his team in action.

Nevis and Brewer were appalled by what they had just observed. Such a performance, they believed, could prove disastrous in a state where people expect to hear the candidates say a few words to a gathering, or exchange some small talk one-to-one. The citizens would not want to be used as extras in a media contrivance. Nevis offered the observation that, if Muskie ran the rest of his primary campaign like the just-concluded media event, he would be in trouble before long.

Such a performance also drew a cost from other areas of the campaign, such as organization. The more time, attention and resources given to the candidate's grand tours (Muskie state coordinator Maria Carrier remarked that each trip was "like planning for the Second Coming"), the less would be given to time-consuming and less sensational nuts-and-bolts work, such as canvassing.

That January 6th, the team of television consultant Robert Squier, Muskie and associates had presided over an event suited for a Massachusetts, New York, California or Pennsylvania primary. New Hampshire voters had been courted many times before and they knew how to test a would-be president. Edmund Muskie would soon undergo that test. Muskie had big plans: New Hampshire would be the opening wedge to a big win leading to other big wins or strong showings in Florida, Wisconsin, Massachusetts and Pennsylvania. But Muskie's "New Beginning" soon dissolved into no beginning at all.

Two decades earlier some people on the Eisenhower for President team conducted a poll prior to the New Hampshire primary. The results were so encouraging, those responsible for its compilation refused to show it to Sherman Adams and his cohorts. They feared that overconfidence would cause the organization to allow matters to drift, allowing Robert Taft to break through with an upset.

Edmund Muskie should have done the same thing as the Eisenhower team. In September of 1971, he had a 55-page, legal-sized document compiled assessing the opinions of 313 people who planned to vote in the Democratic primary. The poll's positive results brought many a smile as it circulated through the Muskie camp. One match-up showed Muskie had 42%, Hubert Humphrey 14%, Edward Kennedy 13% and George McGovern only 4%. Since Humphrey and Kennedy would not be contestants in the eventual ballot, the more meaningful match-up between Muskie and McGovern projected a landslide—Muskie held 53%, McGovern only 6%. The rest were scattered or undecided.

The narrative of the poll (which was done by Anna Navarro of Washington, D.C.) was resplendent with encouraging commentary to match the figures. The very first observation set the tone for the later campaign: "The situation in New Hampshire is very encouraging. Senator Muskie has a large and solid lead....Muskie is in excellent shape in New Hampshire, and that his popularity in the state is strong enough to resist an intense campaign, as long as he does not ignore the state."

In a statement that fueled the simultaneous overconfidence and cautiousness that proved the bane of the campaign, the poll advised, "Our strategy in New Hampshire should clearly be to show voters that the senator appreciates their support, and to refrain from doing anything that might offend anyone."

Muskie was urged to stress his New England heritage. "New Hampshire voters are primarily attracted to Muskie because of his personality," the poll continued. "The qualities that they most appreciate are his honesty and straightforwardness, his Yankee background and his concern for the common man."[3]

---

[3] As any white, Anglo-Saxon Protestant of long ancestry in New England would curtly point out, Muskie is not a "Yankee." His father, Stephen Marciszewski, a tailor, immigrated from Poland in 1903 to flee the Czarist tyranny. Upon his arrival at Ellis Island in New York, officials

In the poll's analysis of the candidate's negative aspects, the most damaging dimensions of his image were his perceived "wishy-washiness" and that "he talks too much." Also, "other negative mentions, of much smaller significance, include criticism of Muskie's stand on issues, of his being overly political and of his reputation as having a bad temper."

When he had traveled to the state in December of 1967, Eugene McCarthy told his supporters not to take a poll, for the results would prove too discouraging. Edmund Muskie would have been well advised to have followed in McCarthy's footsteps years later, but for the opposite reason—the results proved too encouraging. Maria Carrier, in bemoaning the poll's impact, called it "a blueprint for disaster."

The efficiency and effectiveness of a campaign is often most easily measured by monitoring its press operation. Muskie, it became clear, botched things up from the very beginning. On October 9th, half a year before the vote and before he was a declared candidate, Muskie flew into the city of Keene to show the flag. A small group of press people awaited him at the Keene airport, expecting to interview him for 10 or 15 minutes, as was promised by Muskie's staff. Some reporters had traveled as far as 40 miles for the brief press conference. As it turned out, they failed to capture a word out of the senator's mouth; upon leaving the plane, Muskie's advance men guided him away from reporters to shake hands for a few minutes with supporters. Then he was shuffled into a waiting automobile and driven off. The media people stood there in disgust, fuming at the treatment they had received. Tom Kearney, news editor of *The Keene Sentinel*, was so agitated by the broken promise that he fired off a letter to Muskie state headquarters, complaining of the treatment the press had received. He said, "I've never seen a candidate kept away from the press so much. Even Nixon granted interviews in his hotel room."

A month later the same "how-not-to-handle-the-local-press" technique was executed once more. Nick Littlefield, a columnist for the *Rochester Courier*, a twice-weekly newspaper

---

were unable to spell his name; they Americanized it to Muskie. The candidate's religion (Catholic), his ethnic heritage and length of his family's residence in the region does not qualify him for the category of "Yankee" in the true sense of the word.

circulated adjacent to the Maine border, had carefully arranged to ride with the senator from Durham to Dover to conduct a one-on-one interview. The day of the trip Littlefield checked with a press aide to verify the appointment and was told that the senator was tired and needed to relax during the ride. Littlefield never got his interview. In his column titled "Muskie Was Nearly Interviewed," he wrote, "The senator's exposure in the New Hampshire press won't be favorable if he remains as inaccessible to other New Hampshire papers as he has to the *Courier*."

What was plaguing the Muskie operation was the belief that his favorable national press coverage would automatically translate into glowing accounts in the New Hampshire media, an inaccurate and dangerous assumption. New Hampshire is a unique place—provincial, isolated and introspective. The citizens generally care little about what is said in Washington or New York. A Tom Kearney, Nick Littlefield or William Loeb has more bearing on a primary candidate's future than a Tom Wicker, James Reston or George Will.

Many of Muskie's problems courting the press can be traced to the fact that he had no press operation in place until after Thanksgiving, long after other candidates started to churn out press releases, radio blurbs and press packets. An operation was finally pulled together, in part because of an assessment made by Gary Gerlach, a fellow at the Kennedy School of Government at Harvard University who began to serve as a make-shift, volunteer press secretary.

A few days each week that fall, Gerlach climbed into his creaking 1964 Chevrolet and drove to Muskie's Manchester headquarters to do what he could. He traveled about the state, touching base with reporters and editors, particularly those who had been rubbed the wrong way by others in the operation. After reaching a state of despair, he sent off a 10-page memo to Boston attorney Joseph Bartlett, who had taken over coordinating Muskie's New England campaign when George Mitchell went off to Washington to serve as deputy campaign manager.

Gerlach laid things out in the open: "The Muskie press effort in New Hampshire is nosediving toward disaster." Editors and reporters, Gerlach said, "have been miffed by abrasive advance men." Muskie was the sole candidate without a full-time, in-state professional news secretary with backup staff and public relations counsel. According to Gerlach, Muskie "apparently is the only candidate without regular press material direct from

Washington going to every daily newspaper, radio station and weekly in the state."

Thanks to poor press relations, a complaint emerged that grew to be one of the main thrusts against the frontrunner: "Muskie is taking the state for granted....For all anyone knows, Muskie's off at China Lake, Maine, duck hunting," complained Gerlach, who also described the mood as "rancid." While Muskie reaped all the national attention, candidates such as George McGovern and Pete McCloskey, who had little national play, were "golden in New Hampshire."

Another problem in the Muskie organization relates to a common criticism of the way presidential primaries are conducted around the nation. Candidates are not mandated to compete in certain areas: they can pick and choose where to run and where to expend their energies and resources. Muskie's all-front strategy carried with it the risk he'd be nickeled and dimed to death—that George McGovern would concentrate his fire power on New Hampshire one week and ignore Florida the next, or that George Wallace would be all over sunny Florida but never show his face in frost-bitten New Hampshire—while Muskie tried to do it all.

As the importance of the first-in-the-nation primary has grown, increasing pressure has been exerted from outside to influence its direction and outcome. The struggle for control within the struggle to win the election is one of the most interesting facets of the fray. The in-fighting and coups between the national staff people and the natives has, on more than one occasion, determined who discovers New Hampshire to be a launching pad and who finds it a burial ground.

The Muskie situation provides a classic example of such a power struggle. There was much to fight over—Muskie had a commanding lead over his party rivals and he ran strongest in the polls against President Nixon. Every politician with a title or a following hankered to climb on board the bandwagon.

The national Muskie headquarters, at 1972 K Street in Washington (or the Taj Mahal, as disgruntled field workers tagged it) teemed with ambitious young workers eager to lend their talents to provincials in states such as New Hampshire and to lecture in the art and science of president-making. Somewhere in the rarefied air of the Muskie hierarchy the decision was made to send many of these people into the primary states. This situation occurs in every primary, but how it pro-

ceeds depends upon who is at the helm in the invaded state and
the quality, sensitivity and astuteness of those sent.   In
McGovern's New Hampshire camp, Joe Grandmaison was able
to maintain control and resist the countless attempts to put the
power into the hands of the Washington heavies. For Maria
Carrier in Muskie headquarters, things did not turn out so well.

To begin with, Carrier's personality differs greatly from
Grandmaison's. She is as quiet as he is vociferous; as gentle as
he is heavy-handed; as calm and rational as he is volatile. When
the time came for funneling political operatives into the state,
Carrier failed to control the invasion.   In contrast to
Grandmaison, she stood in awe of the national staff and the candidate. She believed they knew what they were doing, and soon,
although she kept her title, operation control settled to an outsider, Tony Podesta, a heavy-set, youthful man from Chicago
and veteran of the 1968 McCarthy campaign.

Muskie's main organizational trauma in the critical first
primary—the test that set the tone of his other attempts—was
the unleashing of dozens upon dozens of paid, out-of-state
workers who soon constituted a parallel structure to the locals
Carrier and associates had cultivated. The out-of-staters numbered at least 100 by January, and almost everywhere they went
trouble ensued. One disgruntled Muskie backer, a man with 16
years of political experience in Cheshire County, wrote the
Muskie state headquarters complaining of the rift caused by the
imported workers. In part his lament read: "Ever since the beginning, our efforts, suggestions and plans have been rebuffed,
altered, discarded and ignored. Important decisions affecting the
county and the people in it have been made without any consul-
tation with, or consideration of the opinions or reasonings of the
people at the local level....No campaign has ever been run with so
little regard for the local organization and as a result the people
involved at the local level are becoming frustrated, confused, discouraged and distrusting. Further, we are faced with having, in
January, a group that will dissolve itself before March."

George McGovern, for so long poor in resources and ignored by the national press corps, was beginning to make headway after a full year of campaigning. The cheering mobs and
limousines that Gary Hart had dreamed about still lay in the future, but McGovern tenaciously worked to score a breakthrough.

His problem of inadequate funding turned out to be a
blessing in disguise in some cases. He had to carefully pick and

choose his primaries; selective places like New Hampshire became do or die battles. Once he passed that primary with a good showing, he could move forward. The campaign lacked the money to hire a chartered plane and galavant around the nation as Muskie did, but that too turned out to be an advantage. McGovern had to fly into Boston's Logan Airport on a regularly scheduled flight; every time he did so he scheduled a press conference or conducted a news-generating event before traveling north, thus gaining valuable, free media exposure in the Boston metropolitan area and much of New Hampshire. Muskie, who flew directly to the Granite State, missed out on this bonanza. In addition, McGovern garnered exposure for the April 25th Massachusetts primary and increased his recognition among college youth, who were recruited to canvass in the first primary state as the college youth had done for McCarthy four years earlier.

As McGovern used the Boston media in one way, he had to bypass it in others, and thus gained another advantage. Muskie, through his director of public relations, Ruth Jones of New York City, spent much of his advertising budget, particularly radio, on the Boston stations, trying for a two-state package. It proved to be a mistake. Merv Weston, McGovern's media counsel, made a much shrewder use of his resources by purchasing radio time on New Hampshire stations at a far cheaper price. (Weston later calculated Muskie spent $28.00 to reach a listening audience of a thousand in the state, whereas McGovern spent $2.50 to reach the same number.)

However, the campaign's chief asset was the candidate himself. McGovern differed from Muskie in that he seemed to enjoy stumping. Day after day he was up before daybreak, greeting factory workers arriving for the first shift. Each day the pattern was the same: moving from one town or city to the next, sometimes as many as half a dozen in a day; visiting factories, main streets and shopping centers; holding kaffeeklatsches and receptions, addressing high schools, colleges and senior citizens. And McGovern, unlike Muskie, granted interviews—to radio stations, daily, weekly and student newspapers and television. By the end of his 24 days of stumping (Muskie spent only 13), McGovern had blanketed the state. Grandmaison enjoys recounting one McGovern exchange toward the end. The senator, campaigning in Nashua, greeted one young woman, "Hello, I'm George McGovern. I'm running for president and I'd like your help." The woman gave him a smile and said, "I know, I've already met you three times." McGovern grinned and said, "I know. Eleanor thinks we're having an affair."

Gary Gerlach did not fail to notice McGovern either. "Every other day it seems, I go up and down the Sheraton-Carpenter elevator with George McGovern," he said. "I have shaken his hand four times, talked with him at length twice. The guy's everywhere!" And that was in November.

It had been a rough day for Maria Carrier; when Friday, February 25th was over, she was more than happy to leave the Muskie state headquarters for her home in north Manchester. A bitter argument had been waged throughout the day on how to respond to the instantly famous "Canuck" letter that the *Manchester Union Leader* had published the morning before. The letter was accompanied by one of publisher William Loeb's front-page editorials.

Carrier was convinced there was no need to overreact to the letter or to confront Loeb, a course Tony Podesta pushed for. She had begun a phone canvass of the Franco-American names in the Manchester card file to gauge reaction to the letter in this politically important ethnic constituency. According to Carrier, the constituency advised they ignore Loeb; not to overeact and become embroiled in a shouting match with him. Few felt the letter had any validity.

The "Canuck" letter was signed by a Paul Morrison of Deerfield Beach, Florida, who has never been identified.[4] In the handwriting of a young boy, Morrison wrote to the *Union Leader* that he had overheard a Muskie aide visiting a drug rehabilitation center in Fort Lauderdale, Florida, tell someone Maine did not have any blacks, "but we have Cannocks [sic]." Morrison claimed he asked Muskie what the man meant and "Mr. Muskie laughed and said come to New England and see."

Loeb, in commenting on this "scoop", could not restrain himself as he wrote in boldfaced type the same day the letter appeared:

[4] While the authorship of the Paul Morrison letter has never been conclusively determined, the Nixon re-election campaign was its most likely source.

If Paul Morrison, the author of the letter, hadn't taken the trouble to write about his experience with Senator Muskie in Florida, no one in New Hampshire would know of the derogatory remarks emanating from the Muskie camp about the Franco-Americans in New Hampshire and Maine—remarks which the senator found amusing....We have always known that Senator Muskie was a hypocrite. But we never expected to have it so clearly revealed as in this letter sent to us from Florida.[5]

The following day reporters traveling with the senator who had accompanied him to the Florida drug rehab center searched their memories to recall any such conversation. None could. They joined Muskie aides in an intensive search to locate Paul Morrison. None could. In the meantime, Loeb ran a reprint of a small *Newsweek* article that contained some quotes from Jane Muskie in a racy *Women's Wear Daily* story that had appeared in mid-December. Mrs. Muskie was quoted as having said "Let's all tell dirty jokes" and "Pass me my purse—I haven't had my morning cigarette yet."

On that busy Thursday Tony Podesta was in frequent contact with the national headquarters and with deputy campaign manager George Mitchell, who was traveling with the senator in Florida. Mitchell heard out Podesta's plan to take on Loeb, and the Muskie confident approved the idea "to show a fighting Ed Muskie." He admitted "those things are great ideas when they succeed and bad ideas when they fail. I'm frank to acknowledge at that time it seemed like a good idea and I discussed it with Muskie and he agreed."[6]

[5] In its March 2nd edition, *The Boston Globe* examined the use of the word "Canuck." It failed to find any Franco-American who took offense at the term. The Canadian counsel-general in Boston, a French Canadian, could not understand what the fuss was about. He said the word is used in his country much like the term "Yank" is used here. The *Globe* article pointed out that World War 1 Canadian soldiers were commonly called "Johnny Canuck." The hockey coach of the Vancouver Canucks, whose team was playing the Boston Bruins in the Hub that evening, was quoted as saying, "I was very surprised to read the newspaper accounts of Muskie's use of the term. The word 'Canuck' is wholesome in every way."

[6] Muskie, in an interview in the June 11, 1975, edition of the *New Hampshire Times*, would concede the decision to go after the paper was "a

The debate on how Muskie should respond centered on where he would do so. He would fly into Manchester that night after a day of stumping in Florida, and would be in New Hampshire for only a few hours the next morning—a day long remembered by those following the 1972 presidential race.

Earlier in the week Muskie had been scheduled to visit a Concord supermarket to chat with shoppers about the state of the economy. With growing concern over the letter, the Concord trip was scrubbed. Instead a press conference was scheduled for the Carpenter Hotel.

After Carrier arrived home that evening, she received a call that Tony Podesta had revised the Muskie schedule one last time. The scene for the verbal confrontation with William Loeb would be literally at his front door: Muskie would walk from the hotel to the *Union Leader* building a few blocks away on Amherst Street the next morning. What Podesta had in mind was one dramatic scene to turn the flagging campaign around and to repair some of the damage caused by the letter.

For months the Maine senator had been forced on the defensive—pushed from the left by McGovern and shoved from the hard right by William Loeb and Sam Yorty. He had been attacked from both sides at once for his refusal to debate the other Democratic candidates. He had been charged with taking the state for granted by not campaigning there enough. He had been pronounced wishy-washy and spineless for his long, vague responses on vital issues. And he had been attacked by McGovern for his late and tepid opposition to the Vietnam War while repeatedly pilloried by Loeb for "Moscow Muskie's" alleged appeasement of the Communists.

Muskie was subjected to what one professor of journalism at Columbia University considered "the most sustained, unprofessional, gut-level attack directed towards any individual in modern journalistic history." Two weeks before the furor over the Canuck letter erupted, Muskie tried to take the offensive by issuing a strange challenge—he wanted to debate Loeb. Of course, he had plenty of things to discuss with the reactionary

---

bad tactical mistake on my part, to attack that paper, to give it the basis for follow-up stories. I should have ignored it, and gone directly to the people. Loeb loves to be attacked. He's just that kind of person."

publisher, but in light of his continued refusal to debate Democratic challengers, the offer looked foolish.

The scene that Saturday morning looked foolish as well— a one-man "debate." While the Democratic frontrunner trudged through the snowy, cold streets of the Queen City, William Loeb sat warm as the proverbial toast in his palatial 30-room mansion in Prides Crossing, Massachusetts.

Carrier felt uncomfortable, not only due to the falling snow and harsh winds. She thought that wheeling a flatbed truck to the newspaper's front door and having the man most likely to be the Democratic standard-bearer denounce Loeb was undignified. For a time she sat up on the truck bed but she "felt so dumb" she got down. As the speakers droned on defending Muskie's record and detailing how he had appointed more Franco-Americans to state government than any other governor in the Pine Tree State, Carrier exchanged pleasantries with reporters, asking and being asked why in the hell they were out on such a miserable morning.

Muskie began to deliver his remarks after a series of preliminary speakers, including the director of the same Florida drug treatment center who stated he had heard no conversation such as that related to in the Canuck letter. The heavy snow made it appear he wore a George Washington wig. He said he had been close to Franco-Americans all his life; being Polish-American, he knew first-hand the pains and indignities of being a minority. In the early portion of his flatbed speech he became so emotional he had to pause a few times to maintain his composure.

At one point he said Loeb "has lied about me and my wife" and "he has proved himself a gutless coward." Then, according to *Time*, "'This man doesn't walk, he crawls,' sobbed Muskie. He tried to regain his composure, then said loudly, 'He's talking about my wife.' Muskie calmed himself; unfortunately for him, however, his breakdown was caught by CBS-TV cameras and shown around the country."

David Broder, one of the top political reporters in the nation, saw it this way for *The Washington Post*:

> With tears streaming down his face and his voice choked with emotion, Senator Edward S. Muskie (D-Maine) stood in the snow outside the *Manchester Union Leader* this morning and accused its publisher of making vicious attacks on him and his wife, Jane. In defending his wife,

Muskie broke down three times in as many minutes—
uttering a few words and then standing silent in the near
blizzard, rubbing at his face, his shoulders heaving, while
he attempted to regain his composure sufficiently to
speak.

Curiously though, some of the initial wire service reports
made no mention of "weeping" or "heaving." In its UPI account of the incident, *The Keene Sentinel* called the speech "the
most fiery rhetoric of the New Hampshire primary campaign."
According to that account, Muskie was "visibly shaken" and
had become "choked up," but he was hardly portrayed as the
broken figure Broder wrote about.

Two experienced wire service reporters who filed accounts
with no mention of crying later tracked down how such differing
accounts of the event were possible. Joe Zellner of AP and John
Milne of UPI, both based in Concord, had stood quite close to
Muskie, watched his reactions carefully and reported no tears.
However, wire service editors began to yell when their accounts
lacked the tears that others were indicating, and soon AP joined
the rest of the pack.

Zellner admitted Muskie had water trickling down his
face, but so too did everyone else there—from the falling snow.
However, Zellner "never saw wet eyes." Milne's story agrees.
Zellner found out later what had happened: "I was told by a
couple of correspondents that they asked a Muskie aide if he
was crying and they were told yes. It was going to be a plus to
show him human in that way."

For a brief time it seemed the event might indeed work to
Muskie's advantage. The Muskie entourage left for Hartford
where the candidate was to attend a large banquet. George
Mitchell remembered people telling the senator that the television
report (which they had not seen) had proved him a man who
could show emotion, a man who cared about his family.
Mitchell: "It looked for a brief moment like it wasn't going to be
too bad. But then the negative reaction began to set in."

Aside from the tears or no-tears debate, the morning's
scene did raise significant doubt whether the Man from Maine
could tolerate the pressures of competing for the highest office in
the land. One Muskie aide had this to say about his stamina:
"He did get turned off by the ordeal. It was a problem. His wife
was more and more protective and he needed more and more

rest. He never was a hard campaigner and from the start we had to have a lot of rest periods built into his schedule."

George Mitchell believes that another factor accounted for Muskie's behavior. Mitchell was not there for the tour of the drug treatment center, but he was later able to piece together what went on. Even for the jaded, cynical reporters, it had been a moving experience that had brought tears to the eyes of some, Mitchell says. Recalling the Loeb "debate," he said, "Muskie on his speech had said, 'Let me tell you about the drug center,' and he began to describe it in very emotional terms and he became very emotional. The fact is that on two or three occasions before the time he was shown on television 'choking' he'd stopped talking. The emotion was induced by his descriptions and reviving in his own mind and describing to others this very moving experience. He mentioned for not more than a minute his wife and that's when he choked up."

As Richard Nixon once put it: "Timing is everything." On the evening newscast that Saturday the contrast between the two men expected to face each other in November could not have been greater. Of the newscast, Theodore White wrote, "Rarely has the instrument of television been able, without any preconceived political intent, to frame perspectives more strikingly."

The "CBS Evening News" opened with a report on a flood in West Virginia, then switched to a series of reports on President Nixon's precedent-setting journey to Communist China. Color camera work showed Nixon and Premier Chou En-lai visiting fabled Hangchow and throwing goldfish from a moon bridge in smiles and friendship. After Dan Rather and Walter Cronkite gave their reports on the journey to the East, Roger Mudd, anchoring the newscast back in New York, returned to the domestic front. He reported Muskie's morning attack on Loeb, with film clips of Muskie choking up.

Nixon had obviously timed his China trip for maximum media exposure at the outset of the primary season. One of his opponents in the Republican primary, California Congressman Paul McCloskey, was so frustrated by this master stroke of White House public relations that he took to introducing himself on occasion as Mao Tse-tung. Edmund Muskie should have spent the day duck hunting at China Lake.

The eventual beneficiary of Muskie's woeful television performance in front of the *Union Leader* office was Richard

Nixon. The immediate beneficiary, many believed, was George McGovern. It carried shades of his 1958 race to retain his congressional seat in South Dakota, when McGovern was assisted by another disastrous telecast by an opponent, the supposedly unbeatable Republican Governor Joe Foss. Before a statewide audience on election eve, Foss had stood in front of a fireplace in the Governor's Mansion, surrounded by his family and their dog. As he began to read his address from the teleprompter, his young son started to do the same, only a few lines behind. Taken aback by this, Foss went off the cuff. He introduced the dog, who then tried to bite his hand as he went to pat his head. Finally he turned to his wife, "Well, honey, what do you think?" She looked at him, "Think about what, Joe?" Foss answered in exasperation, "The election, the election." He lost to McGovern by 15,000 votes.[7]

More than one observer of the sixth running of the primary sweepstakes said it was a deliberate decision. A warning bell rang that many New Hampshire Democrats heard. It warned that if the favorite Muskie won by a huge margin, longshot candidates might decide to prospect somewhere else in 1976. That would mean a future with less ego massaging, less economic pump-priming, less media bombardment and far fewer opportunities to practice being dour and inscrutable.

A noteworthy decision must be rendered, one that would give state senators in Mississippi, mayors in California, or governors in Georgia and Arkansas hope that New Hampshire provided an early, important primary where anybody could have their shot at winning or producing a good showing. Edmund

---

[7] Another memorable election-eve television broadcast occurred in 1962 in Alabama. Big Jim Folsom, endeavoring to regain the governorship (eventually won by George Wallace), went on statewide television the eve of the primary and might have made the run-off if not for the ensuing debacle. He arrived at the studio quite drunk. The telecast was live and could not be halted. Folsom attempted to introduce his children who were there with him, but he could not remember their names. He affectionately ruffled his wife's hair and finally lapsed into making cooing noises into the camera. An Alabama newsman later said, "Sitting there watching it you couldn't believe it was happening. You couldn't really laugh. You felt like crying."

Muskie must not leave the state until he was bloodied and bowed.

In the last few weeks, it became increasingly obvious that the year of hard work and careful organization was beginning to pay off for George McGovern and his followers. With Joe Grandmaison firmly at the helm, hundreds of college students came up to inform the voters about their candidate, persuade those undecided or leaning, and pull in every supporter they could find on election day.

When Joe Grandmaison had met with George McGovern in a Hanover living room in June of 1970, he was impressed with the senator's knowledge of the fragmented nature of the media in the Granite State. The candidate realized the importance of an early start, gaining a grip on the media and eventually cultivating its full potential.

McGovern's television spots, largely beamed from the Boston stations, were produced by Charles Guggenheim, one of the masters of this craft who had worked with McGovern on the Food for Peace program in the early sixties and the two successful South Dakota Senate races in 1962 and 1968. The television ads forged a link with the candidate's day-to-day stumping, showing him as he was: a man listening to individuals or talking with them in small groups, hearing their complaints and comments about government, responding in his nasal, droning voice on his plans to change things once he had presidential power.

He was aided also by a team of "sparklies" who helped to drum up crowds—people such as Gloria Steinem, Shirley MacLaine, Warren Beatty, Dennis Weaver, Leonard Nimoy and Pierre Salinger. Earlier, before McGovern's recognition rose, Grandmaison had to put the lid on these visits because, "One of the problems we had was the fact most of these people were better known at the time than McGovern. I told the Washington office we could not afford to have Pierre Salinger travel with George McGovern because more people would say, 'Hey, Pierre, who's that fellow you're traveling with?'"

McGovern's media onslaught was marred by the use of a radio spot of questionable campaign ethics. Without identification, a tape of Robert Kennedy speaking eloquently of his colleague's courage and foresight during a campaign stop in South Dakota in 1968 was used. The Muskie campaign complained of phone calls inquiring if Senator Edward Kennedy endorsed

McGovern. (At that point he had not.) Muskie's campaign manager called the playing of the tape "almost intentionally deceptive," and called on McGovern to have it taken off the air. It took McGovern a few weeks to acknowledge they should not be aired and more time to have them finally removed.

McGovern kept the pressure on the frontrunner by keeping a grueling routine of four to six towns and cities a day, often rising before daybreak to greet the first shift at the factory gates. In the final month, the candidate realized that Grandmaison was not targeting enough blue-collar workers, the feeling being that these people belonged to the other candidates. McGovern overruled his campaign manager and began to chase these people with the same zeal and drive he had been using in the college towns and white-collar areas. "This tactical shift came in time to win thousands of votes that might have gone to other candidates," McGovern later stated.

Muskie was criticized constantly for not spending enough time in the state, a matter closely linked to his refusal to debate with his opponents. McGovern pointed out that in 1968 then-vice presidential candidate Muskie had attacked Richard Nixon for not debating Hubert Humphrey: "It ought to be a requirement of law that presidential candidates debate each other," he had said. Under pressure, and to boost the morale of his backers, stop his downhill slide in the polls and avoid giving Nixon an additional arguement against debating Muskie in the fall, he finally relented.

On Sunday evening, March 5th, less than 48 hours before the voting, Muskie, McGovern, Hartke, Yorty and Ned Coll, a young social worker from Hartford, Connecticut, who was also on the ballot, gathered in the studios of WENH in Durham for the debate, which was broadcast to a statewide audience and some parts of the nation.

Forcing Muskie into the debate was a victory of sorts for George McGovern, but just as his nomination would prove a hollow victory in the end, so was the debate. The single memorable incident came when Coll dangled a rubber rat before the cameras, saying it symbolized the nation's problems. The whining Hartke contributed little to the discussion; the paranoid, anti-Communist rantings of Sam Yorty seemed pathetic. The debate was, in the words of one campaign aide, "a travesty, democracy dying a slow death."

The sub-zero weather on March 7th did not keep Democrats at home. They turned out in record numbers—93,847—33,328 more than four years earlier. (Some towns were so inundated with Democrats they ran out of ballots and had to put in a plea for more with the secretary of state's office.) The media also waited in record numbers to broadcast the returns. Virtually no one believed Muskie would lose. All the attention centered on the Man from Maine and whether or not he would break the magical 50% barrier.

Some articles that examined the downfall of Muskie in 1972 looked at the impact of the New Hampshire primary and Muskie's "loss" here. The focal point became the comment by Maria Carrier a few days before the vote: "If he goes below fifty percent, I'll shoot myself." The failure to achieve the magic 50% mark hurt the momentum of her candidate.

In the McGovern camp, Grandmaison had shrewdly poor-mouthed his candidate's chances. Ten percent, the first estimate, was adhered to for quite some time. As the field narrowed in late 1971 and early 1972, he and Hart moved the official line up to 15%. Grandmaison cracked: "At that time we were saying 10 percent is a victory, 15 percent is a mandate and 16 percent is unanimous." On the eve of the primary they jacked up the target to 20 and 25%.

Being able to pull 60% of the vote is regarded by election pros as a remarkable feat. Gary Hart believes that the McGovern campaign eventually pulled 90 or 95% of the vote on March 7th. Of his hometown, Grandmaison said, "In Nashua we had an excellent election day program. We didn't do that well there, but our total vote was within a dozen of the ones and twos our organization had identified. That's remarkable."

The final polling by *The Boston Globe* managed to detect the McGovern surge. A spread of 47% between the two candidates in January had shrunk to only 18% in late February and just 16% on the Thursday and Friday prior to the vote. (The final survey had Muskie at 42%, McGovern at 26% and undecided at 20%, double what it had been a week before.)

Ultimately, both men were disappointed with the returns. Muskie had 41,235 (46.4%) to McGovern's 33,007 (37.1%). Yorty pulled a weak third with 5,401 (6.1%), Mills had 3,563 (4%), and Hartke 2,417 (2.7%). Muskie had failed to win 50%, and the media soon told the world. McGovern, to his aides' dismay was upset at his loss, but the cheering crowd that greeted him in the Manchester Howard Johnson Motel made him realize his strong showing marked him a legitimate contender for the nomination and left the frontrunner shaken.

McGovern did well in the growth areas and academic communities, and in the larger towns and smaller cities his intense organizing proved worthwhile. He even managed to carry three counties. Muskie showed dominant strength in the larger cities and the areas closer to Maine. However, the place he failed to carry well enough to lay claim to a "moral" victory was Manchester. In this bastion of conservative, Catholic, Irish and Franco-American Democratic strength, Muskie had only 38% (6,204) to McGovern's 35% (5,694).

George McGovern is not one to attribute his stronger-than-expected showing to his opponent's emotional outburst during the Loeb controversy. In his autobiography, *Grassroots* (Random House, 1977), McGovern stated his campaign had "outworked Ed in every corner of the state. We were also better positioned on the issues that moved the voters: jobs, tax reform, the war, openness in government and political reform." He contends the notion that Muskie's demise was triggered by the Manchester incident was "a myth concocted in the fertile minds of a few journalists looking for an easy story." In fact, McGovern believes the matter strengthened Muskie:

> In thousands of contacts with New Hampshire voters afterward, I never encountered a single person who was turned against Ed by this experience. Indeed, my polling consultants, Pat Caddell and John Gorman, discovered that Muskie's tearful attack actually improved his position with New Hampshire voters. Gorman estimated that it gave Muskie 3 or 4 additional percentage points in the final state tally. That finding supported the conclusion I was reaching from my own visits with voters.

Yet to attribute the "defeat" of Muskie to Loeb and to dirty tricks from the Nixon camp is to miss the ineptness, mismanagement and over-confidence of the campaign. It is to miss Muskie's lack of campaigning stamina. It is to neglect the fact he never settled on a man to run his national campaign, and that he tried to win without a message, plan or program. The Muskie collapse was a multi-faceted phenomenon, and to give William

Loeb all the credit is to overrate the clout of one reactionary publisher.

Examining Muskie's downfall, John Cole—a highly respected Maine journalist whose career largely parallels Muskie's—believes that political reporters need to better understand and explain the candidates' values, backgrounds and personalities. In that way, he says,

> you can understand, or you can make some reasonably accurate judgements about his political future, or his past or his present.
>
> No one tried to really understand Lyndon Johnson. If they'd understood the man they would have understood what he was going to do in Vietnam.
>
> Muskie was following a predescribed course. He and others rebuilt the Democratic Party here in Maine. They made it into a two-party state. But at the top the pressures would become much greater. That's when you become exposed as it were—every weakness is there—under that kind of pressure.
>
> People close to Muskie and who knew him all those years knew he had those weaknesses. He's stubborn, he likes to argue, he had a good mind, but he doesn't have the fire—you've got to have the force—you've got to have that drive. Look at Ed Muskie today and you can understand why he didn't make it. Now it happens to all of us, now he doesn't have any drive at all. He lacked that extra thing and when you get right down to it—it's that extra sort of drive—I don't know what else to call it—that gets people to the presidency.

The indication that McGovern's fortunes had been boosted was the presence the day after the New Hampshire decision of a chartered plane, a plane that had been doubtful 24 hours earlier due to a lack of funds. With his New Hampshire showing, money began to flow in; the candidate could travel to Florida in his own chartered plane with a full complement of television network crews and so many reporters, that staffers had to be bumped from the flight. The path now lay clear for him to claim the minds, bodies and wallets of liberals across the land.

McGovern had his moral victory, Muskie his Pyrrhic one, but the real winner was Richard Nixon. *Newsweek* quoted one

Democratic leader on the results: "The only person really happy about the Democratic vote is sitting in the White House and laughing at the returns."

Nixon had easily dispatched a challenge from his left by Congressman Paul McCloskey (79,239 or 67.6% to 23,190, or 19.8%). The conservative Congressman John Ashbrook of Ohio had 11,362, or 9.7%. McCloskey, falling just below his goal of 20%, strapped for funds and facing a deadline for filing for his congressional seat, withdrew from the race and set out to win another term in Congress.

Richard Nixon had won his final victory in a New Hampshire primary. He had won a virtually clear path for the GOP nomination, just as he had in 1960 and 1968. His re-election chances were boosted by the bitter Democratic in-fighting, a struggle confused in no small measure by his own camp's spying and sabotage.

Nixon had been the dominant figure in the first-in-the-nation primary for two decades. He had won it more often than anyone else. Why did Richard Nixon have such a hold on the Granite State? The question has puzzled more than one panjandrum of the Republican Party. The more strongly one felt against Nixon, the greater the bewilderment as to how he managed to win the blessing of these Yankees.

The aura Nixon generated had depended greatly on the glow surrounding Eisenhower. When Nixon ran for the presidency in 1960 the taint of his hatchetman behavior and the gutter tactics of his earlier days had been largely forgotten, especially by a Republican-dominated New Hampshire press. In addition, Nixon never neglected the state. A visit by an important person is not soon forgotten in a small state, and Nixon never forgot to come—1952, 1954, 1956, 1959, 1960, 1964, 1967, 1968 and 1971. Former Governor Lane Dwinell, always one of Nixon's most ardent supporters, observed: "In a small state like this you feel the visits more and you appreciate it more, too. He was here more than any other major public figure over those years, including our neighbor John Kennedy." Persistence and perseverance is critical to the selling of any product—and Nixon, one long-time party workhorse says, "always kept coming back, he always kept coming back."

With Senator Styles Bridges' death in 1961 Nixon lost an important ally, yet the slack was taken up by the *Union Leader* and William Loeb, who would later sour on Nixon. However, the residue of support Loeb had helped to create over the years could not be washed away with a few months of newspaper editorials and slanted news accounts, no matter how vitriolic.

Nixon's visits were always models of organization and using time for maximum impact. Teams of advance men swarmed the state to plan every move. The candidate was always well-briefed on current state issues and about the people with whom he'd meet. Every hour was calculated to see those people who would make a difference in the coming election. At the start of his 1952 vice presidential campaign, Nixon made a trip to northern New England to limber up and test his wings. After a speech at Hampton Beach, he held a reception for party people at a beachfront hotel. One person who accompanied him remembers how Nixon used the dentist technique of moving back and forth between two rooms, greeting one group, moving to the next while the first room had emptied and refilled, then returning to continue his flesh-pressing and small talk. This businesslike approach was confirmed when Steward Lamprey, who played prominent roles in the 1960, 1968 and 1972 campaigns was asked what the candidate was like in a non-business setting—did he tell jokes, reminisce about his trying to play football for Whittier College, or tell war stories? Lamprey said he could never recall talking with Nixon in such an informal way: It was always business.

Nixon's New Hampshire campaigns always held two advantages. He was never hindered by a lack of funds, and he could galvanize the Main Street Republicans into his organization. When you combine these prominent people with their communities, their instinctive managerial talents, the scores of party loyalists who stood by the Grand Old Party doing the phone work, the mailers, the election day work and the rallies, one can understand why Nixon was so invincible. (Nixon by himself could not turn on this latter group; his wife Pat often made a better impression on the ladies then he did.)

Nixon held yet one more advantage. George Gilman, a prominent Republican said, "He was viewed as the underdog who represented something other than the eastern establishment. And of course he had the unremitting and provocative support of the *Manchester Union Leader*. He just turned New Hampshire people on as not being one of the elite—one of the intellectual elite. He won the hearts of a lot of good, common, hard-working New Hampshire folks."

1976
Outsider from the South

FOR THE FIRST TIME since 1952, Richard Nixon would not be a candidate (actual or write-in) in the first-in-the-nation primary. That is not to say the disgraced former president would not be a factor, for his trip to China just before the eve of the vote nearly cost his successor, Gerald Ford, the election, his first electoral match outside his old Fifth Congressional District in Michigan.

Neither would Spiro T. Agnew be a contestant. He too was forced to resign in disgrace. The New Hampshire Republicans would never be provided the opportunity many pundits thought certain—that is, to launch the former Maryland governor on his way toward the Republican presidential nomination in 1976.

In 1974 and 1975 the pundits made their campaign calls just as they had in 1970 and 1971, but this time they included a disclaimer: they would not be back for the seventh production of the primary follies. They had had enough. They had finally realized that their attention only made the tiny state more important than it really was. And the bitter aftertaste of the hatchet job executed by William Loeb upon Edmund Muskie in 1972 had to be considered.

If this select group threatened a boycott, the same could not be said about would-be presidents. They arrived earlier, stayed longer, spent more money and came in greater numbers than they even had before. A flood of new residents were there for the courting. In 1950, just before the wanderings of Estes Kefauver, 533,000 people were scattered about the 9,304 square miles of the heavily forested state. By John Kennedy's 1960 campaign, the population had risen to 606,000. The next decade showed an increase of 21%—up to 737,000. (Between 1960 and 1975 New Hampshire became the second fastest growing state on a percentage basis east of the Mississippi, with Florida being the first. By 1976 the population reached 836,000.)

Forty percent of the new arrivals were from Massachusetts, fleeing the high taxes, crime and crowded conditions of the Bay State for the less hectic, more spacious surrounding and lower taxes to the north. Most newcomers settled just over the border, in Hillsborough or Rockingham counties, which comprised as many people as the eight other counties combined. In spite of its booming population, the attraction of hundreds of new industries and a solvent state treasury that thrived without a general sales or income tax (the only state in the nation always able to make that claim), New Hampshire in 1975 and 1976 needed to undergo a year-long siege by its New England neighbors and some journalists to maintain its unique position within the American political system.

The challenge was surmounted—when the votes were tallied on February 24th, the Democratic winner, former Georgia Governor Jimmy Carter, was catapulted into the status of frontrunner. For the seventh consecutive time since the implementation of the modern primary law, the man taking the oath of office on the steps of the Capitol in 1977 had begun his journey with a victory in the nation's premier primary.

Anyone who is even vaguely aware of current events knows that New Hampshire receives a disproportionate share of media coverage. No one had bothered to carefully document it until a Catholic University associate professor of politics, Michael J. Robinson, with the assistance of Karen McPherson, monitored the three television networks' evening newscasts from November 24, 1975, to April 9, 1976. Of the 337 news stories on the first eight primaries, 100 focused on tiny, out-of-the-way, rural, Republican-dominated, Loeb-infested, virtually all-white New Hampshire.

Robinson and McPherson noted that the next two most publicized primaries, Massachusetts and Florida (which, when combined, produced 11 times the number of delegates of the Granite State), together received no greater press coverage. Senator Henry Jackson received his greatest primary victory in

New York in April as millions of votes were cast; however, the following day he garnered only 560 seconds on the network news programs.   New Hampshire, which cast just under 215,000 votes, received a total of 2,100 seconds of network news time the day after its primary.

Every war needs it Thomas Paine, and in the attack on the New Hampshire primary, Neal Peirce filled the bill.   His weekly column, which focuses on local government, appears in up to 140 newspapers across the country.[1]   Although he is based in Washington, Peirce owns a summer home in central New Hampshire on Newfound Lake.   He is also a founder of the *National Journal* and was once the political editor of the respected *Congressional Quarterly*.   In January of 1976, Peirce wrote the most scathing, widely-distributed anti-New Hampshire article penned in modern history.

Peirce's indictment led off with a call for action, for it was "time—long before the results are in—to suggest that we might well ignore New Hampshire.   The reason: The state is so paralyzed in creating decent public policies for its own citizens that any verdict on potential presidents is deeply suspect."

The column also quoted one former New Hampshire governor, who remained unidentified, as saying, "Making state government responsive is a task which the people of New Hampshire have not had the political intelligence to face up to." Peirce responded: "In interviews in all 50 states, it is the severest indictment I have ever heard an American governor, past or present, make about his state."

Peirce refused to let up: "A glance into history shows New Hampshire has never had a very savory public life."   He considered the governor, Meldrim Thomson, then in his second term, a "creation" of William Loeb and "the kind of politician no longer tolerated in the South—or anywhere else in the country." As with virtually every article written about the state since the early fifties, the writer could not resist commenting on publisher Loeb: "A mean, backbiting tone infects political discourse in

---

[1] The Peirce article, printed in late January of 1976, was part of his chapter on New Hampshire, "Majestic Disappointment," in his book *The New England States* (W.W. Norton and Company, 1976).   The book is part of an eight-volume series by Peirce on the different regions of America.

New Hampshire.   For this William Loeb, the extremist publisher
of the dominant *Manchester Union Leader*, bears heavy responsibility.   Loeb fulminates against every progressive reform; his diatribes are so bitter that New Hampshire is probably the only
state in which many decent people are frightened from speaking
their minds or entering public life at all."

The article sent the *Union Leader* into predictable spasms
of outrage.   Even the sedate *Keene Sentinel* was upset.   It editorialized: "We've been discounting the primary for years.   But it's
our primary, and we reserve the right to downgrade it, even to ignore it.   But these omniscient pundits, who do very well ignoring
us for three and a half years of every four, tread on our primary at
their own risk....Peirce has fallen into the trap.   Like other in-
trepid analysts who have bent their typewriter keys against the
granite face of New Hampshire politics, Peirce perpetuates the
Loeb myth."

The paper discounted Peirce's canard of Loeb preventing
candidates from running for public office: "If Peirce cares to
scan the ballots in recent state elections, he'll find no scarcity of
decent people courageous enough to run against Loeb and his
candidates.   And all four of the state's delegates to Congress are
certified defiers of Loeb."

As to the question of whether the Granite State's advice
should be discounted because of its election of Meldrim
Thomson, the editorial concluded: "A fair question.   But we
might just as well ask: 'If the nation's voters twice elected
Richard Nixon as their chief executive, why should we heed their
collective judgment?'"

Throughout 1975 the legislative chambers in every New
England state were filled with discussion and debate about the
New Hampshire primary in particular, and about a new idea—a
six-state, New England regional primary, which could be held the
same day or within a week of the New Hampshire primary.   Two
Massachusetts men were credited with the idea: Barney Frank, a
legislator who had served as a top aide to Boston Mayor Kevin
White, and Mark Shields, a Washington-based political operative
who had worked for Robert Kennedy, Edmund Muskie and Ohio
Governor John Gilligan, at the time a fellow at the Harvard
Institute of Politics.

The plan was a hybrid—an attempt to attain compromise
between the chaos of the individual primaries and the frequently
proposed national primary plan.   It was also a hard-nosed attack

on New Hampshire's point position—a bit of revenge for the job it had done on Senator Muskie (whom both Shields and Frank had backed)—and an attempt to shift much of the cornucopia of attention, clout and money to other New England states.

The Boston Globe, the most widely read paper in the region, immediately endorsed the concept and pushed for it in its editorial page and news sections. Advocates felt such a system would make campaigning less rigorous for the candidates because they could concentrate their time and resources on one region and eliminate part of the mad nationwide dash. Advocates also felt, somewhat naively, that such an arrangement would allow both the candidates and news media to discuss the issues in more substantial detail. Such a format for the first primary would also provide a more representative sample, since it would no longer be limited to a single, overexposed state—or so they hoped.

The New Hampshire governor, publisher Loeb and some of the state's legislative leaders made known their disapproval and vowed to continue independently, moving the primary date up as far as possible to stay first. They had no desire to be drowned in a sea of votes—especially by the populous melting pots of Connecticut and Massachusetts.

William Loeb characteristically colored the new primary plan as un-American. In a June 1975 editorial, he wrote: "The whole concept is really almost completely un-American because we are not a nation of regions; we are a nation of states." Typically finding the imprint of the Kennedy dynasty on this new idea, Loeb believed the cost of such a format for candidates would be tremendous, adding, "This is designed to favor the Kennedy candidacy because money is no object for the Kennedys and their followers. To allow this Kennedy plot to succeed would be to Massachusettize the entire region."

The proposal did meet with some editorial approval within New Hampshire, but that was not enough to convince skeptics in three states to go along with Massachusetts and Vermont, which set their election date on the first Tuesday in March, forcing New Hampshire to leap to the last Tuesday in February.

The feuding and friction between Massachusetts and New Hampshire has been a constant for decades. On being informed that New Hampshire was prepared to move up its date if Massachusetts did so, the then-Bay State Senate president, Kevin Harrington, threatened to "hold the primary between halves of the Rose Bowl" if need be. By September of 1975 Massachusetts made its move to the first Tuesday in March, but by then New Hampshire had protected its position by passing a law to move its election to the last Tuesday in February.

It is as easy to know when the primary is over as it is difficult to decipher when it all began. When the cheers, clapping, shouts of joy and boisterous bedlam are heard in one election night headquarters, and the signs of dismay mingled with curses and crying are heard in another, you know it is only hours until the phone lines are pulled, boxes packed and the candidates push on southward and westward for other primaries—or flee the fray altogether.

When it begins is much tougher to pin down. For the 1976 campaign, it all could have begun as early as December of 1973 when former North Carolina Governor Terry Sanford, then the chairman of the Democratic Party Charter Commission and president of Duke University, conducted a commission hearing, in the state Senate chambers in Concord. Sanford was trying to use the commission much as George McGovern had used his in 1969 and 1970 to expand his contacts among party activists.

Or it could have begun the following month when California Governor Ronald Reagan left his warm state to address a $100-a-plate testimonial for his conservative mate, Governor Meldrim Thomson. Attendance at similar events had been performed thousands of times by Richard Nixon in his long climb to the presidency; Reagan hoped the tactic would work for him, too.

Or it could have started in March of 1974, as Illinois Senator Charles Percy, in his brief exploration of a presidential candidacy (which he abandoned once Gerald Ford replaced Nixon in August), came to Nashua for a party banquet. During his brief visit Percy, realizing the remote chances for success of a moderate in a New Hampshire Republican primary, became the earliest dropout ever by announcing that even though he planned to run, he would bypass the first test and launch his quest in his own state in late March of 1976.

It could also have begun that same month when two Democratic senators, Walter Mondale of Minnesota and Lloyd Bentsen of Texas, addressed a $100-a-plate dinner at the Wayfarer Inn in Bedford. Or possibly the kickoff came when two other Democrats formally announced their candidacies in November and December of 1974, just after the mid-term elec-

tions.   Congressman Morris Udall of Arizona and former
Oklahoma Senator Fred Harris both began their quests even earlier than George McGovern had.

Martin and Caroline Gross are a young, politically active
couple who reside in a white Victorian home just a short distance
from the Capitol in Concord. He graduated from Harvard Law
School and, after clerking for the United States Federal District
judge, joined a prestigious law firm that overlooks the State
House plaza. She is a New Hampshire native who graduated
from Radcliffe in 1963, and since 1966 has worked in a succes-
sion of paid political jobs. In 1968 she worked in the gubernatorial campaign for Walter Peterson and for four years served on
his staff, mostly as the federal funds coordinator. Caroline is a
Republican; Martin is a Democrat.

Their split party alignment does not prevent them from
opening up their home to visiting politicians. In the spring of
1974, Walter Mondale stopped in for a kaffeeklatsch; Jimmy
Carter stayed overnight during the final week of the 1976 test. It
is also not unusual for a few journalists to stop by their Rumford
Street home for an informal evening seminar or discussion of the
mystical workings of the political process in the White Mountain
State. Prior to the '72 primary, a couple of reporters from *The
New York Times* came by to pick the fertile minds of the
Grosses.

The couple remembers the evening as a frustrating experience. As Caroline put it, "I remember we couldn't answer their
questions, for the ones they asked were so flat." These visitors
were trained in environments far different from the primary state;
"one of the questions was, where do you go in New Hampshire
to get something—where is the power?" She asked, "'Well,
what is it you want?'" With little success, they tried to explain to
their guests that this is a fragmented, diffuse and pluralistic state.
Afterward they watched the *Times* for weeks, but never saw mention of the discussion. The reporters had simply stopped writing
about New Hampshire for a time. They had written it off until
they could get a better handle on it.

In contrast to the urban, industrial, highly populated
states in the northeastern region, New Hampshire is a power
vacuum. It has no traditional sources of power or dominant financial force such as New York's Rockefellers or Delaware's du
Ponts. It has no unified, effective labor organization comparable
to Michigan's United Auto Workers.   Nor does it have an

educational institution equal in influence to the University of Wisconsin in Madison. The New Hampshire media are quite fragmented and, since the death of Styles Bridges, who ran the state through his organization, the Republican Party has degenerated into an ever-evolving collection of factions and temporary alliances of officeholders.

After some closer probing and listening, one can grasp the small levers that make the state move. But they are difficult to locate. If one learns how to handle them while shedding a New York, Washington, Texas or California mindset, one can begin to move New Hampshire. To gain the power of the presidency, one must first cope with the anti-power outlook that is common to the primary state.

For the frontrunner, the nationally famous, the media-anointed sure-shot, the first primary can be a rude awakening. A superficial glance makes one believe it is really an overrated election that, if ignored, somehow will pass without too much notice. But as it approaches, the predictions of its demise prove greatly exaggerated once again, and, with a sudden rush at the opening of the election year, it sweeps by, sometimes taking the frontrunner along with it.

For the unknown aspirant, New Hampshire is the great equalizer. For it is here, at a cost of less than $250,000, with the exertion of 20 to 40 days of the candidate's time, with the construction of a grassroots organization—it is here that a David can win with the assistance of a cadre of voters and workers scattered about the hills and mountains. The house-to-house missionary work can mean victory—without the interference of the multimillion-dollar media machine required in New York, Florida, Ohio or California.

A longshot who arrives without a load of preconceptions, who listens and learns and who has the foresight and confidence to invest the start of his future with the local people can find himself launched toward the party nomination with fewer than 30,000 votes.

New Hampshire was almost that kind of story for Morris King Udall, the lanky seven-term congressman from Arizona. No congressman had been elected president since James Garfield in 1881, and none had figured in a presidential race in recent memory. Udall moved in to try to fill the vacuum in the liberal wing of the Democratic Party once Senator Edward Kennedy withdrew in September of 1974 [2] and Walter Mondale decided two months later he did not have the stomach for a two-year presidential quest.

Udall hailed from a small state, working in obscurity in the House of Representatives, winning some fights for progressive legislation, and losing a good deal too. He needed to show early strength to demonstrate to numerous cynics in the national press corps and within the Democratic Party leadership that he possessed the force for a real run at the White House.

If not for, as he put it, a few "tiny, little things," Morris Udall might have been able to start his own long march to the party nod with an early victory. Instead, those little things—a flaw in his campaigning, a miscalculation by his national staff in entering the Iowa caucus in January and the entry of what some considered just one too many liberals—started Udall down the path to an endless series of heartbreaking second-place finishes.

Udall was the first to announce his candidacy—on Saturday, November 23, 1974. By that time he had lined up the support of four of the most knowledgeable and effective organizers: Maria Carrier, state party chairman David LaRoche, and state representatives Dudley Dudley and Joanne Symons, who served as his First and Second Congressional District coordinators respectively.

In the ensuing months this would be the core of the group of workers that constructed an excellent primary organiza-

---

[2] The Thursday, September 19, 1974 edition of the *Union Leader* ran a story by its ace reporter, Arthur C. Egan Jr., that was headlined, "Kennedy Seen Launching Presidency Drive in New Hampshire." Kennedy was quoted as telling close associates he "wants the 1976 presidential nomination" and indicated he would launch his campaign in New Hampshire. The source for this scoop of Egan's was David Douzanis of Nashua, who had learned about Kennedy's opinions the previous two weeks while working as a "runner" in Boston while "the senator was there in connection with the busing issue and other things," he revealed. In spite of his rather lowly position, Douzanis insisted, "I was close to the senator and his people."

Events within a few days made the prediction rather inaccurate. Kennedy conducted a press conference at the Parker House in Boston the following Monday at which he announced his "firm, final and unconditional" decision not to seek the presidency in 1976.

tion. They were turned on at the outset by the meetings Udall conducted in Washington. The candidate seemed to have a fine grasp of what a presidential campaign required. They were encouraged by the caliber of his congressional staff and the presence of Mo's brother, Stewart, who had served as secretary of the Department of the Interior in the Kennedy and Johnson administrations, and who provided reason for confidence: someone experienced in national politics would be in charge of the effort and would also have the full trust of and access to the candidate.

Throughout the winter of 1974-1975 and in the following spring and summer, Udall was moved over the state a few days each month, with the accent on the kaffeeklatsch, where it was hoped he would turn on enough people to engage them in the volunteer grassroots effort.

By the fall some real problems appeared. The national effort was hindered by the absence of any real plan. One person commented: "A theoretically perfect campaign was talked about at the start, but I never saw it happen as the months went by."

Udall was also being pressed and elbowed for funds, workers and media attention by the numerous other candidates trying to grasp the liberal-progressive banner—Fred Harris, Sargent Shriver, Terry Sanford and Birch Bayh, a very late entry in the fall of 1975. Udall was also hindered in the far West, a region he should have been able to call his own. Talk of later entries by Idaho Senator Frank Church and Jerry Brown, the newly elected Zen-Democrat Governor of California, made it difficult for Udall to gather any momentum.[3]

Fred Harris had come within an eyelash of being picked Hubert Humphrey's running mate in 1968. He had served as the Democratic National chairman as a consolation prize, and, rather than face the dubious prospect of trying for another term in the Senate from Oklahoma, he chose in 1972 to embark on a $300,000 six-week presidential campaign that failed to reach the

---

[3] As early as December 1974 liberal activists became concerned that the primary field might be overloaded on the left. A meeting was held at a hotel in Concord to explore the possibility of setting up a liberal caucus to try to unite behind one candidate, as was done in Massachusetts and New York before the 1972 primaries. The dozen people in attendance had already begun to drift off into actual or aspiring campaigns, and the group made no headway; the idea was abandoned.

first caucus.   Harris was back for yet another try in 1976, and this time he shed his high-rolling ways and was conducting a populist, low-budget crusade.

In his initial campaign blueprint mailed to his nationwide supporters in June of 1974, Harris made his hopes for the first test quite clear: "The strength of the campaign will only become visible in the last days before the New Hampshire primary, just when the national press and political officials and observers are beginning to get really interested in what's happening.   The local work in New Hampshire will eventually generate national attention for the candidate, the campaign and the campaign issues."   His goal was to "build a door-to-door, person-to-person iceberg organization in New Hampshire" and to finish in the top three with about 25% of the vote.

During the fall and winter of 1974-1975, Harris held more than 50 coffees and managed to sign up those attending at the rate of 70%.   His forays caused a commotion among the media and political community, for he put both these groups into the deep freeze, failing to keep them informed of his whereabouts unless pressed to do so.

Harris's disdain for the press and the pols was not unusual for a presidential candidate, but in deliberately and constantly ignoring these groups he badly miscalculated.   When it came time to spread his message beyond the living rooms of the counterculture, the campaign structure was inadequate for the task, and access to the media was quite limited.

Harris's low-budget operation desperately needed the free exposure the news media could provide.   However, his established pattern helped candidates such as Carter, Udall and Bayh, who had established a far better rapport, receive more extensive coverage.

The coffees purposely excluded experienced political people—the better for Harris to try to weave his spell on the novices.   His approach overlooked the fact that the political power vacuum known as the New Hampshire Democratic Party had recently seen the infusion of hundreds of people in their twenties and thirties into positions of influence.   If many of these people had been cultivated and fused with the hundreds of idealistic, fresh faces Harris had signed on, they might have developed into an army fit to challenge Jimmy Carter and Morris Udall.

The deliberate absence of any state structure and even a state headquarters, along with his sporadic and poorly publicized visits, soon turned off Harris's first wave of supporters. He soon fell behind, never to regain his early momentum.

Robert Raiche was one of just a handful of prominent politicos who supported Jimmy Carter in the very early days— the Jimmy Who? days. Raiche had served as the minority leader for the Democrats in the House of Representatives from 1967 to 1971, and unsuccessfully sought the gubernatorial nomination in 1972.

At first, Raiche thought Carter was coming from too far back in the field to have a chance. By the spring of 1975, after meeting the candidate on a couple of occasions, he felt 1976 might be the year for a non-Washington figure, so he signed on. Raiche said, "Even though I was much more willing to work for Edmund Muskie in 1972 than I ever was for Jimmy Carter, I was much more involved." He was impressed by the caliber of the people surrounding the Georgian, such as Jody Powell and Hamilton Jordan. He says it was an organization that was "not much in size or depth, but they made up for that in commitment, dedication and a willingness to listen and try and understand the New Hampshire scene. It was a small but tight operation that worked like hell for Jimmy Carter."

Carter's game plan always had New Hampshire as a crucial component, even before he ever visited the state. But when he first arrived as a declared candidate in February of 1975, his schedule called for limited exposure—mostly media interviews and meetings in private homes. Before he left the state that first trip, he passed the word back to his headquarters in Atlanta that on future trips he wanted factory gates and street campaigning scheduled. The reason: the warm reception provided this unknown southerner by Yankees who had been impressed by his sincerity, grasp of issues and engaging campaign style.

Carter and his wife Rosalynn had shaken an estimated 600,000 hands in his successful 1970 gubernatorial campaign. He was now going to try to handshake his way to the White House. Where Estes Kefauver had failed, Jimmy Carter would succeed.

William Shaheen became aware of the existence of Jimmy Carter long before any other Granite Staters. Born and reared in the city of Dover, he attended the University of Mississippi Law

School from 1970 to 1973 after graduating from the University of New Hampshire.

As a student he followed part of Carter's tenure as governor. Shaheen says: "The guy struck most northerners down there as a shining light—especially after he called for the ending of racial discrimination in his inaugural address and when he placed Martin Luther King's portrait in the State House."

After graduation in 1973, Shaheen and his wife Jeanne returned to New Hampshire, both determined to get involved in the coming presidential campaign. William Shaheen did not hesitate to form an opinion and make a commitment the first time he met Carter. The setting was a reception at the Dover Ramada Inn in the spring of 1975. He was turned on by Carter's grasp of public matters and the sincerity he projected.

The fact that Carter was not a lawyer was of no small consequence. Shaheen: "I was tired of seeing lawyers run for office. I thought the nation was too. I thought at the time they might go for a bright, solid businessman." Then and there Shaheen became a convert: "I told him, 'Mr. Carter, I'm pledging my support and the support of my family with as much time and energy as we can muster. We will help make you a star and the next president of the United States.'" But after hearing Carter's promise to never tell a lie, he included this disclaimer, "If you ever lie to me or mislead me, I'll work against you. I'll work for you until I don't think you are any good."

At the beginning of the campaign, Carter wanted to avoid the traditional technique of a top honcho running each state primary effort. He wanted all the primary campaigns to be guided and directed from the Atlanta office. That plan was soon abandoned and Chris Brown, who had recently directed a successful gubernatorial campaign in New Mexico, was brought in to manage the organization.

The summer months were deeply discouraging for the soft-spoken, sandy-haired Brown. He had sent out hundreds of invitations to statewide organizational meetings. Only a handful of devoted souls appeared in response. At times he was so frustrated he would drive to York Beach, Maine, to talk to Shaheen, who was busy running a family summer business, and pour out his disheartening tale.

Candidate Carter brought an unmatched tenacity to the contest. During the months of July, August and September of 1975, while a special election was being held to resolve the tie between John Durkin and Louis Wyman for the United States Senate seat, the presidential campaigns of Udall, Harris and others shifted into neutral. Carter kept plugging along in spite of the fact that many a politician sneered at his aspirations, that his fundraising was going through a difficult phase and that his half year of all-out stumping had yet to reap any concrete results.

One extremely hot day in August, this author witnessed Carter's attendance at a reception for about 40 people on the lawn of a West Concord home. As he arrived, he made it a point as he always did to come up to everyone, shake hands and engage in a moment of small talk.

As he greeted me, I mentioned I had heard a talk of his at Dartmouth College the year before and said I had been impressed. (That was the first time I heard what would become his standard address—describing his background, why he had become involved in politics and how he managed to achieve the governorship without the backing of the political bosses, the Atlanta newspapers or special interest groups; and a rundown on what he had done as governor.)

That August day I asked Carter how, in such heat, with so little to show for his efforts, he managed to push his candidacy against such hopeless odds. It was clear by the expression on his face that the question irritated him a great deal. Carter said he found the challenge stimulating and the best way to learn about the nation he planned on governing. I then threw out the observation, "Well, even if you lose, you've seen enough of the country to write a nice little book about it." The smile on his face quickly disappeared, his face and eyes froze, and he curtly shot back at me, "I've already written a book and I'm not going to lose. Goodbye!"

While others held to the pattern of media interviews, speeches to captive audiences and to coffees, Carter's indefatigable person-to-person, factory gate, main street efforts reached a much larger number of people. He visited, at least once and sometimes twice, every major factory near a Democratic area. Those same places were also visited by his wife, his sons and their wives. Carter and his family campaigned, as one Udall staffer put it, "for a year as though it were the last six weeks of the campaign. That saturation campaigning made him impossible to beat."

Shaheen remembers the Carter visits with some chagrin: "He has more stamina than anyone I've ever met. After his visits I'd be sick in bed just from trying to keep up with him. He would put into his day three times what Mo Udall did. And he could do it continuously. The man is just incredible as far as personal stamina goes. Subconsciously people were saying if this guy works this hard for the chance to become president, think of what he'll put into the job if he ever gets it."

One early October evening I followed the Carter entourage around the city of Nashua. The candidate began the day at 6:00 a.m. and a few hours later he had already shaken the hands of an estimated 4,000 people arriving at the Sanders and Nashua Corporation factories.

The rest of his 17-hour day was crammed with stops at schools, firehouses, a center for the handicapped, more factories, and the mandatory media stops. In the evening he had dinner at a restaurant downtown before a handshaking tour of the shops along the main street. Afterward he made a speech in a hall in a low-income section of the city, and for the nightcap attended a reception in the home of the attorney who was his city chairman.

Most candidates use street campaigning as a prop for media coverage or as a filler in the schedule. It is not uncommon for them to spend as little as 15 minutes to visit a few stores and then move on. To his campaign, Carter brought a diligence that was the trademark of his entire drive. It was more than a tactic for him; it was a ritual that was the heart and soul of his meet-the-people crusade.

With me in tow as the solitary reporter, Carter entered a store, accompanied by two Secret Service men to protect his "inner perimeter." He'd stride up to a shopper and, while extending his hand, say, "Hi, I'm Jimmy Carter, governor of Georgia. I intend to be your next president." The surprised shopper would be handed a green brochure as he flashed his soon-to-be-famous million-vote smile. There would be a brief exchange, always some small talk, and he would move on until he greeted every shopper or worker in a store. On the street, he stopped pedestrians between shops, repeating the process inside another store. He was brisk and unruffled and, while I tailed him for almost an hour, no one asked him any question about an issue.

While this tour took place, Chris Brown stood on a corner on Main Street passing out brochures in the evening air and announcing the location of Carter's next speaking engagement. It was surprising to see how many people took the literature while commenting they had already seen or heard him earlier in the day. If one had rolled out of bed in Nashua that morning, it would have been virtually impossible to fall back into it without having met or heard about the visit of the peanut farmer from Plains, Georgia.

At the conclusion of his walking tour, a stocky tractor operator came up to introduce himself. He told Carter that everyone in his family backed him and that he reminded them of John Kennedy and what he had tried to do. Carter beamed a smile and thanked the man for the support and the compliment. They stood there, shaking hands, until the man departed around the corner into the night. Carter remained to shake still a few more hands.

The Udall camp was not caught unaware of Carter's efforts. But they stuck to their "coffee strategy," finally—during the last six weeks—turning the Arizonan out onto the streets. The results were quite discouraging. Joanne Symons comments on the reasons her candidate did so little and started so late on the streets and at the factory gates: "He's a very, very shy man. Unfortunately, people got the impression he was cool and distant." She feels his use of jokes was an attempt to break through his shyness, but others looked upon his humor as a sign he was not serious about running for president.

As for his stiffness, Symons comments, "You could really see it at the factories. He'd never done them down in Arizona. He didn't have an industrial district. The first factory gate in his life was at Sanders in Nashua. He was always so uncomfortable. We went through a paper mill in Groveton and Mo said to me, 'Why do I have the right to stop these people from their work? Why should I push myself on them like this?' That's an unusual thought for a presidential candidate." Especially one competing against the Big Grin from Georgia and the champion backslapper of the Midwest, Birch Bayh.

In tracing other reasons for the defeat, Udall's people believe that the late decision to enter the Iowa caucus badly damaged his prospects to overtake Carter. Symons says: "The problem was Iowa. That was the worst decision that was made by his staff in Washington. That he ever bothered to go there, when Jimmy Carter had been there for a year, was stupid. And that he spent badly needed money in Iowa and, more important, valuable time. We were all screaming, 'What's he doing in Iowa? Get him back here because we can win here.' It was really going those last two months. We were beside ourselves—my God, we might win. If he'd won here, if he'd beaten Jimmy Carter, I think Carter would have been dead—I really do."

The famous Carter luck never meant more to him than in the ideological imbalance of the first primary. The absence of just one other liberal from the ballot—either Harris or Shriver or Bayh—could have meant enough votes for Udall to win, many contend. Alternatively, the presence of someone to the right of Carter—either Senators Lloyd Bentsen or Henry Jackson—might have drained off enough support to cost Carter his first victory.

Bentsen's absence was not a surprise. He simply did not have the heart or stomach for an all-out effort. Jackson, however, gave the question much time and thought. His absence from the field in both 1972 and 1976 makes all the second-guessing about what might have been that much more provocative. In 1972 he seemed a certain entry, but he pulled back. He realized his low recognition required an intense person-to-person campaign, hardly his forte.

Jackson was also caught in a bind on how to deal with Loeb's newspaper. If he courted and gained the endorsement of the *Union Leader*, he would have a vehicle to spread his name all over the state. Yet a strong showing or win with that support would taint him across the nation.

By 1976, Jackson's staff repeated the debate of four years earlier. He reached the same decision—no entry. In his account of the 1976 election, *Marathon*, Jules Whitcover noted how Jackson later regretted his decision:[4]

> The problem we were up against was that Carter had a strategy of appearing to go everywhere. We felt that by trying to go everywhere, you could end up nowhere. It was our feeling that the choice was Massachusetts; it was the kind of state that would provide the kind of acceleration in the campaign effort that would more than offset not going into New Hampshire. Also, New Hampshire involved a long, tedious, one-on-one type of campaign, whereas Massachusetts did not. If we had gone all-out in New Hampshire, I think we could have won, because we had a good media campaign

[4] *Marathon: The Pursuit of the Presidency 1972-1976*, by Jules Witcover. Viking Press, 1977.

going in Massachusetts, and with it could hit New Hampshire.

So Jackson excused himself from the beauty contest and instead gave his blessing and a sizable chunk of money to the group of people running as delegates favorable to him. (He spent $44,268; each delegate was offered $1,000 to promote themselves.) It was as doomed an approach as could ever be devised. By this action he left the area to the right of center to Jimmy Carter, while the liberal running the strongest—Mo Udall—was left fighting for elbow room with Birch Bayh, Fred Harris and Sargent Shriver.

On November 20th, 1975, 65-year-old Ronald Reagan, speaking before the National Press Club and a live national television hook-up, announced his decision to challenge President Ford. He refused to attack the incumbent by name, and focused instead on the "buddy system" of the free-spending bureaucrats and politicians infesting the nation's capital. His anti-Washington rhetoric proved a great crowd-pleaser in the primaries, something Jimmy Carter was also able to capitalize on. But Reagan was, according to *Newsweek* magazine, "embarrasingly unprepared on the defense budget and the latest FBI scandals, among other issues, and he seemed far keener on problems than cures."

Reagan soon departed on a two-day, six-state tour that touched down in some of the crucial early primary states. That first night, after a stop in Florida, the candidate was ushered into the convention center of the Wayfarer in Bedford, where unusually tight security was in effect. (There had been a fake gun incident earlier that day in Miami.) The hall was jammed with 1,000 people, evidence enough of the serious challenge the Californian presented to Gerald Ford, for all the other Democratic aspirants running at that time could not have attracted as many people or media coverage if they all appeared at the same time and place.

After Reagan read his prepared remarks, which were identical to his announcement of that morning, he opened the program to questions from the floor, requesting only that the persons asking the questions not be from the news media and that they state their name and place of residence. This "citizens' press conference," or, as the candidate put it, "let's have a dialogue—not a monologue," would become the cornerstone of his New Hampshire operation. It was an idea of his campaign manager Hugh Gregg, which was opposed at first by Reagan's press secretary Lyn Nofziger.

It turned out to be a format that uniquely served Reagan's purpose. Because of his prominence, the crowds he attracted and the large entourage traveling with him, it was impossible for him to seek out the voters in the one-on-one or small-group fashion that the Democrats could (or had to). The conferences enabled him to reach hundreds of people at once and provided an opportunity for him to be seen and heard without hiding behind a prepared text. Since the press was not allowed to participate, the questions on controversial topics lacked the forcefulness and continuity the media might have delivered. (Reagan did allow access for the reporters because, unlike Nixon, he did not travel isolated in a private car, but rode on a bus. Members of the press corps were summoned one at a time for a personal interview.)

That first night in Bedford, Reagan was peppered with a series of pointed questions by members of the People's Bicentennial Commission, a group that plagued candidates in both parties for the duration. But the strongest opposition was not even in the hall. It was Illinois Senator Charles Percy, who released a statement saying in part: "I believe Ronald Reagan has neither an adequate understanding of complex national and international issues, nor the required vision, to effectively lead our country at this critical time in our history....I believe a Reagan nomination and the crushing defeat likely to follow could signal the beginning of the end of our party as an effective force in American political life."

Percy, a Ford backer, was a victim of an earlier right-wing adventure by the GOP. His loss for the governorship of Illinois in 1964 was attributed to Barry Goldwater's hindrance at the top of the ticket. Percy's statement honed in on what was bothering some Republicans in New Hampshire and across the nation. Would Reagan prove to be another Goldwater? Would he be able to arouse a fervent following and capture the nomination? Was he lacking intellectual strength and a sufficient understanding of the complexities of the modern age?

During the question-and-answer session, Reagan was asked about the Percy statement and what he would do to accommodate the centrist elements of his party. He cracked, "Moderation should be taken in moderation," and the audience broke out in laughter and applause. He recited a litany of his accomplishments as governor, a record he pointed out was supported by many Independents and Democrats. He added, "If you're lying on the operating table and the man is standing there with the scalpel in his hand, I'd like to know he has more than a moderately successful record." More laughter and applause and, for at least that one evening, Reagan had routed Percy and dispelled the Goldwater problem.

After this initial foray, Reagan flew west and then home to California to spend much of the month of December relaxing and being briefed on the national and international issues he would face after the New Year, when the presidential race would be in full bloom.

For the first time since 1952 there was a true two-man race in the GOP primary. Gerald Ford would never be regarded as a liberal Republican, but he was certainly more attractive to that segment of the party than Reagan. Subsequently, the moderate-liberal grouping had a figure to rally around, and a conservative challenger who was embraced by their bitter archrivals, Loeb and Thomson. This inviting target, combined with the managerial genius of Ford's national political director, Stuart Spencer, enabled them to win their first victory over the Loeb-Thomson cabal in six years.

The Ford organization was not hampered by the internal rifts that plagued Reagan's as Hugh Gregg and Mel Thomson struggled for control. To this day the Thomson adherents feel scorned and blame Reagan's defeat in large part on the way Thomson was kept at a distance. Thomson's administrative assistant, Marshall Cobleigh, said: "I think the single biggest mistake they made was trying to keep arm's length from the governor." Cobleigh acknowledges that his boss was a controversial figure and was "considered a cross to bear. Yet six months after the thing, he won by 50,000 votes. If they'd embraced him, rather than keeping him at arm's length, he might have been able to transfer a couple of thousand more votes to Reagan."

It is highly unlikely that if Reagan had spent 19 days strolling arm-in-arm with Thomson he would have gained thousands, or even hundreds, of votes. However, it is certain the slashing, hard-hitting scattershot rhetoric that Loeb and Thomson employ so often, and that Reagan began to use after his early primary defeats, could have had a greater impact. But his strict adherence to the 11th Commandment (Thou shalt not speak ill of any fellow Republican) possibly proved a greater mistake than anything else.

Stuart Spencer, Ford's political director, along with the Ford Committee's press secretary, Peter Kaye, secured a copy of a little-noted speech Reagan had given on September 26th in Chicago. When Reagan flew back to New Hampshire after New Year's to spend two days in the rugged, frigid and sparsely populated North Country, the Ford people were all set to paint him with a bright, bold Goldwater-colored stripe down his back and all over his budding candidacy. It was called at times Reagan's millstone, his tarbaby or just "that figure." In the September speech the former California governor had told an audience in Chicago:

> Federal authority has clearly failed to do the job. Indeed, it has created more problems in welfare, education, housing, food stamps, Medicaid, community and regional development, and revenue-sharing, to name a few. The sums involved and the potential savings to the taxpayers are large. Transfer of authority in whole or part in all these areas would reduce the outlay of the federal government by more than $90 billion, using the spending levels of 1976. With such savings it would be possible to balance the federal budget, make an initial $5 billion payment on the national debt, and cut the federal personal income tax burden of every American by an average of 23 percent.

The director of research for the Ford Committee looked at the speech and called it "completely out of touch with reality." Assessments of its impact were calculated and shipped north to the only state in the Union always without a general sales or income tax and thus quite vulnerable to any drastic change in the flow of federal revenues.

A packet of press releases was prepared, and over the Christmas holidays the Ford people studied, wrote and waited. A Ford staffer later said, "I don't think Ford could have won without that issue. It killed Reagan and threw him completely off guard."

Upon his arrival that first week in January, Reagan was greeted by a storm of controversy and constant questioning about the speech, much of it orchestrated by the Ford people.

As he was flying in from Los Angeles, state Senate President Alf Jacobson and Speaker of the House George Roberts, both Republicans and Ford advocates, attacked the proposal and invited the former governor to testify before the legislature, an invitation Reagan declined. Arriving at the Manchester airport, Reagan said, "The people of New Hampshire, I understand, are worried that I have some devious plot to impose a sales or income tax on them and, believe me, I have no such intention and I don't think there is any chance they may be getting one."[5]

The chairman of the state Senate Finance Committee said a transfer such as the one Reagan suggested would cut at least $100 million in federal funds expected for the state. Speaker Roberts wanted to know what specific taxes Reagan "would dump on the state of New Hampshire in order to justify his $90 billion scheme to reduce the federal budget." He accused him of "talking in terms of vague generalities regarding his ill-thought-out scheme, and he's insulting the intelligence of the New Hampshire voters with his Hollywood-style rhetoric."

Roberts pointed out that New Hampshire's state operating budget is almost 50% dependent on federal funding. If that were ever substantially cut, the pressure on the state and local governments to make up the difference would be enormous.

In placing a fire under Reagan, Roberts, who could easily pass for a middle linebacker on a pro football team, said, "We just turned that tax issue upside down on him and we kept saying that the $90 billion scheme of his would force a sales or income tax, one or the other or both, upon us. It cost him the primary and drove him crazy. Everyplace he went his conservative supporters, who were adamant for him, were just as adamant against a sales or income tax. He just couldn't get out from under it."

Reagan drew fire from another quarter—a fellow Californian and Republican officeholder, Pete Wilson, the mayor

---

5 A clear, not-so-simple way existed for Reagan to escape from this trap of his own devising. He could have conceded that the budget cuts would have meant fewer federal programs, while a larger financial tax base would have shifted to the states, which could in turn lay new levies to pay for the programs preserved. But resistance to any broad-based tax is gospel in New Hampshire, and the team of Loeb-Thomson would have disowned Reagan if he had ever advocated such a scheme.

of San Diego. The youthful executive of the state's third largest city was regarded as a real comer in the GOP. He made a quick trip to the state and got some licks in against Reagan. Wilson said the budget proposal would force homeowners to pay 10% more in property taxes. He acknowledged that Reagan had a good record as governor, but his performance in fiscal management had been overrated. He said the state budget had risen from $4.6 billion to $10.2 billion during his eight-year tenure and the number of state employees had risen from 113,000 to 128,000. Another Reagan proposal was lambasted, for Wilson regarded the idea of using the stock market as a place to invest Social Security funds as "forgetful of the plight of elderly people on fixed incomes."[6]

Everybody who was anybody in the administration or the Republican Party who was backing the president wanted to come up and help out good old Jerry Ford. However, the invasion by surrogates is often a hairpulling time for the campaign managers.

According to John Michels, the Ford campaign manager and a former two-term legislator (he was first elected in 1968 via a mail campaign while he was serving in the Army in Vietnam), many of the guest appearances for Ford had the impact of someone trying to fill in for Johnny Carson during his frequent absences from the "Tonight Show."

Said Michels: "Much of it turned out to be the biggest waste, for it took all our resources. Pete Wilson came up. That was a *complete* waste. First of all, nobody knew who Pete Wilson was. What we were doing with him I still don't know. Surrogates are more a curse than a blessing."

The Ford strategists were working with their own handicaps. Clearly their man lacked the style on the hustings his opponent had, but he could not stay out of the state. The Ford

---

[6] This trip would haunt Wilson two years later. In 1978 he sought the Republican nomination for governor, for the right to take on Jerry Brown. In spite of his innovative leadership and a good media presence, Wilson finished a poor fourth in the primary with only 9% of the vote. The reason he lost so badly is generally thought to be that the Reaganites never forgave him for his New Hampshire trip and attack. Funds and support for Wilson's gubernatorial bid never materialized from the dominant conservative forces. In 1982 he defeated Governor Jerry Brown for a seat in the United States Senate.

polling showed that his visits around the country helped him in the immediate area in which he campaigned; but when a wider sample of voters was polled, it was found that his visits detracted from the aura of the presidency and made Ford look like just another politician grabbing for votes.

In plotting the Ford itinerary, his handlers had to be extremely careful. His day-long swing through the populous southern tier on September 11, 1975, five days before the Durkin-Wyman special Senate election was held, was supposed to aid Louis Wyman. It backfired rather dramatically. In the towns and cities Ford visited, the Wyman candidacy gained 994 votes over the previous total, yet Durkin's total jumped 8,088. In its election day survey of 1,768 respondents, NBC discovered that "the warm welcome received by the president reflected voters' reactions to the institution of the presidency and perhaps affection for Ford, more than it mirrored potential support for Wyman."

Ford's targets had to be selected with extreme care, yet he never penetrated two Reagan strongholds: the North Country or Manchester, where he feared he would awaken the slumbering conservative electorate.

Ford did campaign, but he spent less than three days in New Hampshire and drew mixed reviews. He demonstrated a detailed grasp of the federal budget as he spent an hour answering questions from town and city officials in Concord. He also was lauded for the manner in which he handled some tough questions thrown his way when he addressed students at the University of New Hampshire. However, his prepared remarks were vintage Ford—deadly dull. Yet the two trips did fire up his organization and deflated any arguments being made that he was ignoring the state the way Johnson did in 1968.[7]

---

[7] Ford's dispersal of pork-barrel goodies became legendary as the primaries wore on. Although relatively restrained at first, by late January he let it be known that former New Hampshire Attorney General Warren Rudman was being considered for a "high administration position." He tried to have him placed as the chairman of the Interstate Commerce Commission, a move blocked by the newly elected senator, John Durkin, who had a seat on the Commerce Committee. He felt that Rudman's role on the Ballot Law Commission, which had shifted his 10-vote margin from the recount into a two-vote victory for Louis Wyman, was suspect. (Rudman would later even the score, defeating Durkin for the United

Much of the problem in Ford's losing the early organizational initiative concerned the desire of the White House to divorce itself as much as possible from the campaign—not to be in a position similar to the role of the White House in the 1972 Nixon re-election.

House Speaker George Roberts recalled that Ford's initial visit as president in April of 1975 to address the state legislature was a propitious time for him to start putting the moves on the Republican legislators, but he failed to do so.

In the spring and summer months, Roberts called the White House to receive information on the planning and organizational groundwork. However, he came up against a rule that no calls about the upcoming campaign could be taken. Roberts said that aides "were held in check, for when I called to make inquiries about what they were doing, they would say, 'I'll have to call you back from another phone,'and they would have to leave the White House and go across the street and call me back."

In launching the Ford effort, his Granite State supporters were severely hampered by any kind of direction from the national headquarters. Requests for campaign materials or information went unanswered. In order to secure a copy of a White House press release for distribution, miles of red tape were necessary. Said Michels: "You couldn't get a thing approved. Even a press release from the White House—we couldn't get it. 'Oh my God, we've got to get a new set of approvals to do so.' They just didn't know what the world was like out there."

The campaign got off to a horrendous start, due to the absence of any overall plan and the fact that the campaign organizers operated on the false assumption that since every other incumbent president had had a great organization, Ford did too. Michels:

> Gerald Ford didn't have an organization. The national campaign didn't know what they wanted to do here. After a while we did things here regardless of what anybody said in Washington. They wouldn't decide on anything.

States Senate in 1980 and handily winning re-election over former Massachusetts Governor Endicott Peabody in 1986.)

So we just went out and did things. The people in Washington just never got their act together.

I always had the feeling that the people in the White House and the Washington headquarters had no comprehension of what the world was about because they were so removed from everything. I didn't feel our enemy was Reagan as much as it was our people in Washington.

One of the reasons hundreds of people rallied to the candidacy of California Congressman Paul McCloskey in his long-shot attempt to damage Richard Nixon's re-election effort in 1972 was their hope that an attractive and articulate candidate would have some appeal within the GOP to something other than the country-club, monied, rural and reactionary constituency that had controlled it for decades. In spite of the fact that McCloskey drew considerable attention as the first politician to present a case forcefully about Nixon's machinations and venal behavior, his pitch fell on deaf ears. One of the consequences was that thousands of new voters were pulled into the Democratic column. In failing to attract these new voters, the Republicans lost access to the one source that could replenish their grassroots organization, which has been withering from old age.
This vacuum would become sorely evident to the Ford campaign hierarchy as they tried in the fall and early winter of 1975 to execute a door-to-door voter identification canvass of the Republican electorate, something the Democratic hopefuls do with regularity. The grassroots missionary work for Ford never happened. One campaign leader said: "Few people could recognize just how hard it was to get a single soul for Gerald Ford at that time. People just weren't willing to commit themselves."
That approach was abandoned and the word was passed to Stuart Spencer that there was no way 1,000 people could ever be collared to witness in the cold and snow before their neighbors for Gerald Ford. One or two contacts could be cultivated in each town or ward to do some work, but there would be no massive army of volunteer help.
So the campaign switched to a phone bank base, which the Reagan forces already had well under way.
After months of misdirection, Ford's organization managed to pull itself together by February. It is credited with out-organizing the Reagan group in the waning weeks. Some con-

tend that a major share of the credit belongs to James Cleveland, the state chairman, then serving his eighth term in Congress. Cleveland was one of the few party leaders left who could bridge the gap between the two factious wings—the blueblood, Ivy League elitists of Peterborough, Concord and Hanover, and the noisy, cantankerous neo-populists led by Thomson and Loeb.

"You don't want anything to happen the last few days" is the way a Ford advisor expressed the hope that nothing would jeopardize their momentum, which had closed the Reagan lead of 15 points in the polls a few weeks earlier into a virtual tie.

The "anything" he was referring to was the departure of the disgraced former President Richard Nixon on a nine-day journey to China. In exile in San Clemente, the humiliated Nixon turned down the invitations of the Chinese Communists until the eve of the first primary. In 1972, many observers had felt Nixon timed his first China trip to dominate the news prior to the New Hampshire vote. His state chairman, former Governor Lane Dwinell, had scoffed, "I don't think he felt New Hampshire was so crucial that he'd time the China trip just so he'd be there on the eve of the primary—that's rather ridiculous." The 1972 trip may have been coincidental; the 1976 trip was not.

Why Nixon timed his journey just prior to his successor's critical first test remains a mystery. Most speculation has centered on the possibility that Nixon wanted to embarrass Ford, to trigger events to bring about a Ford-Reagan deadlock, thus clearing the way for the man he had privately promoted for years: Texan John Connally.

In New Hampshire that final weekend, Ford continued to try to put his opponent on the defensive. He attacked the idea of investing Social Security funds in the stock market as "the best blueprint for backdoor socialism that I ever heard. I want to improve the Social Security system, not cripple it."

The president was faced with some hostile questions about the man he had pardoned. Since Ford regarded the Nixon trip to China as one undertaken by a private citizen, a voter in Keene wanted to know why he "didn't treat him as any other American and have him face criminal charges as any other American would instead of pardoning him." An obviously irritated president answered: "The former president obviously resigned in disgrace. That is a severe penalty."

Of Nixon's trip, a beleaguered Ford supporter was over-heard saying at one stop, "It's just Nixon's way of saying thanks."

As is traditional with closely contested Republican pri-maries, the more conservative hopeful jumps into an early lead as the votes from the small, rural towns and also Manchester (where there are voting machines) first come in. But unless that lead is substantial enough, the tide inevitably shifts in the late night and early morning hours as the larger cities—Keene, Claremont, Lebanon and others—send in their tallies for the more moderate candidates.

Reagan, spending the night at the Highway Hotel in Concord, maintained a narrow lead throughout the early part of the night. Ford watched the returns on the networks from the second floor of the White House with his daughter. The White House chief of staff, Richard Cheney, sent nearly all the Ford aides home early out of concern the close race might provoke panic and harmful commentary to the news media. One middle-level aide who stayed was quoted on how bizarre it was to "sit down here worrying about how the president of the United States was going to do in some precinct with forty votes."

While still in the lead, Reagan addressed a throng shortly before midnight: "We came here believing that if we could achieve forty percent of the vote, that this would betoken a viable candidacy, and that we would go on. If it continues the way it is, we have, of course, exceeded our expectations."

At a few minutes before 1:00 a.m., Stuart Spencer in Washington received the first call from New Hampshire that told of a Ford lead—by five votes. A little later the margin shot up to 500, and he broke out the booze and lit a cigar.

Upon rising at 5:30 a.m., Ford turned on the radio and learned that he had won. He was so pleased he had made an impromptu appearance at the morning staff meeting and received a standing ovation. He called his win "a great springboard."

Richard Reeves, a political writer, was certain Ronald Reagan had "won" the 1976 first primary and was probably on his way to the Republican nomination. For three days after the initial vote Reeves read newspapers with photos of the smiling Californian and analyses of how he'd "defeated" the president. His prospects in Florida, good to begin with, now looked even rosier.

There was a catch. Reeves explains: "Unfortunately—at least for Reagan—I happened to be in London. That's the way the British press interpreted Ford's 1,587-vote margin in the first primary."

Eugene McCarthy had lost the first test, and so too had George McGovern (by 7.7 and 9.3 points respectively), yet both were declared "moral victors" by the news media. Ronald Reagan lost by less than 2% and yet he never received—at least from the American press—a similar accolade. How this happened is blamed primarily on two of Reagan's backers: his national campaign manager, John Sears and Governor Meldrim Thomson.

As the returns finally became conclusive in the early morning hours of February 25th, reporters were confused as to how to lead off their stories: Had Ford "lost" even though he won, and had Reagan "won" even though he had lost? They waited for some kind of signal, and the one given greater weight than any other was the depression of the Reagan staff in general and Sears in particular. "We didn't know what to write, and then we saw that *they* (Reagan's top staffers) thought they'd lost," one newsmagazine reporter confided to Reeves later.

The Regan forces, led by former Governor Hugh Gregg, had carefully staked out the 35-40% range to lay claim for a victory. That projection was blown apart by Governor Thomson, for on the single day he was unleashed and allowed to campaign with Reagan, he told a group of reporters that his man would not just win, but he would win handily—with 55% of the vote.

Gregg was livid. He said, "That's absurd and it gives the national media another place to hang their hats if we don't get fifty one percent." (When Reagan returned to the state in October of 1978 to address a $100-a-plate fundraiser for Thomson's unsuccessful attempt at a fourth two-year term, a still bitter Gregg told a reporter: "Had Thomson kept his mouth shut, Reagan might have gotten another handful of votes and actually won. But since he had predicted that Reagan would get fifty-five percent, the press looked at the forty-nine percent and said he lost badly. I believe Thomson cost Reagan the New Hampshire victory.")

That handful of votes Gregg speculated about caused others to consider what might have been. George Will, writing in *Newsweek* in March of 1976, said: "If 794 New Hampshire Republicans had voted the other way, Ford would have limped into Florida a loser. That probably would have meant three percent more of the vote for Ronald Reagan, and a second Ford loss. But that destiny was derailed by those 794 voters, and Ford's presidency has entered a prosperous new phase."

John Sears, who was a participant in a December 1976 Harvard Institute of Politics seminar on the presidential campaign, said: "If we had won in New Hampshire, I think we would have won in Florida [March 9th] and then in Illinois [March 16th]. The week before the New Hampshire primary, our polling showed us ahead in Florida; then on Saturday after the New Hampshire primary, out poll showed us eighteen points down, which gives you some idea of what momentum—or lack of it—can do."[8]

The argument that Reagan was cheated out of a deserved "moral victory" assumes that he was in the same category as Senators McCarthy or McGovern had been. He was not.

The news media had undergone a good deal of criticism for the manner in which they had interpreted the 1968 and 1972 returns. Yet their main motivation in changing their methods for calling this race was not a result of guilt feelings; it had more to do with their use of one of the powers they hold over the race for the White House—the ability to determine the betting line or point spread in the primaries. Virtually no journalist in the country was willing to concede that the Reagan-Ford match was comparable to the McCarthy-Johnson or McGovern-Muskie fights. The point spread had been factored into the previous matches because they initially looked like routs, and it was necessary to do this to attract attention and excitement to what seemed like laughers.

McCarthy and McGovern had as many drawbacks and problems as Reagan had strengths. Both Democrats were held in something bordering contempt by their peers and by politicians at every stratum. Reagan, if not attracting the endorsements of many congressmen or governors, captured the support of some and had the help of a good segment of the middle echelon and the grassroots of the Grand Old Party. Both

[8] The edited transcript of the two-day seminar makes up the book *Campaign for President: The Managers Look at '76*, edited by Jonathan Moore and Janet Fraser. Ballinger Publishing Company, Cambridge, Mass., 1977.

Democrats enjoyed little media coverage at the beginning, and in contrast, the press entourage surrounding Reagan was almost the size of the one that traveled with the president.

Reagan's fundraising and the caliber of his national staff were light years ahead of anything the two senators achieved, and his speechmaking ability, his photogenic presence, his established celebrity status and also his conservative, relatively scandal-free administration of the nation's largest state (a record that probably would have won him a third term in 1974 if he had chosen to seek one) made more than one reporter wonder if he should not be regarded as the favorite in the bumbling, poorly organized campaign for President Ford.

Reagan's failure to achieve a "moral victory" can not really be blamed on the mood of his aides on election night or the loose-lipped boasting of Mel Thomson; it was an informal decision made by the news media after assessing the strengths of the challenger against his lackluster opponent. That judgment was easier to make as the Ford people avoided making any of the bombastic predictions of easy victory made by Johnson's handlers in 1968.

Ronald Reagan had indeed a viable candidacy. It was moving on. But it was not a winning one, and that in the end would help to make all the difference. And the problems he presented to President Ford throughout the spring and summer were no doubt beneficial in helping Jimmy Carter to defeat Jerry Ford in the fall.

1980
Outsider from the West

AS THE NEW HAMPSHIRE primary has increased in significance, so too have the number of challenges to its unique first-place status.

In 1972 Florida's primary alighted on New Hampshire's Town Meeting day, the second Tuesday in March, forcing the Granite State to advance its primary to the first Tuesday in March. By 1976 Massachusetts and Vermont had attempted to implement a New England regional primary, once again forcing the premier primary to be moved up a week; for the first time, it was held in February.

In 1977 the New Hampshire Legislature amended the primary law so that any new challenge was rebuffed automatically. The new law stipulated that the primary must be held "On the second Tuesday in March or on the Tuesday immediately preceding the date on which any other state shall hold a similar election, whichever is the earlier, of each year when a president of the United States is to be elected."

In 1980 the primary's main challenge stemmed from the national Democratic Party. For over a decade, the party had had a fetish for tinkering with the nomination rules by developing commissions to study and recommend changes. Prior to 1980 this group was called the Commission on Presidential Nomination and Party Structure, chaired by Michigan party chief Morley Winograd. The Winograd Commission was the most serious attempt by either political party to end New Hampshire's special status.

The plan eventually adopted by the Democratic National Committee was a 13-week window concept, which limited primaries and caucuses to a time frame between the second Tuesday in March and the second Tuesday in June. However, the plan included a loophole for New Hampshire and Iowa that, in the end, made these two states more prominent, which was certainly not the intent of the plan's advocates.

The window concept was a close relative to a proposal introduced a number of times in the House of Representatives by Arizona Congressman Morris Udall. His plan called for the standardization of the primary laws in all concerned states and the placing of a limit of three or four dates when primaries or caucuses could be conducted.

At a Winograd Commission conclave in Detroit in early September of 1977 the group heard Udall push his idea and call for a reduction in New Hampshire's influence. A non-binding tally revealed that about half the commission members in attendance favored the institution of the 13-week window for the selection of delegates. Advocates hoped such a new restriction would shorten the amount of time devoted to campaigning and influence the media to cover a broader range of elections, especially on opening night. South Carolina party chief Donald Fowler said the window was targeted at the first primary because it was "not a healthy feature of the presidential nominating process." Minnesota Congressman Donald Fraser (later to become the mayor of Minneapolis) was a member of the commission; he not only called for the passage of the window, but argued for sanctions to guarantee that New Hampshire would not be able to circumvent its enforcement.

White House aides on the commission, led by Mark Siegel, originally backed the window concept and the sanctions that Fraser advocated. But by the second day of the Detroit meeting they called a retreat. With an eye cast backward to the lessons of 1976 but shifting forward to the 1980 primary, Siegel and his associates—who controlled many of the group's decisions—decided to call a retreat on the sanctions. By eventually failing to kill the Rule 20 exemption that, if a state party takes "provable, positive steps" to comply with a national rule and fails, they are exempt from that rule, New Hampshire was provided the loophole to remain first in the nation in 1980.

The debate over the window triggered a feeling in the state that a piece of political engineering was being directed from the

rather rarefied atmosphere of Washington—a straight, old-fashioned power play meant to dilute the impact held by such a tiny
state.   The reaction to this power play was best expressed by
one Democratic Party leader, Robert Craig, an associate professor of political science at the University of New Hampshire: "I
know there are a lot of people on the commission who consider
themselves experts.   Some of these people are experts at telling
other people what to do, and I don't know if they're very expert
at politics."   Senator John Durkin's opinion: "You've got
dreamy-eyed types on the commission that couldn't run for
county sheriff, but they sit there in never-never land thinking that
they're going to cut off the New Hampshire primary for the good
of the country."

The Granite State had a trump card to play, if not to defeat the window outright, at least to maintain the Rule 20 loophole. Often while traveling here in 1975 and 1976 Jimmy Carter
included in his litany a verse advocating the retention of the
state's first primary status.   In Nashua in early November of
1975, he witnessed for the state: "I hope that New Hampshire
is always the first primary state.   I hope that one hundred years
from now New Hampshire still has the first primary.   I think it's
good for the country to have at least one relatively small state so
that the candidates have to go directly to the voters to shake
hands at factory shift lines; go to the high schools, the shopping
centers, beano games and meet the people where they are."
President Carter retained some deep emotional ties to New
Hampshire and he eventually delivered on his promise to help
preserve the primary.

On January 21st and 22nd of 1978 the Winograd
Commission met in Washington for its final session.   The proposals it approved were passed on to the executive committee of
the Democratic National Committee and then the full DNC for
its final ratification.   At that point the fight over the window was
lost—it passed handily 41-12—the wide margin guaranteeing its
final approval by the DNC.

The real struggle was saved for the Rule 20 exemption.   A
petulant Donald Fraser, who, as the chairman of the reform-
minded Democratic Conference, had already given up the fight to
deny the Rule 20 loophole: "Since the commission seems to be
unwilling to impose any sanctions on a state which chooses to
be outside the window, we strongly object to the drafting of
meaningless rules which would require many state legislatures to

change their laws and ask many state parties to break with long-standing delegate selection calendars."

The New Hampshire primary often requires the construction of elaborate organizational structures. The outreach to voters includes door-to-door canvassing, phone banks, literature drops and mass mailings. While radio, newspaper and television ads are also used, candidates still must meet the voters through kaffeeklatsches, at factories, walks along main streets, and countless speeches before service and business groups, schools, gatherings of the party faithful and civic groups.

In fact, the state seems a quaint anachronism untouched by the era of electronic campaigning that has swept the nation. With its enormous population and deep devotion to the television culture, California is New Hampshire's opposite. On the evening of April 2, 1979 the contrasts between New Hampshire and California were dramatically illuminated. The glare of events that night left one humiliated victim, the governor of the Golden State, Democrat Edmund (Jerry) Brown Jr.

The Republican speaker of the New Hampshire House, George Roberts Jr., was in the process of positioning himself for a run for higher office—either the governorship held by Democrat Hugh Gallen who upset third-term Governor Meldrim Thomson the previous November by just 10,700 votes, or challenging another first-term Democrat, United States Senator John Durkin. (Roberts would eventually seek the GOP Senate nomination, finishing a dismal seventh in an 11-man field with just 7% of the vote.) The constitutional amendment to require a balanced federal budget seemed like an ideal issue to exploit in fiscally conservative New Hampshire. Who better to bring attention to the issue than the California governor who had embraced the concept on January 8th in his second inaugural address?

At Roberts's invitation, Brown agreed to appear before the House Constitutional Revision Committee to testify in support of the proposed constitutional amendment to require a balanced federal budget. However, the governor never made it into Representatives Hall, where the hearing was being conducted. Instead, he found his media mask stripped bare. The ordeal he suffered that night proved that a mediagenic presence and facility to proffer up bits of wisdom does not make for a legitimate presidential contender—at least not in the first primary state.

Brown had been on a media roll since he announced in March of 1976 he would seek the Democratic presidential nomination.   In only his first term as governor, Brown managed to finish the 1976 primary season with a flourish, winning the primaries in Maryland, Nevada and his native state and finishing a strong third via a write-in in Oregon.   His success was not sufficient to deny the nomination to Jimmy Carter, however.

Clearly, if Brown's 1980 presidential ambitions were to take root, he had to establish a foothold in the rocky terrain of northern New England.   His trip in early April of 1979 was Brown's first exposure to quaint New Hampshire.   He would never fully recover from events that took place that evening.

Brown's plan to attend the hearing immediately raised the hackles of George Roberts's bitter rival, the colorful House Minority Leader Chris Spirou of Manchester.   Brown did not have the courtesy to inform either Spirou or Governor Gallen (both opponents of the amendment) of his acceptance to testify. In the blunt language that has always been his trademark, Spirou believed the Brown-Roberts alliance was an effort "to spit in our face."   He felt that Brown had managed to align himself with "a person that has kicked our ass left and right up here for the last six years and that's George Roberts."

A flurry of calls between Sacramento and Concord ensued in the days before Brown's arrival.   By the time he departed, he was unaccompanied by any staff; indeed, no one had been dispatched to Concord to advance Brown's activities, yet another in what would be a long series of blunders.

Upon arriving at Logan Airport in Boston, Brown was met by a political operative from a labor union in Washington and driven to the State House in Concord.   His first stop was a courtesy call on Spirou in his third floor office.   Once in Spirou's lair Brown was essentially taken captive.   Spirou later said, "He was a sitting duck for me and I took care of him."

While the two men discussed the situation, the assistant minority leader, Mary Chambers, stood in front of the window and helped block the large press gathering from taking photographs of the two men talking.   Chambers remembers: "Brown looked like a fairly good-sized man going through the door.   The longer he sat in there the littler he—he actually shrank.   It was a phenomenon that I thought was incredible to watch."

While this meeting was taking place, most of the Democratic members of the House Constitutional Revision Committee had walked out of the hearing.   The Democrats hoped to register their discontent with the format for speakers, which did not permit Governor Gallen to speak until about a dozen proponents of the constitutional amendment had testified. (Standard House procedure permitted the governor to speak whenever he took the trouble to attend a legislative hearing, but Speaker Roberts forced the chairman of the committee, Republican Joseph Eaton, to abide by this unusual format.)

Brown and Spirou were still meeting when word reached them of the walkout. Upon hearing this news, Brown asked, "Are you sure?" An aide confirmed it. Brown then asked Spirou to go downstairs and confirm it. He did so, and Chambers says, "at that point the governor turned to me and looked absolutely devastated and said, 'I've got to get out of this. Will you help me get out?' I said, 'Of course.'"

Ironically, Brown now needed Spirou's help, even though Spirou had done a masterful job of putting Brown in the fix he was in. According to Chambers: "He saw Chris as being his buffer, his protector, that was what was funny. All at once he realized he had nobody to handle that howling mob outside, to handle anything. It was completely out of his hands and he was very aware of that. He saw Chris as his one ally—not in terms of the issue at stake that night, but in being a fellow Democrat. He knew he was in a tough spot."

It would only get tougher, for the next step on Jerry Brown's Magical Mystery Tour of New Hampshire was a stroll down one flight of stairs to Governor Gallen's corner office, accompanied by about 75 members of the media.

Gallen was in a tough spot of his own; it would do him little good to help humiliate a fellow Democratic governor. Nor would it be to his benefit if his opposition to the balanced federal budget amendment was looked upon by the electorate in his fiscally frugal state as just one more part of a pattern of big spending, of which the Democrats were so often accused.

If Brown, the former seminarian at the Jesuits' Sacred Heart Novitiate in Los Gatos, California, hoped to find sanctuary in his fellow governor's office, he was in for yet another disappointment. Gallen's press aide, Dayton Duncan, let the press entourage crowd into the office to record every word of an impromptu debate on the budget amendment, with Spirou and Gallen in the negative and Brown in the affirmative. The press corps was now eager to hear Brown's explanation of his decision not to testify to the committee in Representatives Hall.

Following the debate in Gallen's office, Brown beat a retreat out of the public limelight and took refuge in the Executive
Council chambers with the handful of Democratic committee
members, Spirou and Chambers. Meanwhile the press crowded
into the governor's reception office to await Brown's more
detailed explanation of why he was not testifying. It took quite a
while for Brown to leave his sanctuary, as Chambers recalled:
"After a while we wanted to get him out of there. He was staying
in that room to recover himself, that was very clear. He was not
in any condition to go out and face the press."

Finally, with Spirou still at his side, Brown met the media.
In his spin-control attempt, Brown proclaimed his mission was
accomplished. While achieving his objective, to focus attention
on federal spending, he had also managed to avoid snubbing the
governor by not attending the hearing. He also mentioned he
had learned quite a lot about "the complexities of New
Hampshire politics;" "any time spent in New Hampshire," he
said, "is time well spent."

Brown, a complete creation of media politics, had failed to
study the unfamiliar terrain he was entering. He had been
tossed, unprepared, into a state representing the antithesis of
media politics. To Brown, one-on-one meant a politician talking
to a television camera; in New Hampshire, which did not see
candidates for governor and the United States Senate use TV
ads until 1978, one-on-one meant something else altogether.

Brown, criticized over the years for embracing a politics of
"no policy," of offering up vague promises wrapped in slogans
and buzzwords carefully measured to fit TV newscasts, at least
had taken a position on the controversial budget amendment.
Yet it was not a position generally embraced by the Democratic
leadership in New Hampshire or across the nation. Surely there
was no need to secure a forum such as the one Republican
Speaker George Roberts attempted to provide.

The following morning, prior to flying back to the West
Coast, Brown decided to place a phone call to William Loeb, a
final attempt to explain his actions the night before. In response,
Loeb wrote under the heading "California Flake": "Not much
snow falls on California, but New Hampshire today feels that
there is a least one big flake, Governor Jerry Brown." The editorial concluded: "In one evening, like Muskie's few minutes of
weeping, Brown has seriously damaged any possibility he ever

had of getting more than a handful of votes in the New Hampshire primary."

If there was one last way to affirm all the reservations New Hampshire Democrats had about Brown, it was by this one phone call. While Loeb was certainly a key player on the Republican side of the primary, he most assuredly was not among the Democrats. In the end, Jerry Brown proved not to be much of a player at all.

In a column assessing the substantial political damage Brown had inflicted upon his presidential ambitions by one night of blundering about the New Hampshire State House, columnists Rowland Evans and Robert Novak quoted a Californian who had known Brown all of his life: "Maybe Jerry really wasn't ever all that tough, but nobody has leaned on him before."

He was leaned on one evening in New Hampshire; he suffered a political meltdown in the process.

Since the 1952 New Hampshire primary, which essentially dovetailed with his control of the *Manchester Union Leader*, William Loeb had managed to endorse only one winner in a competitive primary—Richard Nixon in 1968. In 1980 Loeb brought home his second winner—Ronald Reagan—a success that turned out to be his last.[1] The narrow 1,587-vote loss Reagan suffered in the 1976 primary versus President Ford had always rankled ardent backers of the former movie actor. When Reagan finally made it to the White House in January of 1981, it was with a rather substantial dept of gratitude to William Loeb and his newspaper in the critical first-primary state, possibly as deep a debt as the one he owed to the Ayatollah Ruhollah Khomeini.

Loeb was not simply a master of promotion for himself and his daily newspaper; he embraced candidates with an enthusiasm and zeal matched by few other publishers in this nation. He was also a shrewd enough armchair political advisor (the visits by presidential hopefuls to his hilltop, 30-room Tudor mansion took on the aura of pilgrimages) to know that Reagan's time was running out. Reagan would turn 69 just a few weeks before the 1980 New Hampshire primary.

---

[1] On September 13, 1981, William Loeb succumbed to cancer in Burlington, Massachusetts.

To have a shot at the GOP nomination, the initial primary was crucial for Reagan. But first his newspaper patron had to clear the field of other conservatives attempting to end Reagan's hegemony over the conservative wing of the Grand Old Party.

The man most eager to seize this mantle from Reagan was Illinois Congressman Philip Crane. Described by Hugh Sidey as a "fellow with John Kennedy's forelock and Barry Goldwater's jaw," this mediagenic former college professor supposedly had informed Loeb he would not seek the presidency in 1980 if Reagan chose to do so again.

Reagan made it perfectly clear that 1976 had not been his final bid. By July of 1979 Loeb editorialized against Crane's possible entry into the race. Proclaiming Crane was "this writer's favorite younger Republican," his candidacy would be "a disaster for the sensible Republicans in the country." The reason? "For instance, if Reagan and Crane were to divide the sensible vote in New Hampshire, you could then expect a liberal Republican, someone such as former Ambassador George Bush...would win the New Hampshire primary."

What was Loeb's concept of a dream ticket? "This newspaper's ideal winning ticket for the Republican Party in 1980 would be for Reagan to declare his candidacy for one term only, and then take as his vice presidential running mate Congressman Phil Crane."

However, while Reagan prepared to mount his third attempt at the GOP presidential nomination (1968 was his first), Crane announced his candidacy on August 1, 1978—before the mid-term elections, the earliest announcement in modern times by a serious contender.

While Crane began to till the vineyards of Iowa and New Hampshire with a missionary zeal only the man in the White House, Jimmy Carter, could appreciate, Loeb occasionally lobbed an editorial grenade Crane's way. On February 2, 1979, with little more than a year before the primary, Loeb noted: "Someone should break the news to Phil Crane that good looks and a Ph.D. are simply not sufficient qualifications for running the United States of America in its present condition."

Loeb accused Crane of betraying the conservative cause, mentioning a fall 1977 meeting between the congressman, Loeb and two of his editors. The congressman "told this writer that Ronald Reagan should be the Republican nominee. He also said that he, Crane, would not run unless Reagan failed to indicate that he would by the fall of 1979. In the late spring of 1978, Crane stayed overnight at this writer's home and said Reagan was the one man who could do the job in 1980."

In spite of these warning shots, Crane pressed on, repeatedly visiting New Hampshire and Iowa and promising to organize all 50 states in the nomination process. By the winter of 1979-80 his campaign began to tap deeply into the organization that had put conservative political novice Republican Gordon Humphrey, an airline co-pilot, into the United States Senate. Humphrey's stunning 1978 5,800-vote upset of 16-year Democratic veteran Tom McIntyre, Estes Kefauver's protege, was one of the first indications of a nationwide Republican ascendancy.

Finally, Loeb's sedate lobbying and subtle arm twisting gave way to a frontal assault. By March of 1979 an onslaught was under way that made his 1972 attacks upon Senator Edmund Muskie seem tepid by comparison.

Page one of the March 8th, 1979, edition of the *Union Leader* was topped off with the headline "The Two Faces of Phil Crane," with "Cleancut Conservative?" or "Party Playboy?" in smaller type above. In an article by Jonathan Prestage of the paper's State House bureau, the lead read: "Phil Crane views himself as a 'missionary' who has meticulously fashioned a public image as 'the virgin crusader' of the national conservative movement, former staff members said recently, but there are two faces to this attractive, charismatic congressman who has a serious eye on the presidency."

The newspaper alleged that Crane's public posture of gentleman and moral crusader was not all it seemed. "Upon closer inspection...the public image shatters and a darker face emerges, many Crane associates reveal."

One associate (unnamed, as were most of the approximately 40 individuals interviewed for this expose) stated, "The boy scout image is a cloak of deception. For God's sake, the guy [Crane] once told a friend he was committed in this life to bedding down 1,000 different women." A former Crane staff member, also unnamed, stated, "He's just too good looking. The women are always throwing themselves all over him, and the party circuit was too inviting."

As the controversy over the story grew, Crane prepared to address the New Hampshire House of Representatives. In an unprecedented move, the House passed a resolution condemning the newspaper for printing "totally unsubstantiated allegations amounting to a grossly unfair and vituperative personal attack" on the congressman and his wife. The resolution also read: "Loeb carefully calculated the publication of this attack to coincide with the appearance of Congressman Crane before the New Hampshire House of Representatives." It also proclaimed the paper's "insulting tactics" were "an affront to Congressman Crane and to every citizen of New Hampshire."

Before and after his six-minute address to the House, Crane received a standing ovation. He expressed his gratitude to the members for their expression of concern and he said "my wife spent a sleepless night, my children spent a tearful breakfast."

In the wake of the *Union Leader's* offensive, Crane attempted to put the best possible foot forward by mentioning that his sudden notoriety was greatly enhancing his name recognition level around the state. In the meantime, the national organization for Crane began to fall into disarray. In early May seven top staffers resigned, a new management team had to be brought into the picture and, while the total amount of funds raised looked impressive on paper, a majority of the collected contributions was being devoured by costs owed to conservative direct-mail wizard Richard Viguerie. By June Crane had let the *Union Leader's* attacks rattle him sufficiently to proclaim at a news conference that the Manchester newspaper's reporters would be barred from covering any of his campaign activities.

Crane pressed on through the fall and winter, but the damage had been done. William Loeb was not the only reason Crane's candidacy failed to achieve critical mass in the premier primary, but it was a leading one. His candidacy was doomed in spite of his arduous stumping, mediagenic qualities, his touching base with thousands of party activists within the state and nation, and his embrace of the conservative philosophy gaining currency in the country. He tallied just 2,618 votes, fifth place with only 1.8%. This newer version of Ronald Reagan never caught on in the first primary state, leaving the genuine article one less obstacle in his path.

William Loeb could always be counted upon for voluminous amounts of Kennedy-baiting whenever a member of America's leading political family entered or hovered around the edges of a New Hampshire test. As Senator Edward Kennedy began his intra-party challenge to President Carter in 1979, Loeb periodically took an editorial potshot at the Bay State's senior senator. However, the defeat Kennedy finally suffered in an adjacent state, where Carter tallied 47%, Kennedy 37% and Governor Brown just 9.6%, had little to do with the *Union Leader* attacks. It had a great deal to do with the failings of Ted Kennedy as a candidate and campaigner, along with events well beyond his control.

Carter's vacillating leadership on a host of issues, combined with his poor track record for handling an economy hampered with its high inflation and steep interest rates, sapped the president's strength. In the spring of 1979 two veterans of every New Hampshire primary since 1968, Executive Councilor Dudley Dudley and former Democratic state chairman Joanne Symons, launched a Draft Kennedy campaign to challenge the president.

These two liberal Democrats generated considerable media attention for their "candidate." The course they embarked upon—essentially to run a myth and not a man in the primary— would have been better than what actually occurred: the senator became a declared, active candidate. The first evidence Kennedy was moving toward challenging the president was his decision to address 1,000 Democrats assembled in a state convention on the campus of New Hampshire College, just north of Manchester, on September 30, 1978.

Senator Kennedy is one of the last great hall orators remaining in America. Unfortunately our political system now produces politicians who have the physical attributes and training to be polished TV pitchmen, not the full-voiced, podium-pounding, fiercely partisan orators that men such as Hubert Humphrey and Edward Kennedy best personified.

At the state convention, Kennedy began with an opening line that ignited the first of many roars from an electrified crowd: "I suppose you wonder why I'm here." (Upon his arrival at the Manchester airport Kennedy was asked by Roger Mudd of CBS if his trip to the state meant that "you want to be president." The senator replied: "No, I expect President Carter to be the nominee, and I will support him.")

In his address, which was interrupted a dozen times by applause, he stated, "President Carter deserves great credit for his leadership [on human rights] and especially for his achievement at Camp David that has brought peace closer for Israel and all the nations of the Middle East." Since the audience missed this cue to applaud the president, Kennedy had to start leading the applause, finally managing to coax the crowd to its feet.

A May 1979 *Boston Globe* poll measured the depth of trouble in which the president was mired. The poll indicated that, while the president could easily dispatch a challenge from Governor Brown, 57-35%, the 646 New Hampshire Democratic primary voters polled provided Senator Kennedy with essentially the same margin over Carter, 58-36%.

On the morning of November 7, 1979, speaking in historic Faneuil Hall in downtown Boston, Kennedy declared his candidacy. He stated in part, "For many months, we have been sinking into crisis. Yet, we hear no clear summons from the center of power. Aims are not set. The means of realizing them are neglected. Conflicts in directions confuse our purpose. Government falters. Fear spreads that our leaders have resigned themselves to retreat.

"This country is not prepared to sound retreat. It is ready to advance. It is willing to make a stand. And so am I."

As he announced his candidacy, larger events began to overwhelm this Kennedy, for whom many had waited a dozen years to seek the Oval Office. Dudley Dudley, who became the co-chairman for the Kennedy state campaign, said, "We had a great campaign right up until that day. It was terrific. There's something to be said for running a campaign without a candidate—no arguments—it's beautiful." She added, "As soon as he announced he ran right into a stone wall. He had the Roger Mudd interview, he had Afghanistan and there was then the loyalty to the president aspect over the hostages being taken—all of which happened within ten days of his announcement."[2]

The Mudd interview on CBS was remarkable not only for showing a soon-to-be-announced candidate's inability to articulate the reasons he sought the presidency; it was also remarkable in that, even though Kennedy had been a national figure for more than two decades, it was essentially the first time he had ever

---

[2] While the famous interview with Roger Mudd and the storming of the American embassy in Teheran, Iran, took place on the same day—Sunday, November 4—the Soviet invasion of Afghanistan did not occur until December 27. Clearly all of these events managed to throw Kennedy's challenge of the president off its course.

been interviewed in such a format and at such length. While Mudd and CBS surely deserve a kudo for providing the senator an opportunity to expound upon his views in something other than 30-second "sound bites," it was also a testimonial to the shallowness of network coverage of presidential politics in an era in which this medium has come to play such a significant role.

Of course television was never kind to Kennedy that primary season. The clips of his hesitancy and near-complete lack of verbal grace when speaking without a text reinforced many of the doubts voters held about his ability to be the next president. Kennedy had a long line of ghosts behind him—the assassinations of his two older brothers and the haunting Chappaquiddick accident. (In a draft of his televised speech that attempted to explain the circumstances surrounding the death of Mary Jo Kopechne in the senator's car on July 18, 1969, the phrase "I will never seek the presidency" had been deleted.) The senator had spent much of his zest for campaigning on other crises. While he tried in his speeches to arouse his audiences to a greater sense of hope and confidence in the nation's future, it was clear Kennedy lacked confidence in himself to lead this nation as he stumped the countryside in an ineptly run campaign.

While the Massachusetts senator surely had his problems, so too did the former peanut farmer from Georgia. The Iran hostage crisis began to drag on, week after week, as the election year commenced. Once he announced his determination to remain in Washington until the hostage crisis was resolved, the president did not campaign in his own behalf. His last visit to New Hampshire had been a six-hour trip in late April, with stops in Portsmouth, Manchester and Bedford.

Jeanne Shaheen directed the Carter campaign that year, along with the man who had run the first primary campaign in 1976, New Mexico political consultant Chris Brown. Shaheen said: "That was a long campaign because when we started we were about thirty points down in the polls in the summer of 1979. That's when the movement to draft Kennedy started. Actually we argued long and hard to try to get Carter to come to New Hampshire and do some campaigning; we were never successful at that. What was easier for voters to understand after the hostages were taken and there really was a crisis."

The plan to have the president visit the state once a month during the final months before the primary was scratched.

In his place a number of surrogates arrived, led by Vice President Walter Mondale and First Lady Rosalynn Carter.

In the spring of 1979, when Governor Gallen informed members of his staff he would support the president's re-election, some staffers cautioned him not to be so enthusiastic in supporting a president with substantial problems. Gallen had narrowly won office that previous fall, and it was certain he would face the three-term governor he had just defeated, Meldrim Thomson, once again in November of 1980. (Gallen won a second term against Thomson by 70,258 votes.)

Gallen was not much of a believer in polls (on the night he first won the governorship, ABC News had to admit its early-evening projection of Thomson winning a fourth term was a wrong call). As a small-town businessman and political moderate, Gallen had an affinity with Jimmy Carter. In 1975 Carter had asked Gallen to run as a delegate candidate in his behalf but Gallen had declined, fearing that such a commitment would alienate supporters of other presidential hopefuls in his attempt to win the gubernatorial nomination after failing in 1974.[3]

The governor made it clear to the president he would be better off stumping the state rather than remaining a captive in the White House. However, once Carter made that decision, it spurred his partisans onto greater efforts in his behalf.

The treasury of the United States proved to be the best possible stand in for the president. Dayton Duncan, a former newspaperman who served as the governor's press secretary and later chief of staff, said of the windfall that began to descend upon the White Mountain State the winter of 1979-80: "It doesn't make any difference what party the president is—but a sitting president who is being seriously challenged for re-election within his own party for the primary is one of the best things that can happen to New Hampshire. That was true when Gerald

---

[3] Carter operatives had helped funnel $20,000 from the Democratic National Committee in 1978 to aid Gallen in purchasing air time on Boston television. This was the first time television was used for a New Hampshire state race; it was to become a standard practice for candidates for governor and the United States Senate who had sufficient campaign funds.

Ford was president as a Republican and Ronald Reagan was challenging him in 1976, and it was true in 1980."

In 1979 New Hampshire became the first state to secure federal money to help citizens pay winter fuel bills. The distribution of $1.28 million began in early December; the remainder, $13.2 million, was made available later that winter.

Interior Secretary Cecil Andrus stopped in Concord to help raise a solar wall for which the Department of Energy had provided a $75,000 grant. The wall was attached to a new headquarters for the state's largest conservation group. The grant was all the more remarkable since an earlier request for only $49,000 had been rejected by the DOE.

Federal money helped fend off the Kennedy threat. For a time in the fall it appeared the popular mayor of Nashua, Maurice Arel, was flirting with the idea of endorsing Kennedy. Calls from President Carter—calls that were aided with something tangible for Arel's city—managed to prevent Arel backing the senator. The Department of Housing and Urban Development announced Nashua would receive an $850,000 housing grant.

Kennedy toured the American Skate factory in Berlin in November, yet he could only leave campaign brochures. The First Lady proved to be a bit more effective in this remote North Country city. She stopped into the same plant the next day for a tour. Within hours of her departure, it was announced that the company had garnered a $1.5 million loan guarantee from the Commerce Department.

New Hampshire also secured $34 million for highway improvements, $3.2 million for a Concord-to-Boston commuter train that proved to be a failure, $1.2 million for a downtown Concord redevelopment project, $4 million to revitalize downtown Berlin, plus small business relief funds to assist ski resorts hampered by a generally snowless winter.

In reporting on the windfall, *The Boston Globe* noted in one news account: "Candidates in the New Hampshire presidential primary are restricted to spending $264,000 in campaign funds, but, a Carter aide says, according to a memo prepared for domestic affairs advisor Jack Watson, the president is tossing an additional $70 million in government funds into the state for an array of projects that Gallen wants, and that will hardly diminish Carter's political fortunes in New Hampshire."

On the evening of the Carter victory in the 1976 Granite State primary, CBS anchorman Walter Cronkite called the president "Now clearly the frontrunning" Democratic candidate. Since the Massachusetts primary followed by just a week, Cronkite pontificated that the former Georgia governor was well-positioned for that test "since New Hampshire and Massachusetts are a pair." (In spite of all the favorable media spin Carter's New Hampshire win had generated in 1976, the two adjacent New England states did not prove to be "a pair." Carter finished fourth in the Bay State race, trailing Senator Henry Jackson, Congressman Morris Udall and even Alabama Governor George Wallace.)

In the first primary Kennedy (who had lost the Maine caucuses earlier in the month to Carter) proved to have little appeal as a regional favorite son. He was able to carry only three of the 13 cities in the state and just five of the 15 largest towns. All of those were near or on the border with Massachusetts. Once again the Cronkite "pairing theory" between Massachusetts and New Hampshire had been disproved.

The sizable victory (by 10 percentage points) helped set up a string of Carter primary victories that was not halted until Kennedy carried New York and Connecticut on March 25th. Kennedy withdrew on August 11th, the day after the national convention opened. The president won 24 of the 34 Democratic primaries and the nomination on the first ballot.

If George Bush had been able to replicate his stunning upset of frontrunner Ronald Reagan in Iowa on January 21st— 33,350-31,348—in the Granite State primary, Reagan's political fortunes probably never would have recovered. His money, which was being spent by national campaign manager John Sears in copious amounts, soon would have dried up. Even for the buoyant former movie actor, it would have been difficult to counteract the press's write-off of his prospects after the Iowa debacle. Bush would have been in position to lock up the nomination by the time of the Pennsylvania primary on April 22, if not before.

Reagan and his partisans were stunned by what had happened in the Hawkeye State. Given the facts that Reagan refused to participate in a debate sponsored by the *Des Moines Register*, and his eight stops in the state meant he had spent fewer hours campaigning there than George Bush had spent days, his "taking the state for granted" attitude led the voters to take Reagan for granted in return.

This setback proved to be a blessing for the Reagan candidacy in the end because it knocked his campaign off its complacent track. It also proved to be a bane for George Bush, who had traveled 350,000 miles in 328 days of stumping in 1979, but was not prepared to cope with his sudden surge of notoriety.

Every sudden star in the American political firmament needs to be prepared for a sudden escalation of media coverage. Michael Robinson, professor for the media analysis project at George Washington University, has labeled the practice "compensatory journalism" because of "the tendency by the news media to treat frontrunners more critically, challengers less critically and emerging frontrunners most critically of all."

Following the Iowa returns, Bush—rather than firming up ideas and policy proposals to back up his candidacy—tried to simply keep running on his resume. While his resume is impressive in its scope, the only elective office he had ever won was in 1966 and 1968 in the Seventh Congressional District in Texas. He had managed to lose his bids for the United States Senate in Texas in both 1964 and 1970; the latter effort (a narrow loss to Lloyd Bentsen) was still a matter of controversy for Bush.

On February 7, 1980, the *Los Angeles Times-Washington Post* News Service published the story that Bush was implicated in the Townhouse Operation, a secret fundraising scheme by President Nixon to assist some GOP candidates in the 1970 election. The contributions were of questionable legality since the group responsible had failed to register as a political committee. Bush reportedly received $106,000 from this multi-million secret fund.

This front-page story threw Bush on the defensive for the first time, but it was not truly news at all. It had first been reported by the States News Service on May 21, 1978 and in New England by *The Boston Globe*. But Bush was not then an "emerging frontrunner," so the story had drawn little attention in 1978. Now it was generating the kind of attention the Bush candidacy preferred to do without.

Congressman Phil Crane, regarded as a threat to Ronald Reagan, had been destroyed by William Loeb. George Bush had, from his upset victory in Iowa, leaped ahead of Reagan in polls in the first primary state, and was now poised as an even greater threat to Reagan's nomination.

In 1964, *Time* had written of Bush's failed effort to unseat liberal Democratic Senator Ralph Yarborough: "Bush stands strong for right-to-work labor laws, cutbacks in foreign aid, increased tariffs.   He stands against the 1963 nuclear test-ban treaty and the 1964 Civil Rights Act.   He is an attractive, articulate Goldwater Republican."   Despite the general perception of Bush's conservativism, Loeb often tried to portray the former ambassador to China and chairman of the Republican National Committee as a leading light of the Eastern liberal establishment. In reality, he was really positioned a bit more toward the moderate wing of the GOP.

As the primary entered its concluding weeks, Bush found the competition for the center of the Republican Party a spirited match against Tennessee Senator Howard Baker (who had cast a crucial vote for the Panama Canal treaties to earn the enmity of the New Right) and Illinois Congressman John Anderson, who had staked out some pronounced liberal positions.[4]

While Crane's anemic 1.8% of the primary vote can be traced in large measure to William Loeb's attacks, Senator Robert Dole, the vice presidential nominee just four years earlier, could blame only himself for his paltry 597 votes.   Never very adept at delegating authority, Dole proved once again that a candidate cannot be his own campaign manager and expect to succeed.   Nor should someone who had served in the Senate since 1969 (with four earlier terms in the House) try to build his candidacy around an attempt to inform voters of the details of every piece of legislation with which he had ever been involved.

Texan John Connally (2,239 votes, 1.5%) was determined to prove the truth of the adage that trying to run everywhere, you end up running nowhere.   His strategy of forsaking any meaningful effort to prospect for delegates elsewhere, pratically in the South, showed that unless a foothold is established, a candidate cannot gain momentum.   Connally managed to raise and spend $11 million (refusing to accept federal matching funds) and ended up with one delegate—67-year-old Ada Mills of Clarksville, Arkansas.

4 The 22.8% of the vote reaped by Baker and Anderson—12.9% for Baker and 9.9% for Anderson—did far more damage to Bush than the combined 3.7% of the three other conservatives—Phil Crane, John Connally and Robert Dole—did in eroding Reagan's conservative base.

The candidacy of Senator Howard Baker was hampered by his inability to spend enough time on the stump. (He had given serious consideration to resigning from the Senate to campaign full-time, which former officeholders Reagan and Bush were able to do.) To kick off his campaign in the state, Baker came to Concord on Friday evening, November 2nd, the day after his formal declaration of candidacy in the nation's capital. At a free Tennessee-style barbecue, more than 1,500 people jammed the national Guard Armory in Concord to hear the minority leader of the Senate Republicans.

In his address, Baker praised the role the voters would soon play: "To a remarkable degree, you know the eyes not only of the United States will be on New Hampshire come next February but indeed the eyes of the world will be on this state and your community."

Even a politician with brains can have a blind spot when it comes to trying to hawk the wares of his own profession. Baker proved that. He said, "I am a politician. I am proud of being a politician. The great decisions of our time will be made in the political arena. I know Washington well enough to change Washington, and Washington has to be changed by somebody who knows how to do it." This event was an ideal opportunity for Baker to light a fire under his late-starting drive. However, his speech was flat, he appeared tired and drawn, and he managed to deliver what could only be considered the political kiss of death—a Washington speech.

Baker soon departed for Maine to attend a Republican State Convention. There he competed in a straw vote he was favored to win thanks to support from popular Senator William Cohen. He lost the straw vote. His campaign in New Hampshire never made any headway, and his inability to use the Senate deliberations on the SALT II agreement (which he opposed) worked to cripple his candidacy.

Congressman John Anderson managed to stake out some distinct progressive positions that attracted liberal and independent voters who were not enamored of the ideology of the other GOP candidates. While having compiled a generally conservative voting record in the House on economics and fiscal policy, Anderson's advocacy of a 50-cent-per-gallon increase on gasoline and diesel fuel, energy conservation, federal funding for congressional elections, pro-choice on abortion, support of the Equal Rights Amendment and advocacy of the Panama Canal treaties and SALT II agreement left him positioned as the sole progressive candidate among the Republicans.

Anderson felt Bush was "Ronald Reagan in a Brooks Brothers suit," and said, "I'm not going to permit him to be moderate in the Northeast and conservative wherever else it suits his purpose."

Anderson began to make some headway in smoking out Bush's "moderation" when considerable controversy arose over comments Bush had made to Robert Scheer of the *Los Angeles Times* on January 24th. Scheer had mentioned the futility of a nation gaining the upper hand in the nuclear weapons race. Bush replied, "If you believe there is no such thing as a winner in a nuclear exchange, that argument makes a little sense. I don't believe that." Scheer then asked: "How do you win in a nuclear exchange?" Bush: "You have a survivability of command in control, survivability of industrial potential, protection of a percentage of your citizens, and you have a capability that inflicts more damage on the opposition than it can inflict upon you. That's the way you can have a winner, and the Soviets' planning is based on the ugly concept of a winner in a nuclear exchange."

Any conservative background Bush may have had, or hard-line posture when it came to discussing a nuclear exchange, did not enthrall William Loeb, however.

The Bush campaign's troubleshooter, Judd Gregg, son of former Governor Hugh Gregg and then a member of the Executive Council for the southwestern part of the state, handled the details of the upcoming Nashua debate and endured the onslaught the *Union Leader* inflicted upon his candidate.

Of the role the statewide daily played, Gregg stated: "They like their role of being the burr under the saddle of the American presidential process and they especially like the fact that the national media hates it—that they're so influential. And in that race they were extraordinarily influential. Every day—front page, two, three, four stories just banging the heck out of George Bush or pumping up Ronald Reagan. So they were very, very effective."

By allocating sufficient time to travel the state (10 days of campaigning, nine fewer than in 1976), Reagan not only dispelled charges of taking the state for granted that had hit with such force in Iowa, but he answered any questions regarding his age or stamina.

Gerald Carmen, then the owner of an auto-parts operation in Manchester, served as Republican state chairman from 1975 to 1979 and headed the Reagan effort in the state that winter. Carmen later recounted: "The press was writing him up as they do today as too old, not active enough, he doesn't work as hard as he should and all that type of thing. We were getting in the bus at seven-thirty or eight or nine in the morning and going to ten or ten-thirty at night. He was bouncing off that bus while the news people were coming off that bus dragging their you know what. He had more energy and grit than they did."

The Bush-Reagan debate in Nashua on Saturday evening, February 23rd has taken on the aura of a legendary event in the history of the first primary.

George Carmen remembered, "When we challenged George Bush to a debate right after Iowa, we were down twenty-two points. We were desperate for some kind of an event which would act as a catalyst to showcase President Reagan. We didn't expect them to accept, because the risk was on them. They were ahead, they didn't need the debate....We needed the debate. At the time the debate came we didn't need it anymore."

The *Nashua Telegraph* attempted to both fund and sponsor the debate between Bush and Reagan but was denied the right to pay for it by the Federal Election Commission because such a contribution was considered a corporate contribution, and thus illegal. Jon Breen, the newspaper's editor, commented whether the Nashua event was the turning point in the primary: "I think it already turned. I have difficulty as a newsperson, as an impartial observer believing that that many votes—if I recall it was about a 48,000 vote plurality [it was actually 39,540 votes]—that that many votes swing on an event such as that. I think the momentum was already there for Reagan. Ronald Reagan was going to win the primary anyway. I don't believe that he won the primary that night in Nashua."

Of the decision to sponsor the debate, Breen says, "It seemed like a good idea at the time...Ronald Reagan and George Bush were far and away the frontrunners. What we were interested in was a debate that would highlight these two people."

Certainly if the GOP field had been cluttered with five other contenders the *Telegraph* would have had a legitimate reason to close down the debate to the two who had finished on top in Iowa.

However, John Anderson, Howard Baker, John Connally, Phil Crane and Robert Dole were not chopped liver. The event only helped to reinforce the elitist image that Bush had tried to dispell in more than a year of campaigning. Bush's failure to insist the debate be opened up to Anderson, Baker, Crane and Dole, is all the more remarkable after his own national campaign manager, Jim Baker, informed Breen the Bush camp would not be opposed to opening up the format. However, their failure to insist upon such a change permitted Reagan to take command of the evening's proceedings. In addition, Bush and his campaign handlers made a tactical error in refusing to pick up half the $3,500 tab once the FEC made its ruling, thus setting the stage for Reagan's famous "I've paid for this microphone, Mr. Green" confrontation with Jon Breen.

After the debate, Bush departed for Houston, repeating the error made in 1976 when Reagan was shipped off to Illinois two days before the vote.

The steamroller for Reagan peaked perfectly. He won in a landslide: 72,983 to 33,443 for Bush, 49.8%-22.8%. Reagan was able to win the state's most populous vote center, Manchester, 7,297-913, or 74.8%-9.4%. In other communities surrounding the Queen City in which the *Union Leader* had a considerable circulation, the returns were equally impressive for the Californian over his eventual running mate: Bedford 67.6%-14.3%, Derry 64.6%-15.0%, Goffstown 77.6%-7.3% and Hooksett 78.2%-7.0%.

In 1976, while carrying the state by just 1,587 votes over Reagan, President Ford had carried nine out of the state's 13 cities. In 1980 Bush could carry just three—Lebanon, Portsmouth and Somersworth. Time and again Bush was displaced from other cities and the state's most populous towns by the strength of the vote that Howard Baker and John Anderson reaped, while the anemic returns for conservatives Connally, Crane and Dole did no damage to Reagan's control of the conservative voter bloc.

Concerning the primary's outcome, Judd Gregg expressed this view; "You have to remember Ronald Reagan in 1976 running against an incumbent president got 50 percent of the vote in New Hampshire. He lost by 1,500 votes or something. And that vote didn't change. He kept that 50 percent. It was hard in 1976 and it was hard in 1980 and that really was the bottom line."

Once the two winners of the primary, Carter and Reagan, were nominated, New Hampshire's record of always having its primary winner go on to win the presidency was secure once again.

1984
Doomed Democrats

WHEN THE PRIMARY LAW was revised in 1949 it permitted a direct judgment by voters on the candidates—not simply the selection of delegates. Since then the pattern has been well established: Every man elected to the presidency since 1952— Dwight Eisenhower, John Kennedy, Lyndon Johnson, Richard Nixon, Jimmy Carter and Ronald Reagan—first won the primary in New Hampshire. The Granite State is the only state among the 13 states continuously conducting primaries since 1952 (California, Florida, Illinois, Massachusetts, Nebraska, New Jersey, Ohio, Oregon, Pennsylvania, South Dakota, West Virginia and Wisconsin) that can make that claim. The final two competitors for this status fell by the wayside: Oregon in 1976, when Democratic voters cast their lot with Idaho Senator Frank Church rather than Jimmy Carter; and Pennsylvania in 1980, as its Republican voters selected George Bush over Ronald Reagan.

In spite of (or perhaps because of) its unique status, the premier primary has not endeared itself to powerful interests within the national Democratic Party. Once again the Democrats embarked upon an examination of their nominating rules before the 1984 presidential contest. This time the examining group, the Commission on Presidential Nomination, was headed by North Carolina Governor James Hunt.

The window concept was again a matter of deliberation. The Hunt Commission retained the rule, yet the suggestion to shove both Iowa and New Hampshire into the 13-week time frame starting on the second Tuesday in March lost by a vote of 23-25.

In its final report, the Hunt Commission proclaimed it had "left in place the 'window' established in the 1980 rules, requiring primaries and first-tier caucuses to be held no earlier than the second Tuesday in March and no later than the second Tuesday in June. Specific and limited exemptions would be granted to Iowa, which could hold its caucus no more than 15 days before the 'window' opening, and New Hampshire, which could hold its primary no earlier than the first Tuesday in March."

Governor Gallen helped in the retention of this exemption, traveling to Washington to lobby commission members before the final vote on the rules. Since the Iowa caucus had been moved from the third Monday in January to the final Monday in February (the 27th), the linkage between the first caucus and first primary became that much stronger.

Yet in landing upon a March 6th date, the New Hampshire primary collided with Vermont's primary scheduled for the same day. New Hampshire's law stated that the primary had to be held "on the Tuesday immediately preceding the date on which any other state shall hold a similar election." The Vermont test was such an election according to the state's attorney general and New Hampshire Secretary of State William Gardner, responsible for running elections in the Granite State. Gardner said, "Since New Hampshire law requires our state to go one week ahead of any other state holding a similar election, it was my opinion that Vermont's primary was a similar election, therefore requiring us to schedule our primary one week before according to our law. This decision was the same as had been made in 1976 and 1980."

However, due to the ineptitude of Gallen's chief of staff, Peter Goelz, and New Hampshire's representative on the Hunt Commission, hotel magnate Walter Dunfey, this oversight of the Vermont date meant a lengthy wrangle with Democratic National Chairman Charles Manatt. This lawyer from California worked feverishly to pressure the first primary state to vote on March 6th rather than on February 28th. The battle did little to dispel the widespread impression that the Democrats are a party of nitpickers; after all, the fate of the Republic did not rest on New Hampshire's voting one week before the DNC rules specified.

Many of the public and party relations problems New Hampshire suffered prior to the 1984 decision (which in the end was held on February 28th) were brought about not simply by the spat with Chairman Manatt, but also by the behavior of the Democratic state chairman, George Bruno. Bruno, an attorney, seemed to think the primary was one constant opportunity to empty the candidates' treasuries, surely a boon to his debt-ridden party but of no benefit to the state's image.

In speaking before a conference on the presidential nominating process at the Gerald Ford Library in Michigan in April of 1985, Manatt said of the first primary state:

> This is no way to pick a president. In 1984 candidates had to pay, according to a price list, to put up banners or posters at a New Hampshire party event. They even had to pay a price to speak. Perhaps there is a rough justice in that, at least for some political speakers we have all heard; but such practices degrade not only the candidates but the process. They do not advance the cause of picking a nominee; they exploit it. New Hampshire makes no more sense as the first primary for selecting a Democratic nominee than Massachusetts would as the first primary for the Republicans.

Since New Hampshire is the only state in the nation that has never enacted a general sales or income tax, preferring to fund state government by a hodgepodge of revenue sources aimed at out-of-state visitors, the state's "don't tax me, tax the man behind the tree" philosophy is blatant. With such a fiscal system as a backdrop, the animosity national political reporters, commentators and political leaders feel toward "unrepresentative" New Hampshire's exploitation of the primary for financial gain is strong. Such feelings flare to even greater heights when a party is burdened with a chairman such as George Bruno, who no doubt would fit more comfortably as a ward heeler in the Cook County Democratic machine than as the chief of a state party.

Manatt's fixation upon a mere week's difference in scheduling stands as a classic example of misguided priorities. A new problem was beginning to confront the candidates seeking the Oval Office, and it was not the exhaustion they faced spending time stumping in Iowa and New Hampshire. More states were moving their primaries into March, most settling on the "official" starting date, the second Tuesday in March.

In 1968 just 2% of the Democratic delegates had been picked by the second Tuesday in March. In 1972 that figure rose to 6%, by 1976 to 9% and by 1980 it was 14%. In 1984, with the advent of an electoral extravaganza called Super Tuesday, nine states would vote on that single day; Alabama, Florida, Georgia, Hawaii, Massachusetts, Nevada, Oklahoma, Rhode Island and Washington. In 1984, 19% of the Democratic delegates were chosen by the second Tuesday in March. The nation had embarked upon a path leading toward a national presidential primary.

The phenomenon of holding more and more primaries on or near the window—a process called frontloading—created a new set of problems for the candidates, problems that were ignored while Manatt and his staff tried to end New Hampshire's rebellion. However, any expectation that frontloading would diminish the luster enjoyed by states such as Iowa and New Hampshire proved fruitless, for as the 1984 primary approached the pollster for the Democratic frontrunner, former Vice President Walter Mondale, proclaimed New Hampshire "the Mount Everest of Democratic primaries."

In 1984 President Reagan became the first president without a significant challenger in the New Hampshire test since Lyndon Johnson ran in 1964. (The president would eventually reap 86.4% of the vote versus Harold Stassen and three unknowns. However, for the first time in the primary's history the Democratic turnout beat the Republicans—102,180-78,399 braving a snowstorm to cast ballots.)

Given the absence of any meaningful match on the GOP side, and since there was no Democrat with suitable conservative credentials, the *Union Leader* decided that the next best thing was to stir up a write-in for Reagan among the Democrats.

Those around William Loeb had studied the master of manipulating out-of-state media. As the primary approached in 1984 it seemed as if Loeb were reaching up from his grave, still able to concoct an aura around his newspaper that enhanced its potency. The media, particularly the Boston-based news operations and national press corps, followed the write-in campaign for Reagan as if it were certain to result in an outpouring of votes. In the end it achieved 5%, less than the Democratic winner,

Colorado Senator Gary Hart, reaped among Republican voters writing in his name—5.3%

In 1982 and 1983 the candidate who tilled the vineyards of the White Mountain State with the most diligence was California Senator Alan Cranston, first elected in 1968. Cranston said at the end of his address announcing his candidacy on February 2, 1983: "So, today, I leave the starting line. The finish line is not Election Day, November 6, 1984. That will only be the starting line of the campaign that really counts—to heal our nation—and to bring ourselves and our children out from under the dark shadow of nuclear war. It is essential and possible to win this campaign—and to banish nuclear weapons from the face of God's earth."

Cranston was never able to garner his followers from beyond a small core of anti-nuclear activists and environmentalists (it was alleged he had a lock on the L.L. Bean vote), and he finished a dismal eighth with just 1,025 votes, 2.1%.

While Cranston may have hailed from the most media-oriented of states, with his bald head (he dyed the little hair that remained in an attempt to improve his television presence) and gaunt appearance, he was probably the most unmarketable candidate, visually, in the television age. (Cranston was once told by a supporter: "You're a great guy but you look like an undertaker and you have a voice like a dial tone.")

On primary day he had insisted he would be in the race until the Maine caucus the following Saturday. However, the New Hampshire returns were so discouraging and his debt so sizable ($1 million) the senator called a press conference on the morning after the primary to tell reporters and a number of sobbing supporters: "The race is over for me. I know the difference between reality and dreams. I know when to dream and when and how to count votes."

The aspirant who finished just below Cranston in ninth place was Reubin Askew, governor of Florida from 1971 to 1979. While he had compiled a record of accomplishment as governor of the fastest-growing state east of the Mississippi, he drew just 1,025 votes, 1%. (It should be pointed out that at a July 1983 Manchester City Democratic Committee picnic, Askew managed to draw more support in a straw vote—1,066—than he finally did in the election. That outcome had been distorted by the presence of many Amway distributors backing Askew who were in the area for a convention.)

Askew, who billed himself as "The Different Democrat," was simply too far to the right to be a force in the primary's outcome, just as Cranston was too far to the left. On the morning he filed for a spot on the ballot with the secretary of state, Askew was approached upon departing to sign a petition supporting a freeze on the production of nuclear weapons. He refused. The issue was the centerpiece of the Cranston candidacy and a concept embraced by all the other major Democratic candidates.

Minutes later in a press conference in the State House press room Askew had to explain his advocacy of a constitutional amendment to permit Congress to set a single national standard on abortion, thus restricting the courts' ability to intervene. He was peppered with a flurry of questions from women reporters who did not share his zeal for such an amendment. Later that same day the former governor attended the dedication of a plaza in Manchester named for a former mayor, an Askew supporter. In order to do so he had to cross a picket line, a move that hardly endeared him to his party's most significant constituency, organized labor.

Like any other former southern governor dreaming of the White House, Askew had to contend with the Carter albatross. However, there was a Southerner who was well-positioned by the nature of his national political experience, stature and campaign abilities, it was South Carolina Senator Ernest Hollings, first elected to the Senate in 1966 and governor of his native state from 1959 to 1963. Clearly the contender with the most authoritative physical presence, with silver-white hair and parade ground posture, this graduate of The Citadel was the type of Sun Belt Democrat who could be a formidable opponent to President Reagan in the fall, but would not emerge as the nominee to do so.

Endorsed by more newspapers than any other Democrat in the first primary state, Hollings was hampered by a rich Charleston drawl that often made his speeches difficult to decipher and the absence of any meaningful organization. But he had a refreshingly straightforward manner of saying exactly what was on his mind; his independence would make his selection as a vice presidential nominee the acid test of courage for any presidential candidate. Yet Hollings received only 3,583 votes, just 3.5%, 1,475 fewer votes than the write-in for President Reagan.

If the primary process is one that weeds out candidates as bright and experienced as Hollings, it also weeds out a candidate such as Ohio Senator John Glenn, a senator since 1975 and the first American to orbit the earth. Glenn garnered a media buildup in 1983 that has rarely been matched in modern American politics. However, the media hype meant little when it came time to cast votes in 1984. In Iowa Glenn placed a humiliating sixth with just 3.5%; eight days later in the Granite State, he finished third with 12,088 votes, or 12%. The national press spent all of 1983 concentrating on a two-man race—Mondale versus Glenn. Only half of that equation was fulfilled.

Chris Brown returned to the state after the Carter campaigns of 1976 and 1980 as a consultant to the Gary Hart candidacy. He visited every six to eight weeks to assist in Hart's organizational work. Regarding Glenn's effort, Brown observed,

> John Glenn had more potential than he ended up realizing. A lack of attention to grassroots organizing in Iowa and New Hampshire was clearly a problem. There was a lot of reliance on polling and media and he had the money to indulge in some of that. My clear impression was that while he had some good people...I think this is a case where maybe too strong a national bureaucracy and maybe poor national decisions...hurt.

People are not drawn to work in a campaign by its television ads; nor are activists drawn to a candidate who lacks a concise and forceful message. Glenn had the money for the ads but he had no message to impart. Nomination hopefuls face the chore of running on two tracks simultaneously—organizing in key early matches such as Iowa and New Hampshire, while at the same time running on a national track by fundraising, recruiting a national staff, filing delegate slates in primary states, organizing caucus states and developing positions on pressing national issues.

A candidate must also project an aura of decisiveness and leadership. Hollings said of his colleague Glenn, "Here comes Senator Glenn, who now as a result of his inexperience, is orbiting the issues faster than he orbited the earth. He's running around here with a tax increase. Well, he was the one that cut taxes in July—the $33 billion tax cut for the rich in July had John Glenn's vote and support. And he comes out after that and he starts wanting to raise taxes. So he's going two different directions. He went two different directions on SALT, and he went two different directions on acid rain."

Glenn had received a warm reception from 600 Democrats when he addressed a fundraiser for Governor Gallen in Bedford on November 20, 1981. One of the reasons Glenn generated favorable reviews that night was that people expected less of him; his keynote address to the 1976 Democratic National Convention in New York City had been such a bomb any coherent speech would have been favorably received.

It would be another 10 months before Glenn would step back into New Hampshire. In those months no spadework was done to pull together a core of supporters, as was being done for Mondale, Cranston and Askew. Once he did hit the hustings Glenn had trouble making the transition from Ohio senator to national candidate, looking beyond the parochial concerns he had tended for almost a decade to address broader national interests.

During the spring of 1983, 189 New Hampshire towns endorsed resolutions at Town Meeting advocating a 50% reduction in sulfur dioxide emissions to help alleviate the acid rain problem. Glenn's native state is a leading producer of sulfur dioxide, material linked to the creation of acid rain. Senator Glenn urged caution and more study in addressing the problem. He accused his fellow candidates of "overpromising" on the issue, stating, "Am I going to join them in that just for political advantage? No."

That stance generated considerable negative editorial comment in newspapers around the state; within weeks Glenn announced he would support legislation to reduce acid rain by limiting smokestack emissions of sulfur dioxide after all. However, he had not decided what those limits should be.

By the fall of 1983 the debate had been joined between "Real Democrat" Walter Mondale and purported "Electable Democrat" John Glenn. Glenn often attacked President Carter's "failed, disastrous policies," while Mondale repeatedly castigated Glenn's votes for President Reagan's tax and budget cuts and military spending increases in 1981. (A study by *Congressional Quarterly* had indicated that, in 1981 when the major elements of Reaganomics were put into place, of 128 votes Glenn had backed the president on 54% and opposed him on 41%.)

Glenn's attacks on the Carter record (and by implication on Mondale) turned the race between the two frontrunners into a

referendum on Carter's record versus Reagan's. While Jimmy
Carter surely had his failings as president, it was inane for Glenn
to frame the debate in such a context; after all, Democrats, not
Republicans, would decide upon the nomination he was seeking.

The Democratic race was as much a contest to try to put
distance between the candidates and Carter's reign as it was an
attempt to challenge the Reagan Revolution. Southerners such
as Askew and Hollings had to field countless queries as to
whether the nation was ready for another Southerner in the Oval
Office. Hollings in particular enjoyed pointing out the hypocrisy
of reporters who never pestered Californian Alan Cranston with
the question of whether the recent presidencies of others from
the Golden State (Herbert Hoover, Richard Nixon and Ronald
Reagan) doomed his prospects.

In the end it was Senator Glenn who had the background,
personality and political style that was most reminiscent of the
man from Plains. He shared not just the small-town upbringing
and the tour of military duty (Glenn had been a Marine Corps
officer for 23 years, Carter a Navy officer for seven), but both had
been businessmen for a time and had relatively short stints in
politics before seeking the presidency.

They also shared a "go it alone" attitude that demonstrated little of the gregarious nature that is supposed to be part
of the makeup of every politician. Profiles of the former astronaut
sounded similar to those of Carter: a persistent attention to
detail, a moderate view of the role of government, few if any ties
to the major interest groups of the Democratic Party such as organized labor, and an affinity for technical matters.

In spite of Glenn's attacks on Carter's record,
Congressional Quarterly noted, "The Ohio senator was consistently high in his support for Reagan's predecessor. In both
1977 and 1980 he backed Carter more often than any of his
Senate colleagues currently seeking the presidential nomination."

The Mondale-Glenn in-fighting climaxed in the three-
hour debate at Dartmouth College on Sunday, January 20th,
aired nationwide by the Public Broadcasting System. During
most of the debate among the seven Democratic aspirants,
Glenn's presence was rather passive, consisting of the canned
answers he had given hundreds of times during the course of the
campaign. With about 30 minutes to go, Glenn interrupted a
Mondale answer on his economic program to accuse the former

vice president of providing "the same vague gobbledygook of nothing we've been hearing all through this campaign."

At this point Mondale jumped up and shouted at Glenn, "There's just been about a six-minute speech here—all of it baloney." Yet it was Hart who, speaking up after Jesse Jackson, chided the two: "Quarreling between the two of you as to whose mistakes were the worst is not going to win the election or govern this country."

It was this above-the-battle poise, a concentration on the future rather than a fixation on the past, that Hart had marketed in kaffeeklatsches around the state since December of 1982. This posture had earned Hart favorable reviews when 1,200 Democrats had gathered at New Hampshire College on October 29th to attend a mid-term convention. For months, Hart had articulated the issues and been ignored by the national press. According to his state campaign director, Jeanne Shaheen, in spite of his being written off repeatedly in 1983 by the national press, "We were doing well in New Hampshire even though we were still at two percent in the polls. We had events and the rooms were full, lots of people were showing up. We had lots of volunteers. If you don't read the national press, which a lot of people in New Hampshire don't, if you were just looking at what we were doing in New Hampshire, things were going great."

By comparison to Mondale, Cranston and Askew, Hart had started a bit late in laying the groundwork for his organization. Yet Hart could afford to start later than the others, for he already knew—from his experience as George McGovern's national campaign manager in the early seventies—the rhythms and texture of New Hampshire's primary. The most critical first step was not to stump the state drumming up support in large groups, but to first make sure a capable core group, a board of directors as it were, was put in place. From that base a candidate started to move out in concentric circles to more and more groups of activists.

Any campaign that could achieve what Hart's did in October—canvassing 20,000 homes—was clearly a candidacy on the move. Yet such an accomplishment was given short shrift, for the national press was fixated on yet another straw poll, this time on October 1st in Maine, in which Mondale won with 51%, Alan Cranston tallied 29% and Hollings and Glenn finished a poor third and fourth. Due to lack of resources and little if any enthusiasm for straw polls, Hart bypassed the Maine event.

Hart was not simply on the ground organizationally, he had formulated substantial policies unmatched by most of the others. His ideas on military reform alone, honed from years of service on the Senate Armed Services Committee, could—and later did—help fill a book.

It was, however, a case of Hart putting out too much for the public to digest. Asked about this problem at an editorial board meeting of the *Concord Monitor,* he replied, "I haven't been trying to reach average voters. I've been trying to reach activists in New Hampshire and Iowa and other places where I sensed the level of wanting to know whether the next nominee of this party knew what the heck he was talking about was very high."

The Dartmouth debate managed to sharpen the message Hart was directing toward the electorate—the "new ideas for a new generation of leadership" theme that had been lost in a mass of position papers and policy pronouncements. As January gave way to February there was little doubt that Hart was the major threat to Walter Mondale in the first direct test of voter sentiment.

As far back as July of 1983 the Mondale hierarchy had evidence New Hampshire would be more formidable than conventional wisdom held. Their pollster, Peter Hart, had conducted a survey among 500 likely participants in the Democratic primary. Mondale came out in a virtual tie with Glenn, 37%-36%.

After Governor Gallen's defeat for re-election by just 13,072 votes in 1982 and his subsequent death on December 29, 1982 of liver and kidney failure, Dayton Duncan had planned to leave politics. However, by fall of 1983 Duncan had signed on as deputy national press secretary for Mondale. He later recounted New Hampshire's importance to his candidate: "It was going to be one of Mondale's toughest states. We never had any illusions about that. We figured that Mondale could probably at most get about thirty-five percent of the vote in New Hampshire."

The defeat and death of Gallen left a vacuum in Mondale's New Hampshire organization; although enough people were committed to the Minnesotan, no in-state politician had the strength to guarantee local input into its strategic deliberations.

For the first time in his career, Fritz Mondale did not have a springboard from which to achieve office. Governor Orville

Freeman of Minnesota had appointed Mondale special assistant to the state attorney general in 1958; by 1960 Freeman had appointed him state attorney general. After Senator Hubert Humphrey was elected vice president to Lyndon Johnson, Governor Karl Rolvagg appointed Mondale to serve in the Senate. He won re-election in 1966 and 1972 by 110,000 and 240,000 votes, respectively. In the summer of 1976 Georgian Jimmy Carter needed to strengthen his links with the northern, liberal and congressional elements of his party. Hence, Mondale became his running mate.

In early October of 1983 the former vice president received the simultaneous endorsement of the AFL-CIO and the National Education Association, considered the most politically effective unions in the country, for his presidential bid. At the outset of the race, the AFL-CIO endorsement was possibly more detrimental than beneficial to Mondale. Other than Iowa, a caucus state susceptible to having well-organized constituencies attend caucuses (it should be noted the Iowa vote is not a secret ballot; therefore, union members who supported someone other than Mondale would be known), the calendar in late February and early March worked to the advantage of an anti-establishment, insurgent hopeful, a role Gary Hart was eager to play. New Hampshire on February 28th, the Maine caucus on March 4th, the non-binding Vermont primary on March 6th and the Wyoming caucus on March 10th—all had scant tradition of politically vigorous labor organizations.

Of the impact Iowa had on New Hampshire that year, Chris Brown stated, "It was amazing that based on a forty-eight to sixteen percent finish that he [Hart] would have gotten that much of a boost from the media as he did."

All the work that the Hart partisans had put in for more than a year suddenly began to pay off that final week. Hart began to surge in the polls, previously closed checkbooks opened up, media attention and crowds gathered that were undreamed of just weeks before. Jeanne Shaheen said: "We knocked on about 80,000 doors and we'd handed all this literature to people, yet there were a couple of questions on people's minds. One was we couldn't win." The national press harped on that point without ceasing. Once Hart exceeded expectations in Iowa, Shaheen added, "it made him suddenly this national figure and he became a personality to them."

Hart's financial woes, which had put him on the brink of withdrawing in 1983, were suddenly over. Shaheen:

> When people report on your campaign they talk about the fact that you don't have the money to run ads on television, which was a big concern for us in 1984. One of the things that had really dogged the Hart campaign was the lack of funds....And once we went on TV that answered that criticism and so all the stories about Hart not having enough money to run a campaign ended at that point.

Since Iowa, the Hart campaign had been able to heighten the perception that it was now just a two-man race. Advertisements began running with the headline: "Only two candidates can now make this statement: 'I am running to *win* the Democratic Nomination for President.'" Hart: "I believe my strong showing in the Iowa caucus makes this election a two-person race between me and Walter Mondale. But if you listen to the experts, you would think this nomination process is all over. Over, before a single vote is cast in New Hampshire. I disagree. The race has just begun."

Senator Hart was far more aggressive in stumping the state (he would spend 57 days in New Hampshire, Mondale 51 and Glenn just 37). Time and again Hart's campaign showed a greater understanding of how the media influenced voters in the first primary.

While Manchester has the largest single concentration of voters (14%), Concord is New Hampshire's media capital. Not once during the primary did Mondale conduct a press conference in Concord, which ultimately became the city that awarded the highest percentage to Hart—45%. (Mondale was able to win only three of the 13 cities, Berlin, Nashua and Portsmouth. Hart carried the cities by a vote of 16,304-14,880.)

Mondale had the trait of never saying anything newsworthy whenever he spoke (the most memorable line of his candidacy was spoken by his media advisor—"he dares to be cautious"). When he did have something of significance to say, his flat monotone and lifeless delivery deflated whatever verbal punch he attempted. For example, during the campaign, Mondale repeatedly advocated annual summit meetings between the leaders of the United States and the Soviet Union. His idea drew virtually no notice, yet when Senator Howard Baker mentioned the same idea at Dartmouth's commencement exercise in June after the primary, the proposal drew much greater attention.

In the final week of every primary campaign, the New Hampshire electorate sifts through the candidates, narrowing the choice down to those with a chance of winning or coming close to doing so. In 1984, as in primaries past, the collapse of some candidacies aided those who shared a similar outlook on the issues. The failure of the Cranston and McGovern candidacies surely aided Hart, who was also assisted by the storm of controversy engulfing the Reverend Jesse Jackson.

Jackson began the presidential election year on the highest of notes: his role in the release on January 3rd of Navy flier (and former Portsmouth resident) Robert Goodman from the Syrians after his December 4th capture while on a bombing mission over Lebanon. Because of so much media attention swirling around him, Jackson showed surprising strength in the polls released in January and February. However, once the media reported on his reference to Jews as Hymies and New York City as Hymietown, first reported in *The Washington Post* on February 13th, his descent began.

Any aspiration Jackson had held of reaching the 10% mark scored by Fred Harris and Jerry Brown in the 1976 and 1980 New Hampshire primaries was ended. At a Manchester synagogue the Sunday night before the vote, Jackson called his remarks "insensitive and wrong" and thus quelled the controversy, but the damage had been done. His loss of support was one more reason Hart's surge went unabated.

In what was labeled a Last-Chance Forum, about 500 people showed up at the National Guard Armory in Concord on Friday to hear the candidates—almost all of them. Everyone but Cranston and Mondale availed themselves of the opportunity to address one of the largest gatherings of the election, this one sponsored by the State Employees Association.

In his remarks Hart pitched his New Ideas/New Generation of Leadership theme and also stressed the idea that the nomination race was not predetermined, but in fact the voters—starting in New Hampshire—were the ones with the ultimate say in the matter. Hart also stated: "I believe the policies of Ronald Reagan are working toward the destruction of this nation and all mankind. I don't believe in the 1980s we ought to send our sons to die for a cause we do not understand in

Lebanon or become the bodyguards of dictators in Central America." (One reporter wrote of Hart's performance that night, "He has gotten his Kennedyesque stance perfected to the point where he is beginning to look from a distance less like Gary Hart imitating JFK, and more like John F. Kennedy lip-syncing Gary Hart recordings.")

The Mondale camp managed to borrow a page from the efforts of Reagan in 1976 and Bush in 1980. As he departed the state for Maine, Vermont, Massachusetts and Washington, D.C., Dayton Duncan recalled: "The last three days leading up to the primary he wasn't in the state much. That was not because of overconfidence that he thought he had the state wrapped up; quite the contrary, the idea was that in the last two or three days the candidate's presence in the state itself is a drain on the organization."

While the concept was to utilize the visits to the neighboring states to maintain an electronic link to New Hampshire via television news reports, one had to wonder who the strategists were who thought up the visual the day before the vote: Mondale not only collecting the endorsement of one more politician, but also having that pol, Boston Mayor Ray Flynn, shown touring Boston harbor with the candidate. The eve of the primary featured the former vice president in the nation's capital as the featured speaker at a $1,000-a-plate fundraiser for the national Democratic Party, hardly the proper finishing touch before a primary with a long tradition of embracing upset-minded insurgents.

Hart had caught the media wave just at the right moment—and he rode it to victory in New Hampshire. It was a wave created partly out of his own message, encapsulated in his call for "New Ideas." It was also abetted by Mondale's inability to project any theme, message or personality on the ads and news reports pouring out of television sets in the homes of Granite Staters.

On the morning of the primary *The New York Times* reported that "Walter F. Mondale now holds the most commanding lead ever recorded this early in a presidential nomination campaign by a non-incumbent, according to the latest *New York Times*/CBS News Poll." Mondale was the choice of 57% of the 1,410 people interviewed nationwide who said they were likely to vote in a Democratic primary or caucus. Jackson was second with 8% while Glenn and Hart tied with 7% each.

Debate over political polling often revolves around questions of reliability and relevance. Never in the history of American politics would a poll published on the front page of *The New York Times* in the morning prove so unreliable and irrelevant by nightfall.

After 102,180 New Hampshire Democrats and Independents braved a day-long snowstorm to render their judgment, Hart carried all but one of the 10 counties (Coos being the sole holdout) with a margin of 37,702 to Mondale's 28,173. (Glenn finished third with 12,088, Jackson fourth with 5,311 and McGovern fifth with 5,217.)

Hart secured an outpouring of support from an electorate *The New York Times* described as "younger, better educated, better off, more liberal, more white, more politically independent than likely Democratic primary voters elsewhere in the nation."

New Hampshire was not an anomaly. Within the two-week time span between the New Hampshire primary and Super Tuesday, Hart won a total of 10 primaries and caucuses and, if not for a 22,000-vote loss in Georgia, would have forced Mondale's withdrawal from the race.

The message that the New Hampshire voters had tried to send to the national Democratic Party was not heeded, for the nomination system had been constructed in such a fashion as to cushion the blow an insurgent such as Hart could deliver to an establishment-blessed candidate like Walter Mondale. Hart's sudden notoriety was wasted; too many states were frontloading toward the beginning of the window. Therefore, it was too late to have complete delegate slates, something the well-funded Mondale campaign had been able to accomplish with an assist from the AFL-CIO.

The frontloading also meant any candidate emerging as quickly as Hart simply lacked the time to pull together any coherent national campaign system, although many of Hart's later problems can be blamed on his attempt to be both candidate and campaign manager.

From New Hampshire in 1984 a message was sent: while Walter Mondale was a decent, experienced and compassionate politician, the voters in the first primary and later all across the land decided not to turn away from their desire for a minimalist approach to government. Ronald Reagan so clearly personified that desire. Nor were they interested in turning out of office a president with a remarkable skill at communicating his ideas in favor of a politician who had few if any new ideas.

The Granite State proved once again to be the bellwether state. Again in 1984, the voters of this small state showed a remarkable prescience at the outset of the presidential race to determine the nation's final decision.

Appendix

The New Hampshire Presidential Primary

	PRIMARY WINNERS	NOMINEES	PRESIDENT
1952:	R - EISENHOWER D - KEFAUVER	EISENHOWER STEVENSON	EISENHOWER
1956:	R - EISENHOWER D - KEFAUVER	EISENHOWER STEVENSON	EISENHOWER
1960:	D - KENNEDY R - NIXON	KENNEDY NIXON	KENNEDY
1964:	D - JOHNSON* R - LODGE*	JOHNSON GOLDWATER	JOHNSON
1968:	R - NIXON D - JOHNSON*	NIXON HUMPHREY	NIXON
1972:	R - NIXON D - MUSKIE	NIXON McGOVERN	NIXON
1976:	D - CARTER R - FORD	CARTER FORD	CARTER
1980:	R - REAGAN D - CARTER	REAGAN CARTER	REAGAN
1984:	R - REAGAN D - HART	REAGAN MONDALE	REAGAN

*Write-in.

General Election Results for President in New Hampshire

	REPUBLICAN	DEMOCRATIC	THIRD PARTY AND OTHERS	
1900	McKinley/Roosevelt 54,799 59.3%	Bryan/Stevenson 35,489 38.4%	Others 2,076	2.2%
1904	Roosevelt/Fairbanks 54,163 60.1	Parker/Davis 34,074 37.8	Others 1,924	2.1
1908	Taft/Sherman 53,149 59.3	Bryan/Kern 33,655 37.6	Others 2,796	3.1
1912	Taft/Butler 32,927 37.4	Wilson/Marshall 34,724 39.5	Roosevelt-Progressive 17,794 20.2. Others 2,516	2.9
1916	Hughes/Fairbanks 43,725 49.1	Wilson/Marshall 43,781 49.1	Others 1,621	1.8
1920	Harding/Coolidge 95,196 59.9	Cox/Roosevelt 62,622 39.4	Others 1,234	.8
1924	Coolidge/Dawes 98,575 59.8	Davis/Bryan 57,201 34.7	LaFollette-Progressive 8,993	5.5
1928	Hoover/Curtis 115,404 58.7	Smith/Robinson 80,715 41.0	Others 638	.3
1932	Hoover/Curtis 103,629 50.4	Roosevelt/Garner 100,680 49.0	Others 1,211	.6
1936	Landon/Knox 104,642 48.0	Roosevelt/Garner 108,460 49.7	Lemke-Union 4,819 2.2 Others 193	
1940	Willkie/McNary 110,127 46.8	Roosevelt/Wallace 125,292 53.2		
1944	Dewey/Bricker 109,916 47.9	Roosevelt/Truman 119,663 52.1	Others 46	
1948	Dewey/Warren 121,299 52.4	Truman/Barkley 107,995 46.7	Others 2,146	.9

General Election Results for President in New Hampshire (continued)

	REPUBLICAN	DEMOCRATIC	THIRD PARTY AND OTHERS
1952	Eisenhower/Nixon 166,287 60.9	Stevenson/Sparkman 106,663 39.1	
1956	Eisenhower/Nixon 176,519 66.1	Stevenson/Kefauver 90,364 33.8	Others 111
1960	Nixon/Lodge 157,989 53.4	Kennedy/Johnson 137,772 46.6	
1964	Goldwater/Miller 104,029 36.4	Johnson/Humphrey 182,065 63.6	
1968	Nixon/Agnew 154,903 52.1	Humphrey/Muskie 130,589 43.9	Wallace-American 11,173 3.8 Others 633 .2
1972	Nixon/Agnew 213,724 64.0	McGovern/Shriver 116,435 34.9	Schmitz-American 3,386 1.0 Others 510 .2
1976	Ford/Dole 185,935 54.7	Carter/Mondale 147,635# 43.5	McCarthy '76 4,095 1.2 Others 1,952 .6
1980	Reagan/Bush 221,705 57.7	Carter/Mondale 108,864 28.4	Anderson-Independent 49,693 12.9 Others 3,737 1.0
1984	Reagan/Bush 267,051 68.7	Mondale/Ferraro 120,377 31.0	Others 1,507 .4

Source: *Manual for the General Court,* beginning with Volume 7 in 1901 with all odd-numbered volumes since then.

\# The Carter/Mondale total is inaccurately listed as 147,645 in the Manual.

New Hampshire has four votes in the Electoral College.

Party Vote - New Hampshire Presidential Primary

1952: Total - 136,179 (136,536)*
R - 96,507   70.9%
D - 39,672   29.1%

1956: Total - 99,430 (105,188)
R - 65,479   65.9%
D - 33,951   34.1%

1960: Total - 135,109 (135,216)
R - 81,457   60.3%
D - 53,652   39.7%

1964: Total - 138,430
R - 96,994   70.1%
D - 41,436   29.9%

1968: Total - 168,792
R - 108,273   64.1%
D - 60,519   35.9%

1972: Total - 217,268 (214,961)
R - 123,421   56.8%
D - 93,847   43.2%

1976: Total - 214,968
R - 119,880   55.8%
D - 95,088   44.2%

1980: Total - 261,243
R - 148,091   56.7%
D - 113,152   43.3%

1984: Total - 180,579
R - 78,399   43.4%
D - 102,180   56.6%

Source: *Manual for the General Court.*
Volumes 33, 35, 37, 39, 41, 43, 45, 47 and 49.

* The figures in parentheses are the total vote for both parties as shown in the Manual. In 1952, 1956, 1960 and 1972 these figures are inaccurate. County results are the first figures listed and are the ones used. In 1972 the vote in Ward 4 in Manchester is missing from the Manual, and it is included in these figures.

1952: Candidate Tally

		% OF TOTAL VOTE	% OF TABULATED VOTE
REPUBLICAN: (4)		96,507	92,865
Dwight Eisenhower	46,661	48.3	50.2
Robert Taft	35,838	37.1	38.6
Harold Stassen	6,574	6.8	7.1
Douglas MacArthur	3,227*	3.3	3.5
William Schneider	230	.2	.2
Others	335	.3	.4
	92,865		
DEMOCRATIC: (2)		39,672	36,252
Estes Kefauver	19,800	49.9	54.6
Harry Truman	15,927	40.1	43.9
Douglas MacArthur	151*	.4	.4
James Farley	77*		
Adlai Stevenson	40*		
Others	257	.6	.7
	36,252		

Source: *Manual for the General Court.* Volume 33.

* Write-in.

** The total vote is the number who participated in either the Democratic or Republican primary. The tabulated vote is what was tallied for the candidates. The discrepancy in these figures is attributed to the fact that a number of people would vote in the delegate selection part of the primary–but not the presidential preference poll; or their vote was a write-in not counted for Others. The tabulated vote percentage is used in listing the election results.

In 1977 the legislature voted to remove the delegates' names from the ballots; therefore, in 1980 and 1984 only the percentage of tabulated votes is listed. Percentages are calculated for only those who received more than 100 votes. The number in parentheses after Republican and Democratic is the number of candidates listed on the ballot.

1956: Candidate Tally

		% OF TOTAL VOTE	% OF TABULATED VOTE
REPUBLICAN: (1)		65,479	57,064
Dwight Eisenhower	56,464	86.2	98.9
Others	600	.9	1.1
	57,064		
DEMOCRATIC: (1)		33,951	25,646
Estes Kefauver	21,701	63.9	84.6
Adlai Stevenson	3,806*	11.2	14.8
Others	139	.4	.5
	25,646		

Source: *Manual for the General Court.* Volume 35.

* Write-in.

1960: Candidate Tally

		% OF TOTAL VOTE	% OF TABULATED VOTE
REPUBLICAN: (1)		81,457	73,031
Richard Nixon	65,204	80.0	89.3
Nelson Rockefeller	2,745*	3.4	3.8
Paul Fisher	2,388*	2.9	3.3
John Kennedy	2,196*	2.7	3.0
Henry Lodge	141*	.2	.2
Styles Bridges	108*	.1	.1
Others	249	.3	.3
	73,031		
DEMOCRATIC: (2)		53,652	50,899
John Kennedy	43,372	80.8	85.2
Paul Fisher	6,853	12.8	13.5
Stuart Symington	183*	.3	.4
Adlai Stevenson	168*	.3	.3
Richard Nixon	164*	.3	.3
Others	159	.3	.3
	50,899		

Source: *Manual for the General Court.* Volume 37.

* Write-in.

1964: Candidate Tally

		% OF TOTAL VOTE	% OF TABULATED VOTE
REPUBLICAN: (5)		96,994	92,853
Henry Lodge	33,007*	34.0	35.5
Barry Goldwater	20,692	21.3	22.3
Nelson Rockefeller	19,504	20.1	21.0
Richard Nixon	15,587*	16.1	16.8
Margaret Smith	2,120	2.2	2.3
Harold Stassen	1,373	1.4	1.5
William Scranton	105*	.1	.1
Norman LePage	82		
Others	383	.4	.4
	92,853		
DEMOCRATIC: (0)		41,436	30,777
Lyndon Johnson	29,317*	70.8	95.3
Robert Kennedy	487*	1.2	1.6
Henry Lodge	280*	.7	.9
Richard Nixon	232*	.6	.8
Barry Goldwater	193*	.5	.6
Nelson Rockefeller	109*	.3	.4
Adlai Stevenson	16*		
Hubert Humphrey	11*		
Others	132	.3	.4
	30,777		

Source: *Manual for the General Court.* Volume 39.

* Write-in.

1968: Candidate Tally

		% OF TOTAL VOTE	% OF TABULATED VOTE
REPUBLICAN: (9)		108,273	103,938
Richard Nixon	80,666	74.5	77.6
Nelson Rockefeller	11,241*	10.4	10.8
Eugene McCarthy	5,511*	5.1	5.3
Lyndon Johnson	1,778*	1.6	1.7
George Romney	1,743	1.6	1.7
Willis Stone	527	.5	.5
Harold Stassen	429	.4	.4
Paul Fisher	374*	.3	.4
Ronald Reagan	362*	.3	.3
Herbert Hoover	247	.2	.2
David Watumull	161	.1	.2
William Evans	151	.1	.1
Elmer Coy	73		
Don DuMont	39		
Others	636	.6	.6
	103,938		

		% OF TOTAL VOTE	% OF TABULATED VOTE
DEMOCRATIC: (4)		60,519	55,470
Lyndon Johnson	27,520*	45.5	49.6
Eugene McCarthy	23,269#	38.4	41.9
Richard Nixon	2,532*	4.2	4.6
Robert Kennedy	606*	1.0	1.1
Paul Fisher	506*	.8	.9
Nelson Rockefeller	249*	.4	.4
George Wallace	201*	.3	.4
John Crommelin	186	.3	.3
Richard Lee	170	.3	.3
Jacob Gordon	77		
Others	154	.3	.3
	55,470		

Source: *Manual for the General Court.* Volume 41.

* Write-in.

The McCarthy total is inaccurately listed as 23,263 in the Manual.

1972: Candidate Tally

		% OF TOTAL VOTE	% OF TABULATED VOTE
REPUBLICAN: (4)		123,421	117,208
Richard Nixon	79,239	64.2	67.6
Paul McCloskey	23,190	18.8	19.8
John Ashbrook	11,362	9.2	9.7
Patrick Paulsen	1,211	1.0	1.0
Wilbur Mills	645*	.5	.6
George McGovern	555*	.4	.5
Edmund Muskie	504*	.4	.4
George Wallace	93*		
Samuel Yorty	55*		
Vance Hartke	32*		
Edward Kennedy	28*		
Others	294	.2	.3
	117,208		
DEMOCRATIC: (5)		93,847	88,854
Edmund Muskie	41,235	43.9	46.4
George McGovern	33,007	35.2	37.1
Samuel Yorty	5,401	5.8	6.1
Wilber Mills	3,563*	3.8	4.0
Vance Hartke	2,417	2.6	2.7
Edward Kennedy	954*	1.0	1.1
Richard Nixon	854*	.9	1.0
Hubert Humphrey	348*	.4	.4
Edward Coll	280	.3	.3
Henry Jackson	197*	.2	.2
George Wallace	175*	.2	.2
Paul McCloskey	133*	.1	.1
John Ashbrook	27*		
Patrick Paulsen	19*		
Others	244	.3	.3
	88,854		

Source: *Manual for the General Court.* Volume 43.

* Write-in.

1976: Candidate Tally

		% OF TOTAL VOTE	% OF TABULATED VOTE
REPUBLICAN: (2)		119,880	110,190
Gerald Ford	55,156	46.0	50.1
Ronald Reagan	53,569	44.7	48.6
Jimmy Carter	591*	.5	.5
Morris Udall	421*	.4	.4
Birch Bayh	228*	.2	.2
Fred Harris	225*	.2	.2
	110,190		
DEMOCRATIC: (7)		95,088	81,525
Jimmy Carter	23,373	24.6	28.7
Morris Udall	18,710	19.7	23.0
Birch Bayh	12,510	13.2	15.3
Fred Harris	8,863	9.3	10.9
R. Sargent Shriver	6,743	7.1	8.3
Hubert Humphrey	4,296* #	4.5	5.3
Henry Jackson	1,857*	2.0	2.3
George Wallace	1,016* ##	1.1	1.2
Ellen McCormack	1,007	1.1	1.2
Ronald Reagan	875*	.9	1.1
Arthur Blessitt	828	.9	1.0
Others	1,447	1.5	1.8
	81,525		

Source: *Manual for the General Court.* Volume 45.

* Write-in.

The Humphrey total is inaccurately listed as 4,596 in the Manual.

The Wallace total is inaccurately listed as 1,061 in the Manual.

1980: Candidate Tally

		% OF
REPUBLICAN: (7)		TABULATED VOTE
Ronald Reagan	72,983	49.8
George Bush	33,443	22.8
Howard Baker	18,943	12.9
John Anderson	14,458	9.9
Philip Crane	2,618	1.8
John Connally	2,239	1.5
Jimmy Carter	788*	.5
Robert Dole	597	.4
Edward Kennedy	287*	.2
Edmund Brown Jr.	157*	.1
Others	21	
	146,534	

Total Vote - 148,091.

		% OF
DEMOCRATIC: (5)		TABULATED VOTE
Jimmy Carter	52,648	47.2
Edward Kennedy	41,687	37.4
Edmund Brown Jr.	10,686#	9.6
Lyndon LaRouche	2,307	2.1
Ronald Reagan	1,958*	1.8
John Anderson	932*	.8
Richard Kay	563	.5
George Bush	415*	.4
Howard Baker	317*	.3
Philip Crane	61*	
Others	21	
	111,595	

Total Vote - 113,152

Source: Since the vote in both parties was recounted, the figures published above are the county-by-county breakdown on page 43 of the *Manual for the General Court*, Volume 47.

* Write-in.

The Brown total is inaccurately listed as 10,706 in the Manual.

1984: Candidate Tally

| | | % OF |
REPUBLICAN: (5)		TABULATED VOTE
Ronald Reagan	65,033	86.4
Gary Hart	3,968*	5.3
Harold Stassen	1,543	2.1
Walter Mondale	1,090*	1.4
John Glenn	1,065*	1.4
Ernest Hollings	697*	.9
Jesse Jackson	455*	.6
George McGovern	406*	.5
David Kelley	360	.5
Gary Arnold	252	.3
Ben Fernandez	202	.3
Alan Cranston	107*	.1
Reubin Askew	52*	
Others	10	
	75,240	

Total Vote - 78,399

DEMOCRATIC: (22)		
Gary Hart	37,702	37.3
Walter Mondale	28,173	27.9
John Glenn	12,088	12.0
Jesse Jackson	5,311	5.3
George McGovern	5,217	5.2
Ronald Reagan	5,058*	5.0
Ernest Hollings	3,583	3.5
Alan Cranston	2,136	2.1
Reubin Askew	1,025	1.0
Others	752	.7
	101,045	

Total Vote - 102,180

Source: *Manual for the General Court.* Volume 49.

* Write-in.

Significant Vice Presidential Votes

1956:	REPUBLICAN	
	Richard Nixon	22,936*
	Christian Herter	2,899*
	Styles Bridges	1,925*
1960:	REPUBLICAN	
	Wesley Powell	9,620*
	Henry Lodge	6,567*
	Styles Bridges	2,438*
	Nelson Rockefeller	2,279*
1964:	REPUBLICAN	
	Richard Nixon	8,152*
	Wayne Green	8,030
	Henry Lodge	6,432*
	Margaret Smith	3,163*
	DEMOCRATIC	
	Robert Kennedy	25,094*
1972:	REPUBLICAN	
	Spiro Agnew	45,524*
	Austin Burton	11,264
	Edward Brooke	7,648*
	DEMOCRATIC	
	Endicott Peabody	37,813
1980:	REPUBLICAN	
	Jesse Helms	28,695
	Howard Baker	2,959*
	Jack Kemp	2,638*
	DEMOCRATIC	
	Walter Mondale	10,231*
	Edmund Brown Jr.	1,556*
1984:	REPUBLICAN	
	George Bush	20,555*
	DEMOCRATIC	
	Gerald Willis	14,870
	Alwin Hopfmann	6,351
	George Bush	1,057*

Source: *Manual for the General Court.*
         Volumes 35, 37, 39, 43, 47 and 49.

* Write-in.

Delegate Results

1952:   March 11   Registered Voters: 317,368

Republican:	Delegates:	14
	Elected:	All 14 were favorable to Eisenhower.
	Top Delegate:	Sherman Adams - 41,767

Democratic:	Delegates:	8 (8 were elected at-large, each with 1/2 vote. 2 were elected from each of the two congressional districts; each had a full vote.)
	Elected:	At-large: 6 were pledged to Kefauver and 2 were favorable to Kefauver. District: 2 were favorable to Kefauver and 2 were pledged to Kefauver.
	Top Delegate:	J. Felix Daniel - 12,791

1956:   March 13   Registered Voters: 323,625

Republican:	Delegates:	14
	Elected:	All 14 were favorable to Eisenhower.
	Top Delegate:	Styles Bridges - 39,214

Democratic:	Delegates:	8 - same system as 1952.
	Elected:	All 12 elected (8 actual votes) were pledged to Kefauver.
	Top Delegate:	J. Felix Daniel - 13,815

1960:   March 8   Registered Voters: 325,885

Republican:	Delegates:	14
	Elected:	All 14 were favorable to Nixon.
	Top Delegate:	Robert W. Upton - 36,977

Democratic:	Delegates:	20 were elected - each with 1/2 vote (10 actual votes).
	Elected:	18 were pledged to Kennedy and 2 were favorable to Kennedy.
	Top Delegate:	Romeo J. Champagne - 15,171

Delegate Results (continued)

1964:   March 10   Registered Voters: 349,667

  Republican: Delegates: 14
         Elected: All 14 were favorable to Lodge.
         Top Delegate: Arthur E. Bean - 30,310

  Democratic: Delegates: 20
         Elected: All 20 were favorable to Johnson.
         Top Delegate: Emmet J. Kelley - 7,812

1968:   March 12   Registered Voters: 363,503

  Republican: Delegates: 8
         Elected: All 8 were pledged to Nixon.
         Top Delegate: Lane Dwinell - 55,950

  Democratic: Delegates: 24
         Elected: 20 were pledged to McCarthy and 4 were favorable to Johnson.
         Top Delegate: Thomas McIntyre - 10,315 (Johnson)

1972:   March 7   Registered Voters: 423,822

  Republican: Delegates: 14
         Elected: 13 were pledged to Nixon and 1 was favorable.
         Top Delegate: Robert P. Bass Jr. - 56,631

  Democratic: Delegates: 20 - each with 9/10 a vote - 18 votes in all.
         Elected: 15 pledged to Muskie and 5 pledged to McGovern.
         Top Delegate: Richard Leonard - 14,116 (Muskie)

Delegate Results (continued)

1976:   February 24   Registered Voters: 443,583

    Republican: Delegates: 21
                      Elected: 18 were pledged to Ford and 3 were pledged to Reagan.
                      Top Delegate: James Cleveland - 49,347 (Ford)

    Democratic: Delegates: 17
                      Elected: 15 were pledged to Carter and 2 were pledged to Udall.
                      Top Delegate: Robert Bossie - 9,728 (Carter)

1980:   February 26   Registered Voters: 509,915

    Republican: Delegates: 22
                      Elected: 15 were pledged to Reagan, 5 were pledged to Bush and 2 were pledged to Baker. All voted for Reagan at the convention.

    Democratic: Delegates: 19
                      Elected: 10 were pledged to Carter and 9 were pledged to Kennedy.

1984:   February 28   Registered Voters: 488,970

    Republican: Delegates: 22
                      Elected: All 22 were pledged to Reagan.

    Democratic: Delegates: 22
                      Elected: 12 were pledged to Mondale and 10 were pledged to Hart.

Source: *Manual for the General Court.*
       Volumes 33, 35, 37, 39, 41, 43, 45, 47 and 49.

Acknowledgments

In the course of researching this book, I spent many days in the Concord City Library as well as the New Hampshire State Library. Each of these libraries contains much of the information on the history of the New Hampshire presidential primary. I am grateful to the staffs of both of these fine institutions for all of their assistance.

Other libraries around the state were also quite helpful. In particular, I wish to acknowledge the Danforth Library at New England College, which contains the Styles Bridges Collection, and the Special Collections of the Baker Library at Dartmouth College, which includes the papers of Sherman Adams, Robert Bass, Charles Tobey and Sinclair Weeks.

I would also like to express my gratitude to the staffs of the Harry S Truman Library in Independence, Missouri; the Dwight D. Eisenhower Library in Abilene, Kansas; the John F. Kennedy Library in Boston; and the Estes Kefauver Collection at the University of Tennessee in Knoxville. The staff people at all of these libraries were of unfailing aid during my visits.

I conducted more than 100 interviews while researching *First in the Nation*. It would take far too long to thank all who submitted to an interview, but I do want to express my thanks to Bernard Boutin, Robert Burroughs, Maria Carrier, Bill Dunfey, Joseph Grandmaison, William Johnson, Stewart Lamprey, Tom and Myrtle McIntyre, Walter Peterson and William Treat for the time they took for their interviews.

New Hampshire was fortunate to have Richard Cooper as a native son. Cooper, who died on September 20, 1985, was a dedicated and compassionate public servant. A longtime leader in the Republican Party, he was not only quite helpful in arranging my two interviews with Sherman Adams (who died on October 27, 1986), but he also provided me access to his own files while acting as a guide through the maze of New Hampshire politics in the 1950s and 1960s.

I would also like to thank John Gfroerer, the Yankee Cable Network news director and my collaborator on the television documentary on the primary, "The Premier Primary: New Hampshire and Presidential Elections," for making available the interviews he conducted for the program.

In the process of researching this book, I accumulated many files of material on these historic elections and, in addition, compiled an oral history, since virtually all of the interviews were taped and preserved. I am very grateful to Stuart Wallace, the former director of the New Hampshire Historical Society, for his willingness to acquire this comprehensive collection, since this enabled me to conclude the research and writing of this book.

I would also like to thank Sally Helms, Anne Nute and Jane Funk for their work in preparing the manuscript, as well as Darlene Bordwell of Editorial Inc., of Rockport, Massachusetts, and Stephen Cox, director of publications at the New Hampshire Historical Society, for their editorial assistance.

Mark Shields, a columnist for *The Washington Post* and a radio and TV commentator, has not always been an uncritical admirer of the New Hampshire primary, but his lively foreword to this book is adequate compensation.

Peter Randall is the publisher not only of this book but also my previous publication, *New Hampshire Notables.* New Hampshire will probably never be known for having a vigorous book publishing industry, but the role that Peter has performed in publishing more than 125 titles is an imprint that will endure for decades to come. I am thankful for all of his help.

While a number of candidates who have trudged through the snows of the first primary are no longer living—Estes Kefauver, John Kennedy, Nelson Rockefeller and Robert Taft— the courage and commitment that all the presidential aspirants have shown provides Americans with a sense of confidence and faith in our democracy. And the efforts made every presidential election by thousands of citizens, not only in the first primary state but in every state of this nation, are a contribution to our democracy for which we should all be thankful.

Charles Brereton
Concord, New Hampshire
September 3, 1987

Bibliography

Adams, Rachel. *On the Other Hand.* New York: Harper & Row, 1963.

Adams, Sherman. *Firsthand Report.* New York: Harper & Brothers, 1961

Alsop, Stewart. *Nixon and Rockefeller.* New York: Doubleday, 1960.

Anderson, Jack, and Blumenthal, Fred. *The Kefauver Story.* New York: Dial Press, 1956.

Anson, Robert. *McGovern: A Biography.* New York: Holt, Rinehart and Winston, 1972.

Bell, Jack. *The Splendid Misery.* Garden City, N.Y.: Doubleday, 1960

Bellush, Bernard. *He Walked Alone: A Biography of John Gilbert Winant.* The Hague: Mouton, 1968.

Bernstein, Carl, and Woodward, Bob. *All the President's Men.* New York: Simon & Schuster, 1974.

———. *The Final Days.* New York: Simon & Schuster, 1976.

Blumenthal, Sidney. *The Permanent Campaign.* New York: Simon & Schuster, 1982.

Burns, James MacGregor. *John Kennedy: A Political Profile.* New York: Harcourt and Brace, 1959.

———. *Edward Kennedy and the Camelot Legacy.* New York: W.W. Norton, 1976.

Cannon, Lou. *Ronnie and Jesse: A Political Odyssey.* Garden City, N.Y.: Doubleday, 1969.

Caro, Robert. *The Years of Lyndon Johnson: The Path to Power.* New York: Vintage Books, 1983.

Carter, Jimmy. *Why Not the Best?* Nashville: Broadman Press, 1975

Casey, Susan. *Hart and Soul.* Concord: NHI Press, 1986.

Cash, Kevin. *Who the Hell Is William Loeb?* Manchester: Amoskeag Press, 1975.

Chester, Lewis, et al. *An American Melodrama: The Presidential Campaign of 1968.* New York: Viking Press, 1969.

Churgin, Jonah. *From Truman to Johnson: New Hampshire's Impact on American Politics.* New York: Yeshiva University Press, 1972

Collier, Peter, and Horowitz, David. *The Rockefellers: An American Dynasty.* New York: Holt, Rinehart and Winston, 1976.

259

———. *The Kennedys: An American Drama*. New York: Summit Books, 1984.

Crotty, William, and Jackson, John III. *Presidential Primaries and Nominations*. Washington, D.C.: Congressional Quarterly, 1985

Crouse, Timothy. *The Boys on the Bus*. New York: Random House, 1974

David, Lester. *Ted Kennedy: Triumphs and Tragedies*. New York: Award Books, 1975.

Davis, James W. *Springboard to the White House*. New York: Thomas Y. Crowell, 1967.

———. *National Conventions: Nominations Under the Big Top*. Woodbury, N.Y.: Barron's Educational Series, 1973.

Desmond, James. *Nelson Rockefeller: A Political Biography*. New York: Macmillan, 1964.

Diamond, Robert, editor. *Presidential Elections Since 1789*. Washington, D.C.: Congressional Quarterly, 1975.

Dougherty, Richard. *Goodby, Mr. Christian: A Personal Account of McGovern's Rise and Fall*. New York: Doubleday, 1973.

Dunfey, William. "A Short History of the Democratic Party in New Hampshire." M.A. Thesis, University of New Hampshire, 1954.

Eisenhower, Dwight. *Mandate for Change: The White House Years*. New York: Doubleday, 1963.

Evans, Rowland, and Novak, Robert. *Nixon in the White House*. New York: Random House, 1972.

———. *Lyndon B. Johnson: The Exercise of Power*. New York: New American Library, 1966.

Fraser, Janet, and May, Ernest, editors. *Campaign 72: The Managers Speak*. Cambridge: Harvard University Press, 1973.

Fraser, Janet, and Moore, Jonathan, editors. *Campaign for President: The Managers Look at '76*. Cambridge: Ballinger, 1977

Gates, Gary Paul, and Rather, Dan. *The Palace Guard*. New York: Harper & Row, 1974.

Germond, Jack, and Witcover, Jules. *Blue Smoke and Mirrors*. New York: Viking Press, 1981.

Goldman, Eric. *The Tragedy of Lyndon Johnson*. New York: Alfred A. Knopf, 1969.

Gorman, Joseph. *Kefauver: A Political Biography*. New York: Oxford University Press, 1971.

Grassmuck, George, editor. *Before Nomination: Our Primary Problems*. Washington, D.C.: American Enterprise Institute, 1985

Gunther, John. *Inside U.S.A.* New York: Harper & Brothers, 1947.

Hadley, Arthur. *The Invisible Primary*. Englewood Cliffs, N.J.: Prentice-Hall, 1976.

Halberstam, David. *The Unfinished Odyssey of Robert Kennedy*. New York: Random House, 1968.

———. *The Best and the Brightest*. New York: Random House, 1969.

————. *The Powers That Be.* New York: Alfred A. Knopf, 1979.

Hart, Gary. *Right from the Start: A Chronicle of the McGovern Campaign.* New York: Quadrangle/The New York Times Book Co., 1973.

Hatch, Alden. *The Lodges of Massachusetts.* New York: Hawthorn Books, 1973.

Hersh, Burton. *The Education of Edward Kennedy: A Family Biography.* New York: William Morrow, 1972.

Hughes, John Emmet. *The Ordeal of Power: A Political Memoir of the Eisenhower Years.* New York: Atheneum, 1963.

Johnson, Lyndon. *The Vantage Point: Perspectives of the Presidency 1963-69.* New York: Holt, Rinehart and Winston, 1971.

Kearns, Doris. *Lyndon Johnson and the American Dream.* New York: Harper & Row, 1976.

Keech, William, and Matthews, Donald. *The Party's Choice.* Washington, D.C.: The Brookings Institution, 1976.

Koenig, Louis. *The Invisible Presidency.* New York: Rinehart, 1960.

Koskoff, David. *Joseph P. Kennedy: A Life and Times.* Englewood Cliffs, N.J.: Prentice-Hall, 1974.

Leary, Mary Ellen. *Phantom Politics: Campaigning in California.* Washington, D.C.: Public Affairs Press, 1977.

Lodge, Henry Cabot. *The Storm Has Many Eyes.* New York: W.W. Norton, 1973.

————. *As It Was.* New York: W.W. Norton, 1976.

Lorenz, J.D. *Jerry Brown: The Man on the White Horse.* Boston: Houghton Mifflin, 1978.

Lurie, Leonard. *The King Makers.* New York. Coward, McCann & Geoghegan, 1971.

————. *The Running of Richard Nixon.* New York: Coward, McCann & Geoghegan, 1972.

MacDougal, Malcolm. *We Almost Made It.* New York: Crown, 1977

Magruder, Jeb Stuart. *An American Life: One Man's Road to Watergate.* New York: Atheneum, 1974.

Mailer, Norman. *Some Honorable Men: Political Conventions 1960-1972.* Boston: Little, Brown, 1976.

Mazo, Earl. *Richard Nixon: A Political and Personal Portrait.* New York: Harper & Brothers, 1959.

Martin, Ralph, and Plaut, Ed. *Front Runner, Dark Horse.* Garden City, N.Y.: Doubleday, 1960.

McCarthy, Eugene. *The Year of the People.* Garden City, N.Y.: Doubleday, 1969.

McDowell, Charles Jr. *Campaign Fever.* New York: William Morrow, 1965.

McGinniss, Joe. *The Selling of the President 1968.* New York: Trident Press, 1969.

Moore, Jonathan, editor. *The Campaign for President: 1980 in Retrospect.* Cambridge: Ballinger, 1981.

Moos, Malcolm, et al. *Presidential Nominating Politics in 1952: The Northeast.* Baltimore: Johns Hopkins Press, 1954.

Moos, Malcolm. *The Republicans: A History of Their Party.* New York: Random House, 1956.

Morison, Elizabeth Forbes, and Morison, Elting. *New Hampshire: A Bicentennial History.* New York: W.W. Norton, 1976.

Nixon, Richard. *Six Crises.* Garden City, N.Y.: Doubleday, 1962.

Novak, Michael. *Choosing Our King.* New York: Macmillan, 1974.

Novak, Robert. *The Agony of the G.O.P.* New York: Macmillan, 1965

O'Brien, Lawrence. *No Final Victories.* New York: Ballantine, 1975

O'Donnell, Kenneth, and Powers, David, with Joe McCarthy. *Johnny We Hardly Knew Ye: Memories of John Fitzgerald Kennedy.* Boston: Little, Brown, 1970.

Orren, Gary, and Polsby, Nelson, editors. *Media and Momentum.* Chatham N.J.: Chatham House Publishers, 1987.

Overacker, Louise. *The Presidential Primary.* New York: Macmillan, 1926.

Parmet, Herbert. *Eisenhower and the American Crusades.* New York: Macmillan, 1972.

Patterson, James. *Mr. Republican: A Biography of Robert A. Taft.* Boston: Houghton Mifflin, 1972.

Peirce, Neal. *The New England States.* New York: W.W. Norton, 1976

Perry, James. *The New Politics.* New York: Clarkson N. Potter, 1968

———. *Us and Them: How the Press Covered the 1972 Election.* New York: Clarkson N. Potter, 1973.

Price, David. *Bringing Back the Parties.* Washington, D.C.: Congressional Quarterly, 1984.

Reeves, Richard. *A Ford, Not a Lincoln.* New York: Harcourt Brace Jovanovich, 1975.

Rovere, Richard. *The Goldwater Caper.* New York: Harcourt, Brace & World, 1965.

———. *The Eisenhower Years.* New York: Farrar, Straus and Cudahy, 1956

Salzman, Ed. *Jerry Brown: High Priest and Low Politician.* Sacramento: California Journal Press, 1976.

Sanford, Terry. *A Danger of Democracy: The Presidential Nominating Process.* Boulder, Colo.: Westview Press, 1981.

Schlesinger, Arthur Jr. *A Thousand Days: John F. Kennedy in the White House.* Boston: Houghton Mifflin, 1965.

Schram, Martin. *Running for President: A Journal of the Carter Campaign.* New York: Pocket Books, 1976.

———. *The Great American Video Game.* New York: William Morrow, 1987.

Shannon, William. *The Heir Apparent: Robert Kennedy and the Struggle for Power*. New York: Macmillan, 1967.

Shields, Mark. *On the Campaign Trail*. Chapel Hill: Algonquin Books, 1985.

Sorensen, Theodore. *Kennedy*. New York: Harper & Row, 1965.

Stavis, Ben. *We Were the Campaign: New Hampshire to Chicago for McCarthy*. Boston: Beacon Press, 1969.

Stout, Richard. *People*. New York: Harper & Row, 1970.

terHorst, Jerald. *Gerald Ford and the Future of the Presidency*. New York: The Third Press, 1974.

Thompson, Hunter. *Fear and Loathing: On the Campaign Trail '72*. New York: Popular Library, 1973.

Truman, Harry. *Memoirs by Harry S Truman: Volume Two - Years of Trial and Hope*. Garden City, N.Y.: Doubleday, 1956.

Truman, Margaret. *Harry S Truman*. New York: William Morrow, 1973.

Tugwell, Rexford. *How They Became President*. New York: Simon & Schuster, 1964

Valenti, Jack. *A Very Human President*. New York: W.W. Norton, 1976

Veblen, Eric. *The Manchester Union Leader in New Hampshire Elections*. Hanover: University Press of New England, 1975.

Whalen, Richard. *The Founding Father: The Story of Joseph P. Kennedy*. New York: New American Library, 1964.

———. *Catch the Falling Flag*. Boston: Houghton Mifflin, 1972.

Wheeler, Michael. *Lies, Damn Lies, and Statistics*. New York: Dell Publishing, 1977.

White, Theodore. *The Making of the President 1960*. New York: Atheneum, 1962.

———. *The Making of the President 1964*. New York: Atheneum, 1965.

———. *The Making of the President 1968*. New York: Atheneum, 1969.

———. *The Making of the President 1972*. New York: Atheneum, 1973.

———. *Breach of Faith: The Fall of Richard Nixon*. New York: Atheneum, 1975.

———. *America in Search of Itself: The Making of the President 1956-80*. New York: Harper & Row, 1982.

White, William. *The Taft Story*. New York: Harper & Brothers, 1954

Whitman, Alden, and *The New York Times*. *Portrait-Adlai E. Stevenson: Politician, Diplomat, Friend*. New York: Harper & Row, 1965

Wicker, Tom. *JFK and LBJ: The Influence of Personality on Politics*. New York: William Morrow, 1968.

Witcover, Jules. *85 Days: The Last Campaign of Robert F. Kennedy*. New York: G.P. Putnam's Sons, 1969.

———. *The Resurrection of Richard Nixon*. New York: G.P. Putnam's Sons, 1970.

———. *White Knight: The Rise of Spiro Agnew*. New York: Random House, 1972.

————. *Marathon: The Pursuit of the Presidency 1972-1976.* New York: Viking Press, 1977.

Witker, Kristi. *How to Lose Everything in Politics Except Massachusetts.* New York: Mason and Lipscomb, 1974.

Wyckoff, Gene. *The Image Candidates: American Politics in the Age of Television.* New York: Macmillan, 1968.

Index

About the author

Charles Brereton is a writer living in Concord, New Hampshire, where he has resided since 1970, shortly after moving to New Hampshire from California.

Mr. Brereton is also the author of the book *New Hampshire Notables*, published for the New Hampshire Historical Society by Peter Randall Publisher in November of 1986. This book features biographical sketches of 422 prominent citizens of the Granite State and is the fourth in a series that began in 1919 with subsequent editions in 1932 and 1955.

Since January of 1980, he has written a column on politics and public affairs for several New Hampshire daily and weekly newspapers.

In the fall of 1979 he wrote *First Step to the White House*, a brief history of the New Hampshire presidential primary which was published by the Wheelabrator Foundation.

Another of his publications is *The New Hampshire Primary Guide*, a compilation of presidential primary returns released in May of 1987. He also published in 1983 and updated in 1985 *The New Hampshire Election Guide*, a collection of state election returns.

Mr. Brereton is also the researcher for a television documentary titled "The Premier Primary: New Hampshire and Presidential Elections," which first aired in March 1987 on the Yankee Cable Network.